Adam Leonas

The Empress Is Naked

From Female Privilege
to Gender Equality
and Social Liberation

Version 1.2.0

2021

Table of Contents

Part 3: The War of the Sexes 113

Part 4: From Prehistoric to Historic Society: What Went Wrong?   171

Part 5: Towards a Solution   203

Author's Note   242

Appendix: Tables 243

Bibliography   245

This page
was intentionally
left blank

Introduction

"The first class oppression coincides with that of the female sex by the male"[1], wrote Engels in 1884. Since then, women's inferior position has been considered an undeniable fact, especially by progressive thinkers. Different political traditions have different viewpoints on the issue, but two of them stand out: Left Feminism which advocates that women are oppressed by Capitalism, and therefore that they will be liberated by overturning it; and Radical Feminism which argues that women are oppressed by "Patriarchy", which is a complex set of prejudices, beliefs and institutions that result in men generally benefiting against women. Therefore, it concludes, the struggle should be against male privilege.

"Radical" Feminism is mainstream

Although the ideological construct of a "Patriarchy" is touting itself as anti-systemic, it has essentially been adopted by the system. Throughout the Western world, the concept of an oppressive patriarchy, as expressed by politicians, journalists and academics, is a key component of the dominant ideology. It is quite difficult to express a different view without being scorned, mocked, and subjected to fierce attack.

Time Magazine characteristically attacks the Men's Rights Movement with these words: "Imagine a kid who got a cone with three scoops of ice cream in it. Good flavors, too. Like peanut-butter chocolate, plus a scoop of cookie dough. In a waffle cone. And then this child whines about the lack of chocolate sprinkles on top. Welcome to the men's rights movement…. it's overwhelmingly a toxic slew of misogyny."[2]

When Doris Lessing, an emblematic figure of feminism in the '70s,

---

1   Engels, Friedrich. *The Origin of the Family, Private Property and the State.* Australia: Resistance Books (2004). p.73
2   "The Toxic Appeal of the Men's Rights Movement | TIME." http://time.com/134152/the-toxic-appeal-of-the-mens-rights-movement

acknowledged the current gender dynamics and attacked the "unthinking and automatic rubbishing of men which is now so part of our culture that it is hardly even noticed"[3], BBC felt obliged to fill its reporting article with the answer of a typical feminist, taking up 60% of the article's length. This is a very mild case of the typical censorship against any statements that are sympathetic to men. There is no counterargument to statements that take women's oppression for granted.

An example from the Washington Post is quite representative of the way the systemic media distort reality when it comes to gender issues. One article was titled "Study: Black girls suspended at higher rates than most boys"[4]. The author had chosen to focus on a specific state, Wisconsin, as an example, where "21 percent of black girls are suspended, compared with 14 percent of black boys, 6 percent of white boys and 2 percent of white girls". But she couldn't actually bury the overall findings, which showed that "black boys are more likely to be suspended than any group, at 20 percent." Black girls are at 12%. White boys are at 6%, while white girls at 2%. Instead of being titled "Boys are suspended more than girls, and blacks more than whites", the article's Goebbelian selection of title and emphasis are clearly more consistent with a feminist alteration of reality.

It is a fact that "Media and courts treat women like delicate little flowers instead of full human beings[5]" – and thus fully capable of evil actions. In a Canadian research about the way newspapers describe the mentally ill, researchers concluded that "the chivalry hypothesis holds ... after examining 1,168 newspaper articles published over six months": "These articles more frequently portrayed women compassionately as victims of circumstances or passions beyond their control. However, this kind of background information was routinely lacking in articles about men, who were routinely portrayed in a more dismissive and contemptuous

---

3   "BBC News | ARTS | Doris Lessing Attacks Feminists."
    http://news.bbc.co.uk/2/hi/entertainment/1491085.stm
4   "Study: Black Girls Suspended at Higher Rates than Most Boys - The Washington
    Post." http://www.washingtonpost.com/blogs/she-the-people/wp/2014/03/21/study-
    black-girls-suspended-at-higher-rates-than-most-boys
5   "Christie Blatchford: Media and Courts Treat Women like Delicate Little Flowers
    instead of Full Human Beings | National Post."
    http://fullcomment.nationalpost.com/2014/07/11/christie-blatchford-media-and-
    courts-treat-women-like-delicate-little-flowers-instead-of-full-human-beings

manner... Portrayals of women appear to be more sympathetic and considered; more frequently being portrayed as 'sad'."

The extent to which "radical feminism" is mainstream is highlighted by the fact that one the most popular feminist in the US is Hillary Clinton, a politician belonging to the core of the Establishment. She has been able to make extensive use of the pro-feminist bias in the American political scene and the media in order to propel her political career.

Another issue that highlights "radical feminism's" conventionality is the pervasiveness of its academic expression, Women's Studies, in education. "By the mid-1970s, there were at least eighty Women's Studies programs across the United States.... There are now ... more than 500 Women's Studies Departments around the world."[6] The most impressive fact is that there are also Men's Studies departments, with a mission... to make men be more like women: "men's studies was formed largely in response to, and as a critique of, an emerging men's rights movement... In many universities, men's studies is a correlation to women's studies or part of a larger gender studies program, and as such its faculty tends to be sympathetic to, or engaged in, advocacy of feminist politics."[7]

Women's oppression: Systemic views

There are many studies on how women are oppressed at work, in the family, in sexual relationships and so on. And it's beyond doubt that women are indeed oppressed. But are they *more* oppressed than men? Are they oppressed *as women*, or as members of a specific social class?

Systemic views cannot admit that men are *also* oppressed because that would be admitting that the system itself is oppressive. These views don't mind, however, assigning to women the status of victims, to which they themselves pretend, along with the positive discrimination that this entails such as alimony[8], early retirement, a milder treatment by the

---

6   'First Women's Studies Department'.
     http://womenshistory.about.com/od/practice/a/womens_studies_programs.htm
7   Wikipedia, Men's Studies. Accessed Jan. 15 2015
     https://en.wikipedia.org/wiki/Men%27s_studies
8   "Of the 400,000 people in the United States receiving post-divorce spousal

courts, exemption from the military service and more. *The practical result is that the system facilitates women's lives in several ways, while men, especially those from lower social classes, have to struggle for everything, and are never given a break.*

Left Feminism

For those in the Left it is almost self-evident that the women's cause should be supported. The hypothesis of a female oppression stands since the era of the Classics of Marxism. The feminists are protesting, and since the Left feels compelled to side with whomever protests against the system, the choice is made. Paradoxically, however, the Left feminist approach has been formulated... by men. It was Lenin himself who described Socialism as the system where every cook-maid can govern. The Left's vision of female liberation seeks a woman who can live as a man. It is doubtful, however, whether that is what women themselves want.

Research in Great Britain (2018) found that only 1 out of 3 women claim that they are feminists[9]. And that comes from the 3rd most feminist country in the world[10]. In the US, only 23%[11] to 38%[12] of women call themselves feminists. Twice as many Americans (23%) consider the term to be an insult rather than a compliment (only 12%)[13], despite the blatant pro-feminist bias in the media. One reason for this rejection of feminism is its outright hostility to men, something that most women are not

---

maintenance, just 3 percent were men, according to Census figures." (data from 2010). 'Why Do So Few Men Get Alimony?'
http://www.forbes.com/sites/emmajohnson/2014/11/20/why-do-so-few-men-get-alimony

9   'BBC - Why so many young women don't call themselves feminist'
https://www.bbc.com/news/uk-politics-47006912

10   After the Scandinavians and New Zealand:
http://www.sofeminine.co.uk/personal-life/women-s-rights-worldwide-d50167c584739.html

11   'Poll: Few Identify As Feminists, But Most Believe In Equality Of Sexes'.
http://www.huffingtonpost.com/2013/04/16/feminism-poll_n_3094917.html

12   'Feminism may be dead: 72 percent of Americans say they 're not 'feminists' - Washington Times'.
http://www.washingtontimes.com/blog/watercooler/2013/may/1/liberated-72-percent-americans-say-theyre-not-femi

13   Ibid.

prepared to accept – at least at its explicit manifestation. The other reason is that women have begun to realize that the male world, i.e. the world of wage – and compulsory – labor are not as rosy as promised, and that the "traditional" female role may not be so bad after all...

Revisiting our convictions

Feminism has been around for almost two centuries[14] and three "waves". All its initial goals at the institutional level have been met. Women have the right to vote. Their position before the law is not only that of men's equal, they are favorable compared to men, particularly with regard to marriage, divorce, property, and of course child custody. In the Western world, the right to abortion has been won.

And yet women still have a *different* position in society than men. Is it worse? Or could it be *better*? Could it be that this "difference" is to women's advantage? Feminist Germaine Greer holds that their different position is largely their choice: "The old suffragettes ... served their prison term [and] lived on through the years of gradual admission of women into professions which they declined to follow, into parliamentary freedoms which they declined to exercise, into academies which they used more and more as shops where they could take out degrees while waiting to get married..."[15]

This is why we need to re-examine the tenets of "female oppression". This is the topic of the first part of this book in which we examine the various areas in which some claim that women are oppressed. We will see that all the supposed disadvantages of women are essentially tradeoffs against much worse alternatives, and that these tradeoffs benefit the great majority of women, if not all of them.

---

14 Charles Fourier, a Utopian Socialist and French philosopher, is credited with having coined the word 'feminism' in 1837.

15 Greer, Germaine. *The Female Eunuch*. London: Farrar, Straus and Giroux, 1970. Summary.

Felix Valloton: The Rape of Europa (1908)

Part 1: Are Women Oppressed?

Introduction

We have been living for millennia in class societies that oppress the majority of people, both men and women. All the female workers are oppressed due to the exploitation of their working power. Women are forced to pay taxes. Their sons are taken away and sent to war. A woman may be sexually harassed. She risks being socially marginalized if she deviates in her sexual orientation, or if she rejects the standard model of marriage and family. She can be subjected to violence at the hands of riot police, or of a hostile army, in case her country is besieged or occupied by foreign powers. The list is not exhaustive, but you get the idea: there are many aspects of female oppression today – and there were also many in earlier periods in History.

The problem is that *men are oppressed as well*. They have the obligation to join the army and fight in wars in which they might get killed, whether their country wins or loses. If they belong to the working class they need to work in order to survive, because no one is going to support them. They too face social marginalization when sexually deviating from the norm. And the list goes on. Some forms of oppression are the same as those affecting women, while others are different.

Therefore, the question whether women are oppressed has an obvious answer: "yes". But the question worth asking is: are women *more oppressed* than men?

The classic feminist view...

The classic feminist view argues that, apparently, women are the most oppressed. Sometimes it may recognize that men have some disadvantages, but those are supposedly offset by their generally privileged position. For example, men may make up 95% of the prison population, but this is not considered as a strong argument for the disadvantaged position of men when on the other hand almost all the heads of state around the world are men. Similarly, men earn more money at work, so supposedly they are the privileged sex, and yet the number of homeless men is three to four times that of women. And so on.

For any undeniable disadvantage of men, another, relative or irrelevant "advantage" is found. More often than not, this advantage is enjoyed by a small minority, the ruling class. In all other circumstances, men pay dearly for it, with longer working hours, with their health, with worse working and living conditions, and so on.

...and the Postmodern one

There is also a Postmodern opinion which is used as a subterfuge by some modern feminists that says that there is no sense in trying to compare oppressions; we just need to fight to abolish them, each instance taken independently from the other.

Such reasoning would have a point if we were, say, an American scholar discussing the oppression in Tibet and East Timor, issues which are not closely related to our daily lives. But in the case of the sexes, the oppressions are correlated: men's military service would be shortened by half if the female population was drafted as well. The abolition of compulsory alimony, and a legislation for joint custody in case of divorce would be positive measures for men but negative for women. The social expectation for the man to buy dinner and drinks is a handicap for men and a privilege for women. And so on.

The burdens of social life need to be assumed by someone – and the less women take up, the more men must do to pick up the slack.

Rethinking our beliefs

The problem with beliefs is that we forget how we acquire them. The knowledge that led up to them gets lost. Where does the strong conviction that women are oppressed come from?

Firstly, as we have seen, it is a part of the dominant ideology. In all the Western world, the pro-feminist bias in the mainstream media is universal and of massive proportions. For those in the Left, this belief probably comes from the opposite direction: since we trust the ideology of the Left, and since it claims that women are oppressed, that's the way is must be. On a personal level, the fact that women in our social circle might complain, while men maintain a stiff upper lip, also has an influence. And of course, the first woman whose complaints one internalizes is one's mother, who has a vastly greater capacity than one's father to affect the unconscious impressions not only of her daughters, but also of her sons.

The other big problem with beliefs is that they block our thinking, preventing us from examining the counterarguments with an independent eye. Can it be, for instance, that men are more sexually oppressed? "Of course not, everyone knows that women are – end of discussion".

However if we leave emotions towards women aside and try to use cold logic, we must accept that "female oppression" is based on some key positions. If these prove to be false, then we have to at least re-examine our beliefs.

The main arguments for women's oppression have to do with the wage gap, the "double oppression" of women at work and in the house, marriage as an institution of female oppression, violence against women, the preferential upbringing of boys versus girls, and several aspects of the quality of life.

In this part we will examine these arguments one by one, to show that historically, socially and sometimes even logically, they do not add up. For readers with a feminist background the following discussion might be difficult to follow, because it contradicts their deep convictions. But they should try to. "It is the mark of an educated mind to be able to entertain a thought without accepting it" said Aristotle. Feminist Hanna Rosin, who believes that nowadays women are advantaged, characteristically writes, "Once you open your eyes to this possibility, the evidence is all around you."[16]

Chapter 1: Work

Wage gap

The most common argument about female oppression at work has to do with the wage gap.

> "The European Commission defines it as the average difference between men's and women's hourly earnings. It is generally suggested that the wage gap is due to a variety of causes, such as differences in the types of positions held by men and women, differences in the pay of jobs men typically go into as opposed to women, and differences in amount of work experience, and breaks in employment. However there is still debate over whether any of the wage gap is due to explicit discrimination, as well as over the extent to which women and men are forced to make certain choices due to social pressure."[17]

In the US women earn on average 79% of what men do[18]. The feminist view argues that this is due to unfair discrimination against the female sex. However, the available evidence overwhelmingly shows that this is not true. The simple answer is that women have the luxury to choose easier, cleaner and more pleasant jobs than men, because the social pressure to be professionally successful, compared to men, is negligible.

---

16   'The End of Men - Hanna Rosin - The Atlantic'.
     http://www.theatlantic.com/magazine/archive/2010/07/the-end-of-men/308135
17   Wikipedia, Gender Pay Gap. Accessed Mar. 21 2014
     https://en.wikipedia.org/wiki/Gender_pay_gap
18   In 2020. This number is in dispute, but we will generously use it as an upper limit for
     our discussion.

"The raw wage gap data shows that a woman would earn roughly 73.7% to 77% of what a man would earn over their lifetime. However, when controllable variables are accounted for, such as number of children, and the frequency at which unpaid leave is taken, in addition to other factors, the U.S. Department of Labor found in 2008 that the gap can be brought down from 23% to between 4.8% and 7.1%. Furthermore, the United States Government Accountability Office found in 2009 that when accounting for diminishing differences in variables including chosen occupation, education, and experience, the variable wage gap among federal workers can be brought to roughly 1–2%."[19]

If women are paid less for the same work, why don't bosses hire only women? Female unemployment should be nonexistent, or in any case much less than male unemployment, but this is not the case. Warren Farrell is a prominent feminist of the '70s who has become the most respected proponent of men's issues. In his book *Why Men Earn More: The Startling Truth Behind the Pay Gap – and What Women Can Do About It*[20], he identifies 25 different reasons why men earn more.

"I discovered that each of men's choices resulted in men earning more; that each of women's choices resulted in women having more balanced lives – and therefore, usually happier lives. The main finding was that the road to high pay is a toll road: the tolls of working more hours, traveling overnight and weekends, moving to undesirable locations, hazardous jobs, unsanitary jobs, night shifts and so on."

Nevertheless, in several jobs, some of which are quite high status, women earn more than men with similar marital status, education and experience. E.g. "In the United Kingdom, single women 'earn as much on average as single men' and 'women in the middle age groups who remain single earn more than middle-aged single males'"[21], a fact that would not make sense if there was discrimination against women. "The

---

19   Wikipedia, ibid.
20   Farrell, Warren. *Why Men Earn More: The Startling Truth Behind the Pay Gap.* USA: AMACOM (2005).
21   J.R. Shackleton. *Should We Mind the Gap? Gender Pay Differentials and Public Policy.* London: Institute of Economic Affairs, 2008. pp. 29–30.

U.S. Census Bureau found that as early as 1960, never-married women over 45 earned *more* in the workplace than never-married men over 45."[22]

In his book *The War of the Sexes*, feminist Paul Seabright, gives evidence showing a smaller representation of women in highly profitable jobs and the existence of a wage gap, and rejects the hypothesis that this is due to difference in talent. He concludes:

> "The different salary dynamics do not appear to be a result of discrimination against women as such: men and women with identical qualifications who make identical decisions about career interruptions do equally well."[23]

He cites a study about the income of MBAs[24], where

> "As the authors put it: 'The data do not indicate that MBA women lose more than MBA men for taking time out. It appears that everyone is penalized heavily for deviating from the norm.' Instead, the story is one in which the rules for getting ahead emphasize long hours of work, single-minded devotion to the job, and a refusal ever to take a break. MBAs (both men and women) work, on average, sixty hours per week after graduation, with investment bankers averaging a startling seventy-four hours per week. The fact that fewer women want to play by these rules puts women at a disadvantage."[25]

The argument about the wage gap eventually backfires on the feminists that use it. In the best case, it shows that they are ignorant. If not, they are deceptive, since they don't make it clear that the wage gap does not concern the same jobs, but has to do with choosing an easier career. Ultimately, it undermines their position about "female oppression", showing that even when they are given every opportunity from an

22   Farrel, Warren. *The Myth of Male Power.* USA: Finch Publishing (2001). p. 29.
23   Seabright, Paul. *The War of the Sexes: How Conflict and Cooperation Have Shaped Men and Women from Prehistory to the Present.* New Jersey: Princeton University Press (2012). Ch. 6.
24   Bertrand, Marianne, Claudia Goldin, and Lawrence F. Katz. *Dynamics of the Gender Gap for Young Professionals in the Financial and Corporate Sectors.* American Economic Journal: Applied Economics 2: 228–55. (2010).
25   Seabright, The War of the Sexes, Ch. 6.

institutional standpoint, women do not need to work in demanding jobs and therefore do not choose to do so, despite the better pay.

Unemployment

Comparison of men's and women's unemployment is a complex issue. The corresponding unemployment rates are of little use taken in isolation.

The most important observation is that unemployment affects men much more than women. An unemployed man is considered a loser by everyone, be it men or women, and this has dramatic effects on his social life and mental health. When he cannot support a family, it is quite frequent to see his friends and family reject him. An unemployed woman can marry. An unemployed man cannot even have a relationship. As we will see, unemployment of the husband often leads to divorce, while a wife's unemployment does not. And of course, until recently, the woman could be exclusively a housewife, supported by her husband. This happens not infrequently even today. The luxury of being a "housewife" is particularly enjoyed in the upper social strata, where women typically do not work. In the US, "almost 70% of the wives of male executives (vice-president and above) do not hold paid jobs outside the home – not even part time."[26] Even in the lower strata, the social expectations dictate that the man is the main family provider, while the wife provides "supplements".

Unemployed men are therefore under incomparably more pressure than women. But aren't unemployed women more numerous? No. The data from Eurostat[27] for 2012 shows that there is 10.7% unemployment for men as opposed to 10.8% for women. In 2009, male unemployment in Europe was higher than female unemployment. In the US today, more than half of the long-term unemployed (56) are men[28]. In countries hit by the recent economic crisis the picture is similar. In Russia, long-term

---

26   Data from 1987, reported in The Myth of Male Power, p. 29.
27   http://epp.eurostat.ec.europa.eu/statistics_explained/index.php/
     Unemployment_statistics
28   'For men, the future doesn't look too good'.
     http://www.capitolhillblue.com/node/52309

unemployment for men is 2.3% versus 2.1% for women[29]; in the Ukraine, female unemployment is also lower[30]. In OECD[31]countries, long-term unemployment for men is 3.2%, higher than women's, at 3.1%.

Chapter 2: "Double oppression"

Left Feminism, contrary to radical feminism's "patriarchy" ideology, understands at least that most men, as members of the working class, are oppressed. However, it claims that nowadays women are "doubly" oppressed: from wage labor, and from their duties at home. This theory certainly does have elements of truth: the second wave of feminism worsened women's position by exposing them to the world of labor. However, when feminists claims that this constitutes a "double" oppression, they do a double sleight of hand: first, they assume that the oppression of women in labor is approximately equal to men's; and second, they suppose that men don't work at home.

As we have seen, however, the fact is that women are much less oppressed at work than men. They can choose easier, more pleasant jobs with more convenient hours, less overtime, less commuting and other advantages.

On the other hand, men, in addition to their job, are also burdened with household chores, a fact rarely acknowledged. Many men now participate almost equally in "female" housework, cooking, washing the dishes, drying the clothes, etc. Some take it so far as do the ironing. They also pay bills, fill tax returns, deal with State bureaucracy, take the children to school. Almost all of them do the "male" chores alone: they repair and paint the house, the furniture, the lighting fixtures, etc., they fix the car and act as the family chauffeur, driving around the children or

---

29   http://www.oecdbetterlifeindex.org/countries/russian-federation
30   'Ukraine: A land of Economic Insecurity'. Accessed Nov. 3, 2014.
      http://www.ilo.org/public/english/protection/ses/info/database/ukraine.htm
31   http://www.oecdbetterlifeindex.org/topics/jobs

even the mother-in-law, and they are expected to carry the heavy loads while shopping and when moving house. Sure, some of these jobs only need to be done once a week or once a month, as opposed, say, to daily cooking; but when you need to do 6-7 different jobs, it's easy to fill each day of the week.

The above is not just a literary discussion, but the result of surveys. In research published in *USA Today* in 2013[32] the details are as follows:

Table 1: Work hours for women and men, USA.

Work hours	Paid work	Home	Total
Women 1965	8	32	40
Women 2011	21	18	39
Men 1965	42	4	46
Men 2011	37	10	47

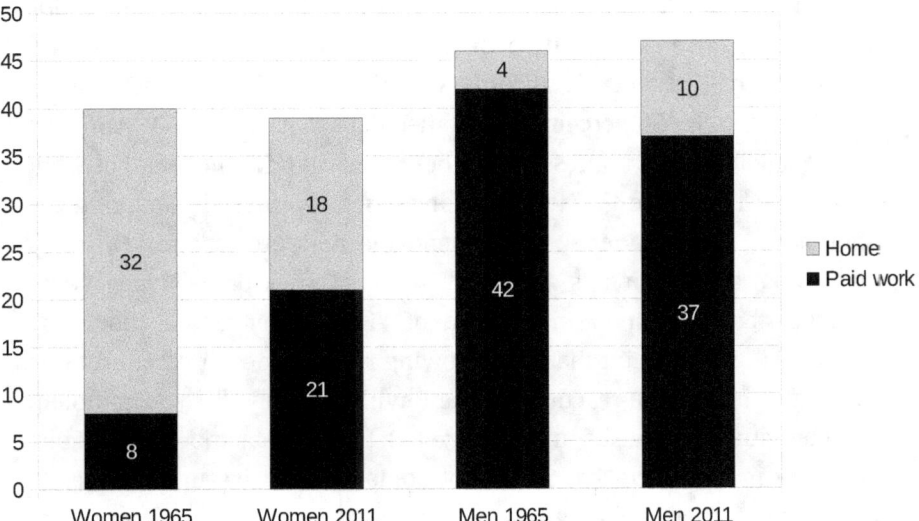

The figures above show that from 1965 to 2011 the total female labor time, in home and outside work, has *decreased* by an hour, while for men it has *increased* by an hour. Furthermore, women now work much longer

32 'Men vs. women: How much time spent on kids, job, chores?'
http://www.usatoday.com/story/news/nation/2013/03/14/men-women-work-time/
1983271

hours in paid jobs than before.

These findings are compatible with the following reading:

One of the ways the system tried to overcome the economic crisis of the '70s was to drive women to work, so that it could extract more surplus value. Feminism's quest for women's economic independence was, in that period, in accordance with systemic needs. Tellingly, the Equal Pay Act was signed into law in 1963: it preceded the feminist movement, rather than being its outcome. At the same time, there was a shift in the economy from the dirty, harsh and unhealthy industrial jobs to the cleaner, easier and healthier jobs in the services sector. The wage reduction of the (until then, male) workers, was another pressing factor for the family budget. All of the above resulted in women's exodus from the house.

The irony is that almost 40 years later, this has resulted in women working fewer hours (39 instead of 40), while men work longer hours (47 instead of 46). Nevertheless, it seems that women were left short-changed: the difference in life expectancy, where they were traditionally way ahead of men, *decreased* in favor of men. The decrease is quite significant too: by 50 percent (for detailed data, see Chapter 7). Women's gain of one hour of work less, does not compensate for the fact that work *outside* the house, i.e. harder work, increased. Women, by entering the labor force, are experiencing first-hand the pressure that for so many years was only a man's reality. That is why women were never wholeheartedly given to the pursuit of "independence". It should be embarrassing to the Left that the following remark doesn't come from its own ranks, but from a reactionary like Phyllis Schlafly: "If you complain about servitude to a husband, servitude to a boss will be more intolerable. Everyone in the world has a boss of some kind."[33] It's much easier to have a harmonious relationship with a husband than with a boss, she concludes.

---

33   Schlafly, Phillis. *Feminist Fantasies*. USA: Spence Publishing Company (2013).

Chapter 3: Family and relationships

Contrary to Feminist assertions, family is an institution that suits women, much more than it suits men. It is much easier for a woman to find happiness and meaning in life in her family role, than it is for a man.

Before the '70s

We will begin by examining the family before the 1970s. Compared to today, things then were simple: the man worked, and the woman took care of the house. Regarding quantity, we already mentioned that women always worked fewer hours. Regarding "quality", i.e. how *hard* the housework is, consider this scenario: you are a student, apparently bored with the idea of doing tedious and uninteresting housework, so the house is a mess. And then, comes the exams season! You need to study Maths or Pathology or International Law. Then you suddenly realize that doing the dishes is not so boring at all, on the contrary, this refreshing play with soap can prove rather pleasant. Mopping becomes a healthy and enjoyable workout. And hanging clothes reveals its therapeutic dimension, one that had eluded you until now. If you need to study Calculus III, you might even feel like hand-washing your underpants.

Women's views regarding the housework was not unlike this scenario. Rather than work, be responsible for the family, have a boss over her head, and be exposed to the rain, the wind and the hot sun, house"work" was always an incomparably preferable option. While her husband worked in real, i.e. unpleasant work, the middle-class housewife killed time with worthless occupations such as embroidery, somewhat like medieval princesses – occupations that could disguise her idleness, bestowing her an arty honorary title. With the invention of the washing machine and other house appliances, the whole debate about "housework" in the past decades has become almost meaningless: a family of four needs, at most, two hours of housework a day.

The tendency of women to avoid real work through their role as homemakers is backed up by recent data. The participation of women in the labor market reached its peak in the US in 1999. The 2000 millennium brought along the economic crisis, which was very effective in demolishing the illusions of self-fulfillment through work. As a result, women started to return home. "The number of women age 20 and older not in the labor pool ... has soared from 40 million in 2000 to nearly 49 million [in 2013]... The participation rate of women in the workplace has dropped from a high of 60.7 percent in 1999 to 58.8 percent [in 2013]."[34] What's more, studies have found that it's the graduates of elite institutions i.e. those that have the most options in life, that have quit jobs at a greater rate. "For feminists, the drop-out trend undermines their argument that women – even our most accomplished and best educated – are victims of discrimination."[35] (Incidentally, this timeless tendency of women avoiding work even when they have received the necessary education, has been responsible for the exclusion of women from higher education in the past. If a society needs doctors and can train only a limited number of students, it needs to be sure that they will indeed work, so that the resources spent on their education are put to good use[36].)

The opportunity to be a housewife was so scandalously advantageous that Simone de Beauvoir wrote in 1975: "No woman should be authorized to stay at home and raise her children. Society should be totally different. Women should not have that choice, precisely because if there is such a choice, too many women will make that one."[37]

So what did the man contribute to the family? His labor force, in case he was a lower-class worker, and small or greater property if he belonged to a higher class. What did the woman contribute to the family? Basically, *her sexual availability*.

In those times, virginity was a woman's treasure. The taboo of virginity aimed at sexually asphyxiating men. Only under that condition could

---

34   'Why Women Are Leaving the Workforce In Record Numbers | The Fiscal Times'. http://www.thefiscaltimes.com/Columns/2013/04/17/Why-Women-Are-Leaving-the-Workforce-in-Record-Numbers.

35   Ibid.

36   For more about the issue see Baumeister, Roy F. *Is There Anything Good About Men?: How Cultures Flourish by Exploiting Men*, USA: Oxford University Press (2010). p. 207-210.

37   "Sex, Society, and the Female Dilemma," Saturday Review, June 14, 1975.

men be compelled to support a woman for the rest of their life, and that was to meet their basic sexual (and, as they believed, their emotional) needs.

The dominant narrative holds that the purpose of the family was so that men could ensure the paternity of their children. To the extent that this was a purpose, it was only a minor one. Take, for instance, 100 men from any historical period, and give them two options: a) free sex throughout their life, with a variety of attractive women, but with unknown paternity, or b) paternity certainty, but strict monogamy forever. What would the score be? We will have more to say about that later[38], quoting related historical examples.

A special reference to the families in the lower social classes, workers and farmers, is perhaps in order. In contrast with the upper classes, women in these lower strata often worked outside the house. We already mentioned that they worked less, and that their work was easier than men's. But that was not their most important benefit. It was the waiver of *responsibility*. Even when they did relatively harsh agricultural work that was similar to men's, the responsibility of the survival of the family fell on the man's shoulders. The penalty for the man who failed to "support his family" was shame and social ostracism, especially in small communities. When urbanization made this customary social control inefficient, and under pressure from women "reformists", the US and the UK instituted draconian laws against those who were marked "home slackers". "Not just jail but jail with hard labor was the reward for indigence"[39].

Dowry

Wasn't it a disadvantage of women that in order to marry they often needed to have a dowry? Well, it would be if they were obliged to gather it themselves. Dowry was an aid from the father of the bride, that until then was responsible for supporting her, to the new man who would undertake this heavy burden. If the father had died, the duty to

---

38   See the section "Paternity certainty and jealousy" in the 4th Part of the book, p.172.

39   Moxon, Steve. *The Woman Racket: The new science explaining how the sexes relate at work, at play and in society.* UK: Imprint Academic (2008). p. 125.

accumulate it fell on the brother. In the custom of dowry the standard pattern of the relationship between the sexes clearly stands out: men have extra burdens, while women have extra privileges.

The myth of the unhappy marriage

There is a classic myth regarding the traditional family that needs to be dissolved. The woman was supposedly forced to marry whomever her father had selected for her, and she then spent her life with someone she did not love, living miserably.

The above cliché is so far from reality that it is only good as a scenario for a third-world film drama.

For example, in India, 95% of marriages are arranged, and the divorce rate is among the lowest in the world. The couple's opinion is taken into account, and the combination of choice and sound guidance leads to arranged marriages in India being better than Western marriages with regard to longevity, satisfaction, and love. "Indeed, the love experienced by Indian couples in arranged marriages appears to be even more robust than the love people experience in 'love marriages.'"[40] The researchers used the "Rubin Love Scale, which gauges intense, romantic, Western-style love.... Love in the arranged marriages they examined started out low and gradually increased, surpassing the love in the so-called love marriage in about five years. Ten years into the marriage, the love was nearly twice as strong."

The reality was that rather than fathers, it was always the mothers that made the match. As old women, they knew. The marriages lasted, they had "love" (we will discuss what that means later on[41]), and were much happier than today. Instead of being oppressed in marriage, women easily found happiness, as much as they could, and certainly much more than the men: in that period, women scored higher than men in tests measuring happiness (data are presented further down).

---

40   Horstman, Judith. *The Scientific American Book of Love, Sex and the Brain: The Neuroscience of How, When, Why and Who we Love.* San Francisco: Joeesy-Bass (2012). Ch. 6.
41   See p. 110 and p. 164.

Today

From the decade of the '70s onwards, women's roles include working outside the house. But unlike men, women's work is optional and can be part-time or intermittent, without resulting in the woman feeling useless and unworthy.

The era that introduced women in the labor market demonstrated the imbalance that always existed between men's and women's burdens: even today, when women work and are financially independent, they still choose men that earn more than thy do. It's a consequence of the sexual imbalance between the two genders: the female sexual availability has an intrinsic value, and women demand from the man to match this value, either with his job or his property.

What novelty the new era has brought is, of course, divorce. In the Western world, divorce rates are huge. The majority of these, about 70%, are initiated by the woman[42]. Of course, a man losing his job is a major factor in divorce cases, while "a woman's employment status has no effect on the likelihood that her husband will opt to leave the marriage."[43] For all their supposed emotionalism and sensitivity, it is shocking with what degree of cynicism women shove the "companion of their life" and father of their children out of doors and sue him for child support when he becomes unemployed. They can then live an "independent" life, not having to support a slacker. Sex they can easily get from the abundance of sex-hungry men. "Half of women have a fall-back partner on standby who has always fancied them", and furthermore "married women are more likely have a Plan B in the background than those who are just in a relationship."[44] The children will be raised together with grandma, and the mother will cover her emotional needs by becoming an emotional vampire over them.

---

42 'Do Men or Women File for Divorce More Often? | Psychology Today'. http://www.psychologytoday.com/blog/homo-consumericus/201311/do-men-or-women-file-divorce-more-often

43 "PsychCentral - Male Unemployment Increases Risk of Divorce" http://psychcentral.com/news/2011/06/22/male-unemployment-increases-risk-of-divorce/27142.html

44 'HALF of women have a fall-back partner on standby who has always fancied them, in case their current relationship turns sour | Daily Mail Online'. http://www.dailymail.co.uk/femail/article-2769593/HALF-women-fall-partner-standby-fancied-case-current-relationship-turns-sour.html

There is, however, a force that opposes the exodus of women from the frame and the protection of the family – the protection, that is, that her husband provides. With families falling apart and women increasingly entering the labor market full time, there has been, since the '70s and for the first time in history a decrease in the difference in life expectancy between women and men, as mentioned earlier. Women through work discover cardiovascular diseases, strokes and cancers that until recently were a "privilege" of her "oppressor" husband.

Procreation

If a man wants to have children, he discovers that he has no reproductive rights whatsoever. A woman can do as she pleases:

a. *Have children with a husband.*

In this case, the main financial burden falls on the man, while the woman is more free to enjoy time with her children, and connect emotionally with them. That, for better of worse, helps in the next case:

b. *Divorce him and keep the children.*

The worldwide rates of child custody awarded to women are overwhelming[45]. In the US, it is around 85%[46]. Dads are left with the obligation to pay for child support, to pay for the mortgage of the house in which they no longer live, and in which now their ex lives with the children and the new boyfriend. In addition, spurned dads have to pay for all the costs of dating in the search of a new partner. It's a situation that can easily lead to burn-out. Despite the stereotype of the tough and resilient man, modern science has recognized that men are more susceptible to stress.

c. *Marry someone who will support her children, and have children by another.*

---

45   In some western countries this is starting to change. E.g. in Denmark and Holland, there is a tendency towards joint custody 50-50, but in practice the arrangements still end up favoring the women.

46   "The Spearhead - The bias against fathers in U.S. custody and child support" http://www.the-spearhead.com/2011/08/22/the-bias-against-u-s-fathers-in-custody-and-child-support

Until recently, men could not verify the paternity of their children. This issue might sound as if it concerned only a few. However, "DNA fingerprinting studies reveal that roughly 12 percent of women get pregnant by men other than their long-term mates."[47] Indeed, given that women are attracted and "typically have affairs with men who are higher in status than their husbands"[48], working class women are much more likely to cheat on their hard working husband: In a study in "block of flats in Liverpool", researchers found that "fewer than four in every five people were the sons of their ostensible fathers"[49] (that is twice the standard rate). "In case this had something to do with Liverpool, they did the same tests in southern England and got the same result."

d. Have children "on her own".

In this case, in many countries the State takes up the role of the provider husband: the woman gets benefits as a single mother. In the UK the situation is so advantageous that a "Jobless mum advise[d] her daughter, 19, to get pregnant – for an easy life on benefits"[50]. The benefits are based on a taxation that burdens working men more, despite the fact that the women in question had summarily rejected them as unfit mates[51].

The women usually sue the naive biological father of their children for support, and this support is usually awarded. There is a widespread sympathy towards "single mothers" who are viewed as wronged creatures worthy of compassion and support. And without doubt, some of them do make heroic efforts in adverse conditions. That is not the general picture, though. A study in Michigan found that "49 percent of *all* child abuse cases are committed by single mothers"[52].

---

47   Meston, Cindy M, and Buss, David M. *Why Women Have Sex: Women Reveal the Truth About Their Sex Lives, from Adventure to Revenge (and Everything in Between)*. USA: St. Martin's Griffin (2010). Ch. 1.

48   Buss, David M. *The Evolution of Desire: Strategies of Human Mating*. USA, Basic Books (2003). p. 91.

49   Riddley, Matt. *The Red Queen: Sex and the Evolution of Human Nature*. UK: Penguin Books (1993). p. 226.

50   'Jobless mum advises daughter to get pregnant for easy life on benefits | Daily Mail Online'. http //www.dailymail.co.uk/news/article-2605677/Mother-two-never-worked-encouraged-daughter-pregnant-council-house-easy-life-benefits.html

51   'He who pays the piper, calls the tune. Or does he?'. http://www.avoiceformen.com/feminism/government-tyranny/he-who-pays-the-piper-calls-the-tune-or-does-he

52   Joan Ditson and Sharon Shay, "A Study of Child Abuse in Lansing, Michigan,"

In all cases, it is customary that the woman polices the child's relationship with the father. There is a general agreement about the value of the "mother" for the child, and a general uneasiness regarding the emotional role of the father, that confuses even men themselves and results in their not asserting their paternal rights. And this despite recent studies that show that the contribution of the father is essential for the mental balance and well-being of the child[53].

Social mobility, marrying up

While a man needs to work hard and get very lucky to achieve social advancement, women get it for free, through marriage. The overwhelming majority marries up, at least a notch. The most attractive women in any social class take it for granted that they will socially ascend through marriage. Only a few marry someone at their social level, while even fewer marry someone socially beneath them[54].

Social correspondence of Women-Men in marriage:
"Invisible" men, unmarriageable women

The above illustration schematically shows the resulting situation. Men

---

Child Abuse and Neglect, 8 (1984).

53   Gottman, John with Declaire, Joan. *Raising an Emotionally Intelligent Child: The Heart of Parenting*, USA: Simon & Schuster Paperbacks (1997). Ch. 6.

54   In the case of women of higher education that marry a man of lower, 58% of them earn less money than him. Consequently, in the US in 2012, only 8.2% of women married someone with both an inferior education and less income.
   "When we look at the newlywed women who married someone with less education, we find that a majority of these women actually "married up."", as the following article characteristically puts it:
   'Record share of wives are more educated than their husbands | Pew Research Center'. http://www.pewresearch.org/fact-tank/2014/02/12/record-share-of-wives-are-more-educated-than-their-husbands

in the bottom of society remain in anonymous obscurity, they are "invisible". The are shunned by all women, even those socially at their level. These "invisible" men are often compelled to take desperate risks in order to climb the social ladder, ending up in jail, drugs, or violence. On the other end, many women of the higher classes "continue to shun marrying 'down' in terms of education, job prestige and income"[55], as is typical for a female. Given that "men are relatively indifferent to women's socioeconomic status when choosing partners"[56], the men socially corresponding to them are taken by women of lower social classes that are simply more attractive.

The conclusion is that women have something more than just their "working power". Women are never proletarians. As feminist Silvia Federici aptly observes in *Caliban and the Witch*, "the body has been for women in capitalist society what the factory has been for male waged workers"[57]. With this she means the means of production (i.e. the reproduction of the working class) and oppression. However, while no worker has control over the factory he works in, women do have control of their bodies. To the extent that they exercise that control, they are small capitalists. Women are the petty bourgeoisie of humanity.

A shocking study[58] shows how easy upward social mobility is for girls – and how hopelessly difficult it is for boys. The title of the article is characteristic: "For Boys, Moving to a Wealthier Neighborhood Is as

---

55 Townsend, John Marshal. *What Women Want – What Men Want: Why the Sexes Still See Love and Commitment So Differently*, New York: Oxford University Press (1998). p. 84.

56 Ibid.

57 Federici, Sylvia. *Caliban and the Witch: Women, The Body and Primitive Accumulation.* New York: Autonomedia (2004), p. 16.
"the body has been for women in capitalist society what the factory has been for male waged workers: the primary ground of their exploitation and resistance, as the female body has been appropriated by the state and men and forced to function as a means for the reproduction and accumulation of labor." The writer, being a feminist, underlines the dimension of the oppression of the female reproductive capacity, underestimating the degree of control that women excercise over it. Elsewhere, she appears to have half-understood that, accepting that "The female body is the big stumbling block that capital has not mannaged to overcome" - as the only means of procreation.

58 Kessler RC et al. *Associations of housing mobility interventions for children in high-poverty neighborhoods with subsequent mental disorders during adolescence.* JAMA. 2014;311(9):937-948.
http://jama.jamanetwork.com/article.aspx?articleid=1835504

Traumatic as Going to War"[59]. The researchers examined the results of programs that encouraged young people to move from poor neighborhoods, and found that "boys who move into more affluent neighborhoods report higher rates of depression and conduct disorder than their female peers." The basic reason is that poor boys "were coded as these juvenile delinquents ... whereas with the girls, it was exactly the opposite. They were embraced by the community – 'you poor little disadvantaged thing, let me help you.'"

Follow-up interviews a decade later showed boys having "higher proportions of major depression, post traumatic stress disorder, and conduct disorder than boys within the control group – rates of PTSD comparable to those of combat soldiers." Girls, on the contrary, reported substantially better health than those that stayed in poor neighborhoods.

Sex

There are no brothels for women. It is a ridiculous concept. If a woman wants to have sex, all she has to do is get out of the house. Among the girls, it is a standard joke when someone complains about the lack of sex, to tell her "why don't you get out and knock on a couple of doors?" Sex itself is so much a given for women, that it's not a big deal. A woman will not sleep with an acceptable man that will cross her way: such men are countless, and there is no challenge in it. She will sleep with the best she can find.

The free buffet

Remember the first time you were at a hotel with a free buffet? On the first day, you fill up your plate with everything and eat until you burst. Since you cannot calculate the correct quantity of food, you take too much food and leave half of it uneaten. On the second day you still eat untill you feel like bursting. Now, you fill your plate with as much as you want, but no more. From the third day onwards, the sense of inflation in

---

59 'Boys report PTSD when they move to richer neighborhoods | New Republic'.
    http://www.newrepublic.com/article/116886/boys-report-ptsd-when-they-move-
    richer-neighborhoods

your stomach begins to bother you. You now leave bread-like food aside, and focus on healthier food. After a week or so, you eat only the best there is, shrimps, fish, fillet, in normal quantities, and you walk past the pasta without looking back.

Sex is like a free buffet for women. There are so many available men out there, and they have so many options that apparently they will choose "the best one". Why settle for a second-rate man? Schematically, this could be summarized thus:

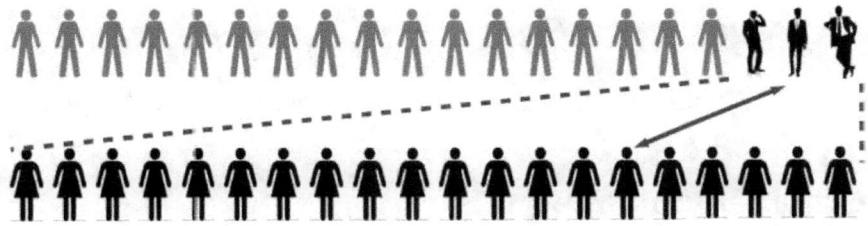

Correspondence of women-men in sex:
Men getting incdequate sex are much more than those that get adequate sex

The situation for the "stronger sex" is not so rosy. The burning issue for men is to find any minimally acceptable woman to relieve their sexual hunger.

The problems of the two sexes are of a different order: What is a given for women, and allows them to take their tastes and wishes further, i.e. a good level of sexual opportunities, becomes a requirement for men, and blocks them and consumes their energy. Women may complain that they are unhappy because they cannot find someone like Brad Pitt to make wild sex to them and love them truly, while shunning the Average Frustrated Chump that desires them. But that chump is much worse off, having no sexual outlet at all...

Here is a business idea: a website where 40 and 50 year-old non-rich men can advertise their sexual availability, without any prospect of marriage, strictly for casual sex with younger 20 and 30 year-old women. Sounds ridiculous? That's because it *is*. But just reverse the sexes, and you are back into reality. There are websites where older women put ads like "if you are young, handsome, athletic, and willing to satisfy me, contact me…”. The writer, despite extensive research, could not find similar sites for men. (If you spot one, please tell him.)

Sex is the means by which women exercise their power. In the 2nd Part of this book, where we deal with Biology, we will extensively examine why men are the most sexually oppressed sex.

Chapter 4: Violence

Another feminist myth is that women are the biggest victims of violence.

Criminal Violance

Criminal violence overwhelmingly befalls on men. Men are generally twice as likely to be victims of *violent* crimes[60]. If we take the most serious crime of all, murder, the probability increases threefold. It is true that most of the perpetrators are also men, but that does not compensate for the fact that if you are born a man you are much more likely to face violence, while if you are a woman you can be more at peace. Feminists, with their typical double logic, tend to not consider violence as a sign of oppression of men because the perpetrators are men, while at the same time considering, for example, female genital mutilation, as a proof of female oppression even though those performing it are exclusively women.

Suicide

With regards to suicide, the situation is even worse for the "stronger sex". "In the United States, the male-to-female suicide death ratio varies between 3:1 to 10:1."[61] In all the countries of the world, with the exception of China, there are more male suicides than female ones – up

---

60   Farrell, The Myth of Male Power, p. 32.
61   Wikipedia, Gender Differences in Suicide, Accessed 20 Jan. 2015,
       https://en.wikipedia.org/wiki/Gender_differences_in_suicide

to 6 times more. And the lower classes have greater suicide rates than the most privileged ones[62]. Therefore, the higher male suicide rates are incompatible with a perception of men as the privileged sex.

War

"Women have always been the primary victims of war. Women lose their husbands, their fathers, their sons in combat..." – Hillary Clinton[63]

It should be obvious that men are the biggest victims of war. However, the cynical gynocentrism of our era denies even that. The death of a man is considered a lesser evil than the loss it creates for his wife. If things were really so, the solution for women would be clear: to go to war themselves. For every woman killed, a husband, father, son, would be saved... *Hic Rhodus, hic salta.*

Furthermore, the myth that men support war while women generally oppose it is not confirmed by research. Women's support for wars is indeed lesser, but comparable to men's, differing about 9%[64]. The unsubstantiated belief of feminists that the world would be more peaceful if it were ruled by women has already been proved wrong. In the research of Oeindrila Dube and S. P. Harish, covering five centuries of European history (15th-20th), queens were found to be 27% more aggressive, i.e. more likely to start a war, than kings[65].

An impressive case of female support to war emerged in the most horrible, until then, war of mankind, the First World War. In the infamous White Feather Campaign, women in Britain gave a white feather, a symbol of cowardice, to those men they found wearing civilian clothes.

62   Kreitman, Norman el at. "Association of age and social class with suicide among men in Great Britain", Journal of Epidemiology and Community Health 1991; 45: 195-202.

63   *Conference on domestic violence in San Salvador, El Salvador (17 November 1998).* Speech is available on http://clinton3.nara.gov/WH/EOP/First_Lady/html/generalspeeches/1998/19981117.html

64   Clemens, Ben. *Men and Women's Support For War: Accounting for the gender gap in public opinion.* E-International Relations, Jan 19 2012. http://www.e-ir.info/2012/01/19/men-and-womens-support-for-war-accounting-for-the-gender-gap-in-public-opinion

65   Dube, Oeindrila, Harish, S.P. *Queens.* Journal of Political Economy V.128 N.7, University of Chicago, June 2020.

in order to humiliate them and send them to war. The campaign was so successful that it created a problem for the government, as officials in critical positions were forced to enlist in the army. It had to issue special signals for the staff, as well as for veterans who were demobilized due to injuries, so as not to be harassed. This story has highlighted a phenomenon that has since been repeated on several occasions: the striking accord of women standing at the far ends of the ideological spectrum, i.e. "traditional" women and feminists, when it comes to male sacrifice. Both Humphrey Ward, president of the National Organization of Women Against Voting, and Emmeline Pankhurst, leader of the Suffragettes, enthusiastically participated and encouraged their followers in action.

Corporal punishment

Regarding corporal punishment, there is no denying that boys get beat up much more than girls. By their parents, as well as by their teachers, when this is allowed. In many countries, corporal punishment for girls is officially forbidden, while boys' is not[66]. In any case, boys' punishment for the same misdeed is harsher than girls' by several orders of magnitude. And beating is not something that belongs to the past: a 2000 US research[67] found that 61% consider it an acceptable punishment, while 37% consider it acceptable even for children under 2 years old. The practice is still applied in schools even in the US, not only in the third world, where it is common.

The view that beating is fit for boys while not for girls is widespread. Let's look at a modern example, the popular tablet app Talking Tom. Basic ways of interacting with the app's male cat is to hit his foot, in which case he screams and hops, to punch him in the belly, when he coughs and puffs, and to knock him on the forehead, when he shouts "awww!". If you hit him many times, he is knocked out with birds fluttering around his head. This is supposed to be funny, and you should

---

66   Benatar, David. *The Second Sexism: Discrimination Against Men and Boys*. USA: Wiley-Blackwell (2012). Chapter "Corporal Punishment".
67   'Survey Gives Children Something to Cry About - TIME'. http://content.time.com/time/nation/article/0,8599,56808,00.html

lol. In the corresponding app Talking Angela with a *female* cat, the interactions are not hits but teases. "That's not tickling!" Angela scolds you. Hitting her in the nose results in a sneeze, as if you had tickled her, while if you insist on hitting her on her head and she falls down, an angry dog-cop appears on the screen, waving his club and growling at you menacingly...

The Hollywood movie industry is full of movies where violence against men is trivialized. A woman's murder is a dramatic event, often calling for merciless revenge. The deaths of dozens of men are presented as a fact of minor importance, up to the point of becoming a subject of ridicule[68]. You may remember the scene from Indiana Jones, where a menacing guy with a cleaver crosses Indiana's path, and Indiana shoots him casually with his pistol. Can you remember any scene in a movie where a woman is executed so summarily?

Judicial system

Worldwide, the judicial system is responsible for the exercise of legalized violence against the citizens who break the law. In the more civilized countries, this violence is limited to the deprivation of freedom by imprisonment. But in countries like China, North Korea, Iran, Yemen and the US, it can even be the death penalty. Given that the judicial system is part of the hard core of the system, the way the courts treat each sex is indicative of the system's overall attitude towards the sexes. Let's look at some typical cases:

24-year-old British citizen Ronnie Lee suffered an unprovoked attack from 21 year old Yasmin T. She smashed a glass on his left eye socket. If it had been "a couple of millimeters" closer to the eye, he would have lost it. Yasmin T. had a record of seventeen (17) previous convictions for assault. She was released on parole[69].

30-year-old American former teacher Jessica H. admitted to having sex

---

68 Farrell, *The Myth of Male Power.* p. 226.
69 'Yasmin T. victim disgusted she walked free | Mail Online'.
     http://www.dailymail.co.uk/news/article-2726219/Yasmin-Thomas-victim-disgusted-walked-free.html

with two underage boys with special needs. In the US, sex with minors is considered as statutory rape. She was sentenced to three days in jail[70].

Judy N. from N. Carolina shot her husband in the head while he slept. She claimed that she had been abused. Although convicted, the governor commuted her sentence, and she served a total of only two months in prison[71].

In all of these cases, the offenders were women and the victims men. If the sexes had been reversed, the punishment would be harsher by several orders of magnitude – and in the last case it would probably have ended with the death penalty. In the US, 98.9% of those put to death are men, and the worldwide percentage is even higher[72].

The case of Billy and Lana H., a couple, is characteristic of the bias of the judicial system[73]. They let their 6-months-old daughter in a locked car and then they took drugs. The baby almost died from asphyxiation. While they were both convicted for the same offense, the man was sentenced to 4 years in prison, while the woman walked free on parole, "to care for the baby".

"Many studies have found that females are likely to be treated more leniently than males at sentencing"[74]. And sentencing is only one of the many parameters we need to examine. "There are various decisional nodes in the criminal justice system. These include decisions whether to arrest, whether to prosecute, whether to allow pre-trial release, whether to accept a plea bargain, whether to convict, what sentence to impose, whether to grant parole and whether to commute a sentence."[75] In comparative studies, it has been found that for the same offenses, women were less likely to get arrested, less likely to be held in custody, and

---

70   'Mom Who Had Sex With Two Special Needs Teens Gets Three Days In Jail | Liberty Viral'. http://libertyviral.com/mom-who-had-sex-with-two-special-needs-teens-gets-three-days-in-jail
71   Farrell, The Myth Of Male Power, p. 190.
72   Benatar, David. *The Second Sexism: Discrimination Against Men and Boys*. UK: Wiley-Blackwell (2012). Part 2.
73   'Parents Convicted Of The Same Crime - Male Gets Jail, Female Gets Off | The Libertarian Republic'. http://thelibertarianrepublic.com/parents-convicted-crime-male-gets-jail-female-gets
74   Benatar, The Second Sexism.
75   Benatar, The Second Sexism.

"were advantaged at every stage of decision about pre-trial release".

So the degree of violence against men is much greater. Feminists and the media, however, emphasize violence against women more, focusing on rape and family violence, which are supposed to be problems that only afflict women. But this is not so.

Rape

The Feminist movement of the '70s argued that the issue in rape was not sex, but violence. Despite this, the term today has broadened to include cases that are at least in a "gray" zone, one that does not involve violence. In the US, for some age ranges, 97% of rape cases are so-called "date rapes"[76]. The legislation is so biased in favor of women, that any woman can at any time regret having sex, decide that she was raped, and persecute a man, fearing no reprisals from the law. As a result, the false rape allegations now account for an unbelievable 40% to 80% of the reported cases, much more than false allegations for other offenses, that range around 2%[77].

And the consequences of that situation are dire. "Following pressure from feminist groups, the Western Australian parliament in 1985 dramatically amended the law relating to rape, first by changing the term rape to sexual assault and then greatly widening the definition of what could be classed as sexual assault."[78] Kevin Ibbs was one of the first to be charged under the new law. While he was having consensual sex with a woman, and when approaching ejaculation, the woman (claimed that she) withdrew consent, and accused him of rape. "The judge found that Ibbs had continued sexual intercourse for about thirty seconds without consent (for which he was later dubbed the 30-second rapist)", and sentenced him to 4 years in prison. He served 6 months. It was finally revealed that the woman who accused him and his wife had plotted to

---

76   Suzanne S. Ageton, Sexual Assault Among Adolescents, Lexington, MA, Health, 1983, p. 155. Referred in Van Creveld, Martin. *The Privileged Sex*. Israel: DLVC Enterprises (2013).

77   Moxon, The Woman Racket, ch. 11.

78   'Australian News Comentary - The diabolical episode of the 30-second rapist'. http://australian-news.net/articles/view.php?id=142

trap him and drive him out of their common house. It took him 14 years to clear his name. Describing how he felt about his acquittal, he said:

> "There is no feeling. I don't know how I'm supposed to feel. I've been exonerated but I'm not jumping up and down for joy. To coin a phrase that I've said for a long time, I'm the original living dead – the tissue on the outside's alive but there's nothing inside. That's it. It's gone for that long that the poison's just eaten it away.... Whenever there's a rape anywhere, you're waiting for the knock on the door. Please explain where you were. I've had the task force come through and luckily I was living with my Uncle and he said where I was.... I haven't seen my daughter for 14 years."[79]

A few years later, Kevin Ibbs committed suicide.

The fear of rape

Apparently no one argues that rape is not a problem. It is just an infinitely smaller problem than the dimensions it is given. Contrary to the widely held view, rape is not necessarily a traumatic experience. Gillian Mezzey, in her review of the related research, concluded that "Even if depression does occur following rape, it lasts on average only two to four months, even including for those who undergo a 'compounded reaction' because of prior psychological or serious medical problems."[80]

The results of an American research are truly shocking for the majority of men, who consider unthinkable to rape a woman under any circumstances:

> "In a study of American students published in 1982, it was found that girls who were exposed to an attempt at date rape were three times *more* likely to resume their relationship with the man concerned if his attempt *succeeded* than if it failed.... [I]f the man succeeded in forcing intercourse, nearly half (40 per cent) later resumed their relationship with him... If he failed, then nearly nine out of every ten of the women (87 per cent) refused to have any more to do

---

79   'ABC Australia - PM - WA man acquitted of rape'.
     http://www.abc.net.au/pm/stories/s265381.htm
80   Moxon, The Woman Racket, ch.11, citing Mezey, Gillian (1985) Rape –
     victimological and psychiatric aspects. The Journal of Hospital Medicine (UK).

with him..."[81]

Anyone oblivious to the fundamental female attraction to male dominance would find the above female preference for "successful" "rapes" as opposed to "failed" ones, completely incomprehensible.

On the other hand, almost all women will claim that they fear rape. What they really fear is the small percentage of forcible rape, that is perpetrated by an unknown (and unattractive) man. What are the causes of this fear? Its extent is not justified statistically. It does not come from some paranoia[82], because the percentages of paranoids in the female population are not so large to justify it[83]. We will explain the reasons later[84].

The data

The exact rates of women's rape are extremely difficult to define, and rape's changing and widening definition is only one of the difficulties involved in quantifying rape cases. Some feminists argue that half of women will be raped in their lifetime. This means that the average man would know hundreds of raped women, which is quite doubtful. Independent studies give much lower rates, one in fifty in the US. In Europe the rates are seven times lower[85]. Christina Hoff Sommers, despite her extensive investigation in *Who Stole Feminism*, was unable to settle on a number. However, she does note the following:

> "According to Stephen Donaldson, president of Stop Prison Rape, more than 290,000 male prisoners are assaulted each year.... [He] has calculated that there may be as many as 45,000 rapes every day in our prison population of 1.2 million men.... If he is anywhere near right, the incidence

81 Baker, Robin. *Sperm Wars: Infidelity, Sexual Conflict and Other Bedroom Battles.* London: Fourth Estate (1996). p.250.

82 Reading about the problems that men have when they walk on the pavement behind a woman, someone could dispute that.
http://np.reddit.com/r/funny/comments/1zzzjq/apparently_guys_really_do_feel_selfc onscious

83 However, an example of a clearly paranoid view is that every sexual penetration is rape, a view that is discussed as logical, if extreme, in feminist circles.

84 See the conclusion Chapter 22: The sexual double standard, p. 133.

85 Hoff Sommers, Christina. *Who Stole Feminism: How Women Have Betrayed Women.* USA: Simon & Schuster (1994). p. 223.

of male rape would be as high or higher than that of female rape."[86]

Inflating the data

Let's look at a specific report about women's rapes, in order to have a picture of the general unreliability that characterizes them.

In *RapeCrisis England and Wales*, we read:[87]

> "Government statistics released in January 2013 estimated that 85,000 women are raped on average in England and Wales every year, that over 400,000 women are sexually assaulted annually".

The first observation is that they do not report the respective numbers for men, which are 12,000 raped and 72,000 sexually assaulted. They are clearly smaller, but by no means negligible, accounting for 12-15% of the victims.

Examining the official data[88] that the article refers to, we see that the 85,000 "rapes" are "including attempts", while the real number excluding attempts is 62,000. RapeCrisis' report, by this "oversight", inflates the official number by 1/3.

The number 400,000, which in RapeCrisis' report is referred as "women sexually assaulted annually", in the official report is referred as "any sexual offence (including attempts)". On the one hand, that is, the failed attempts are reported as sexual assaults. On the other, any sexual *offense* is turned into a sexual *assault*.

Sexual assault is a serious offense:

> "Sexual assault is any involuntary sexual act in which a person is coerced or physically forced to engage against their will, or any non-consensual sexual touching of a person. Sexual assault is a form of sexual violence, and it

---

86   Hoff Sommers, Who Stole Feminism, p.225.
87   'Myths & facts about rape & sexual violence'. Accessed Nov. 3, 2014.
     http://www.rapecrisis.org.uk/mythsampfacts2.php
88   See the Appendix at end of the book, Victims of sexual assault in England-Wales, p. 243.

includes rape (such as forced vaginal, anal or oral penetration or drug facilitated sexual assault), groping, forced kissing, child sexual abuse, or the torture of the person in a sexual manner."[89]

In the UK there are 52 classes of sexual offenses[90], *one* of which is sexual assault, while others include: Engaging in sexual activity in the presence of a person with a mental disorder impeding choice, Controlling prostitution for gain, Sex with an adult relative, Voyeurism, Exposure. There is no doubt that those are illegal actions. But they are not sexual *assaults*.

Apparently the inflation of the data was done on purpose. RapeCrisis deals specifically with this issue, and cannot claim ignorance of the niceties of legal terms. However, the fact that rape is a heinous crime does not justify the falsification of data. This shows a clear intention to show the extent of the problem as being bigger than it really is.

"Rape culture" is above all an idea created in the minds of women – from the system, with feminists on the cutting edge of the issue.

Why are women not afraid of road accidents?

Let's study the numbers a bit more. We will draw some interesting results.

The population of England and Wales is 56 million. Women at the age 16-59 are about 14 millions. With 62,000 rapes a year, the possibility of being raped is 1 in 200. Strangers are perpetrators of rape at most in 10% of the cases. So cases in which a woman is raped by a stranger is 0.5 in 1000.

Let's compare this to road accidents[91]. There are about 1,500 deaths and 20,500 serious injuries per year in England and Wales. Women victims in

---

89   Wikipedia, Sexual Assault. Accessed 30 Jan. 2015.
       https://en.wikipedia.org/wiki/Sexual_assault
90   Wikipedia, Sexual Offences in the United Kingdom. Accessed 30 Jan. 2015.
       https://en.wikipedia.org/wiki/Sexual_offences_in_the_United_Kingdom
91   Reported Road Casualties in Great Britain: 2012 Annual Report, Department for
       Transport ttps://www.gov.uk/government/uploads/system/uploads/attachment_data/
       file/245383/rrcgb2012-00.pdf

the age group 16-59 are correspondingly around 5,000. The probability of a serious accident then is 0.35 in 1000. This is very close to the number we found for rapes. Therefore, if would be logical that women who go out should fear road accidents as much as they fear rape. But this does not seem to be the case. Why then is there so much latent fear of rape?

Behind Rape Culture

The USA is the champion in a phenomenon that appears throughout the Western world, with particular intensity in Anglo-Saxon countries: rape hysteria. Rapes are supposed to be on the rise, and all the media talk about a "rape culture", although the numbers have dramatically *decreased*, e.g. with "forcible rape" having fallen from 0.42 per 1000 people in 1991 to 0.25 per 1000 in 2013[92]. This hysteria is based in dubious data, such as "1 in 5 women are raped", a claim originating from the Centers for Disease Control and Prevention (CDC). These numbers, which have been widely publicized, are the result of shady tactics[93]: the questions in the studies are designed so that they encourage positive answers, which are then considered "rape" even if the interviewee does not consider it so. Interestingly enough, with regards to the same CDC reports, "if being made to penetrate someone was counted as rape—and why shouldn't it be?—then the headlines could have focused on a truly sensational CDC finding: that women rape men as often as men rape women."[94]

Rape hysteria has created an atmosphere of "state of emergency", within which the presumption of innocence has literally been abolished. Students are expelled from their schools simply on the basis of accusations, while lives are destroyed irrevocably when the media

---

92   'United States Crime Rates 1960 - 2013'. Accessed 4 Dec. 2014.
     http://www.disastercenter.com/crime/uscrime.htm. Based on the FBI UCS Annual
     Crime Reports.
93   'The CDC's Rape Numbers Are Misleading | TIME'.
     http://time.com/3393442/cdc-rape-numbers
94   Ibid.

present someone on the front page as a rapist, before he is tried.

The important question about this hysteria is *why*, and especially *why now*. The answer has to do with the economy of sex, and emerges more clearly through the complaints of the Conservatives. The Washington Times, for example, complains that "sex is cheap these days"[95], blaming women for that. Sociologist Mark Regnerus summarizes the problem from the systems' perspective, as follows:

> "Don't forget your Freud: Civilization is built on blocked, redirected, and channeled sexual impulse, because men will work for sex. Today's young men, however, seldom have to. As the authors of last year's book *Sex at Dawn: The Prehistoric Origins of Modern Sexuality* put it, 'Societies in which women have lots of autonomy and authority tend to be decidedly male-friendly, relaxed, tolerant, and plenty sexy.' They're right. But then try getting men to do anything."[96]

Conservative journalist Heather MacDonald

> "sees a clear upside to the 'the new campus sex regime' of 'biased campus sex tribunal[s]' that 'puts boys in danger of trumped-up assault charges heard before kangaroo courts.' She thinks these injustices will 'result[ ] in boys taking a vow of celibacy until graduation,' and, she clucks, 'there is simply no loss whatsoever to society and only gain to individual character' from that. MacDonald goes so far as to bleat that she does not consider college men unjustly accused of sexual offenses to be 'sympathetic victims' because, even though they are not guilty of rape, 'many are guilty of acting as boorishly as they can get away with.' Let's put this in plain language. MacDonald is perfectly content with unjust laws and illegal policies that put college men ... at grave risk, so long as these unjust laws and illegal policies usher in an era of sexual morality in the academy that mirrors MacDonald's personal views."[97]

---

95   'Economy of sex: It 's cheap these days - Washington Times'.
      http://www.washingtontimes.com/news/2011/jun/14/economy-of-sex-its-cheap-
      these-days/?page=all.
96   'Sex is cheap: Why young men have the upper hand in bed, even when they 're
      failing in life.'
      http://www.slate.com/articles/double_x/doublex/2011/02/sex_is_cheap.html
97   'Community of the Wrongly Accused: Repugnant: Heather MacDonald finds an

Thus, the hysteria about "rape culture" is essentially an orchestrated terrorist campaign against men (where terrorism is "the systemic use of terror especially as a means of coercion"[98]). It aims to artificially raise the cost of sex for men, which the system considers to be "low", by making it dangerous. Its ultimate purpose is to force men to comply to the production model as the only way to acquire the sex they need. (The policy of the penalization of prostitution is a similar case which we will discuss later).

At the same time, rape hysteria serves another goal. It gives women absolute freedom and policing duties regarding sex. Woman's sexual freedom continues to be a basic feminist promise and lure, an advantage of her "independence" – that is, her obligation to work outside the house as an employee. "Rape" is the safety valve: if things don't go as planned, if her friends call her "slut" or her husband finds out, she can always *ex post facto* shout "rape", renouncing any liability. Similar is the case with "sexual harassment" in the workplace. Given that many, even the majority of women marry a man they met in a workplace flirt, "When it works, it's called courtship. When it doesn't work, it's called harassment."[99]

Domestic Violence

In feminist circles one can repeatedly hear that domestic violence is the leading cause of death in women.

Feminists and the mainstream media, like The Guardian, argue that "Violence against women is a pandemic more extensive than HIV/Aids. It is the main cause of death and disability globally for women aged 15 to 44"[100]. However, as we have seen, violence afflicts men more. What is implied in these declarations, is that *Domestic* Violence is what hurts

---

upside to the unjust campus rape witch hunt -- it will force college 'boys' to keep their pants zipped'. Accessed 4 Dec. 2014.
http://www.cotwa.info/2014/12/repugnant-heather-macdonald-finds.html.

98   'Terrorism - Definition and More from the Free Merriam-Webster Dictionary'.
Accessed 4 Dec. 2014. http://www.merriam-webster.com/dictionary/terrorism.

99   Farrell, The Myth of Male Power, p. 292.

100 'Lesley Abdela: Trivialising violence against women | theguardian.com'.
http://www.theguardian.com/commentisfree/2008/nov/25/domestic-violence-gender

women more. Kent's Police in Great Britain made a similar claim that Domestic Violence was the "leading cause of death for women aged between 15 and 44."[101] Similar claims can be found in numerous government committees, media reports etc. Could they be lying?

The short answer is "yes".

The first problem is that there is a sympathetic mutation in favor of women of the primary information. So, while initial reports talk about "morbidity (i.e. ill health)", this is "rounded upwards" to "death".

Searching for the source of these reports we arrive at the World Bank. In its report entitled "Gender Based Violence, Health and the role of the Health Sector"[102], the exact wording is

> "domestic violence and rape ranks higher than cancer, motor vehicle accidents, war and malaria in the global estimates of selected risk factors for increased morbidity, disability and mortality, accounting for an estimated 5 to 16 percent of healthy years of life lost by females aged 15 to 44 years of age (WHO, 2002)."

Note that the above excerpt is located in the section examining "The *Economic* Impact of Gender Based Violence", not "The *health* impact...". It is, then, a typical case of economic reductionism.

The first thing to note is that domestic violence is conflated with rape, in order to compare it to cancer and the other causes of death. Similarly, morbidity, disability and mortality are put together. Maybe for economists these practices are common, but they don't help to paint an accurate picture of the problem. It is like claiming that "Slapping and cancer is the leading cause of blackened eyes and deaths worldwide". With a little good will, this is converted to "slapping is the leading cause of death worldwide"...

The World Bank refers to the World Health Organization report, WHO

---

101 'How true are Domestic Violence statistics ? | Robert Whiston'. Accessed Nov. 3, 2014. http://robertwhiston.wordpress.com/2011/06/03/27
102 "Gender Based Violence, Health and the role of the Health Sector", http://siteresources.worldbank.org/INTPHAAG/Resources/AAGGBVHealth.pdf

2002. The corresponding report for 2004[103] however, does not include such conclusions. In any case, if one uses WHO 2004 which includes more analytical data, we can make the following observations:

a. The report is based on 119 heterogeneous studies (p.13) from different countries. Some of these come from women's organizations, which are not exactly famous for their accuracy and objectivity.

b. The economic calculations are essentially arbitrary. As the report itself admits, "Among studies that quantify the value of lost human life, there is considerable variation in the monetary value assigned to one life" (p.9). Similarly arbitrary values are assigned to psychological cost, judicial cost etc.

c. The WHO study completely ignores domestic violence against men, considering it negligible, although as we will see shortly, it is as important or greater than that against women.

A look at WHO's general statistics, beyond domestic violence, is enough to see that the real picture about the main causes of death in women is different: "The three top causes of death for adult women are infectious and parasitic diseases; cancers; and cardiovascular diseases."[104] Cardiovascular disease alone is responsible for about 30% of deaths[105]. Intentional injuries, which include suicide, wars and *all kinds of violence*, comprise only 1,7% of deaths for women. The corresponding percentage for men is more than double, 3.9%.

It seems then that the World Bank and the WHO are using really creative accounting to reach their conclusions. To understand how this is done: "a single homicide is calculated to cost, on average, $15,319 in South Africa, $602,000 in Australia, $829,000 in New Zealand, and more than $2 million in the USA" (page x). Note how "cheap" killing is in South Africa. If we compare these values with the calculated cost of a rape in

103 'WHO | The economic dimensions of interpersonal violence'. Accessed 14 Aug 2014. http://www.who.int/violence_injury_prevention/publications/violence/economic_dimensions/en

104 'Mortality and causes of death - Gender Statistics Wiki'. Accessed 14 Aug. 2014. http://unstats.un.org/unsd/genderstatmanual/Print.aspx?Page=Mortality-and-causes-of-death

105 Wikipedia, List of causes of death by rate, http://en.wikipedia.org/wiki/List_of_causes_of_death_by_rate

the US, $85,000 to $110,000 (p. 22), we conclude that a rape in the US "costs" as much as 6 or 7 murders in South Africa! (6 murders X 15,319$ per life = $91,914). And this knowing that 90% of violence-related deaths happens in countries of low and medium income (p. 1). It seems that the representative of the World Bank in South Africa would prefer to see two daughters, his mother, his grandma and two distant aunts get murdered, rather than having his aunt living in the US getting raped...

In short, a study referring to *arbitrary economic costs* of violence against women which includes no respective costs for men, is used to claim that women are subjected to more violence than men.

Women as the perpetrators of domestic violence

Let us put economic reductionism aside, whether valid or invalid, and move on to the real data. Domestic violence, even if it is not the No. 1 killer, is undoubtedly a serious social issue. But women are not only its victims. They are equally its perpetrators, and in fact even more than men.

In her memoirs (*Life so Far, 2000*), Betty Friedan claimed that her husband Carl used to hit her. It seems that even this emblematic figure of the feminist movement was not spared from domestic violence against women. Later, however, on the "Good Morning America" show, she restored the truth: "I almost wish I hadn't even written about it, because it's been sensationalized out of context. My husband was not a wife-beater, and I was no passive victim of a wife-beater. We fought a lot, and he was bigger than me."[106]

The above anecdotal incident outlines the big picture about domestic violence. In their study "Male Victims of Domestic Violence"[107], Donald G. Dutton and Katherine R. White, show that most studies use selected samples of abused women, and they do not inquire at all about violence from the part of women, resulting in men appearing as the sole aggressors and women as the sole victims. But "When asked about their

---

106 Wikipedia, Betty Friedan. Accessed 10 Sep. 2014.
https://en.wikipedia.org/wiki/Betty_Friedan
107 Dutton, Donald G. and White, Katherine R. *Male Victims of Domestic Violence*, New Male Studies, 2013, Vol. 2, Issue 1, pp. 5-17.

own use of violence 67% of these women reported using an act of *severe* violence themselves against their partner." [emphasis added]. Large scale studies show that about half of the cases of Intimate Partner Violence (IPV) are mutual. The most interesting data involves the cases where only one of the partners is the aggressor, in which it is a consistent finding that women attack non-violent partners about twice as often as men. As for the intensity of aggression and the severity of injuries caused by female violence, contrary to stereotypes, they are equal or more serious than men's. Men report attacks by "choking, using a knife, burning with scalding water, targeting of their genitals, death threats, threats to the family pet, display of weapons," etc.

English writer and activist Erin Pizzey[108] could hardly be considered hostile to women: in 1971 she opened one of the world's first shelters for abused women.

> "Soon after establishing her first refuge, Pizzey determined that much domestic violence was reciprocal, with both partners abusing each other in roughly equal rates. She reached this conclusion when she asked the women in her refuge about their violence, only to discover most of the women were equally as violent or more violent than their husbands. In her study 'Comparative Study Of Battered Women And Violence-Prone Women,' (co-researched with Dr. John Gayford of Warlingham Hospital), Pizzey distinguishes between 'genuine battered women' and 'violence-prone women;' the former defined as 'the unwilling and innocent victim of his or her partner's violence' and the latter defined as 'the unwilling victim of his or her own violence.' This study reports that 62% of the sample population were more accurately described as 'violence prone.'"

The results of her research were not very well received by the feminist community:

> "Pizzey says that it was after death threats against her, her children, her grandchildren, and the killing of her dog, all of

---

108 Wikipedia, Erin Pizzey. Accessed 10 Sep. 2014.
      https://en.wikipedia.org/wiki/Erin_Pizzey

which she states were perpetrated by militant feminists, that she left England for North America."

Women as the perpetrators of domestic violence... also against children

As women are more aggressive against their partners, they are more aggressive against their children[109]. A large scale study in the US, examining 718,984 cases of child abuse, showed that 58% of the offenders were female. A similar survey in Canada showed approximately equal proportions of women and men offenders for various kinds of child abuse, with biological mothers ahead of biological fathers in physical (47% vs 42%) and psychological (61% vs 55%) violence. And of course, boys were subjected to greater physical violence from their mother than girls.

Boys who are subjected to violence from their mothers are three times more likely to exercise violence themselves in their relationships. This violence then, which is returned back to women, is not a product of "patriarchy", but has been instigated by women themselves.

Chapter 5: Upbringing and social expectations

At which age does society begin to be more violent against boys than against girls? Unfortunately, the violence begins even before birth. Mothers consider their unborn girls more "sensitive" and the boys "tougher", adjusting the attention they give to their bellies. As infants, girls enjoy more hugs and caresses, and they are talked to more softly. The "toughening up" of men begins very early indeed!

The typical classroom could also be considered especially designed to help girls and hinder boys. It requires the restriction of movement,

---

109 Data from Dutton, Male Victims of Domestic Violence, p.13.

something that for boys, especially of younger age, is almost impossible. Two and a half times more boys than girls are diagnosed as "hyperactive"[110], a rate of 12-13%. The problem of overdiagnosed ADHD, which many experts identify, as well as that of overprescribing sedatives, affects mainly boys.

Separation from the mother

Separation from the mother is perhaps the greatest source of trauma and pain for a child. A degree of pain is necessary in life, because pain is what matures a person – when given in careful doses. But when it is either too much, or too little, it is destructive for the individual.

In so-called "traditional" societies, the "society" of men is very distinct from the "society" of women. The latter includes children. It is only the boys that need to transcend from one to the other. This transition is so important that there is always a ritual to mark it, and there is substantial help from the whole community to the boys that undergo it:

> "In 'primitive' societies, [the leader of the mythopoetic men's movement in the US, poet Robert] Bly writes, the boys are pretty much raised by the women until early adolescence. When it is time for the boys to leave the sphere of female influence and move into the men's world, the men of the tribe stage a raid. They put on their war paint, enter the village, and steal the boys away. The women, on cue, weep, protest, and do their best to hang onto the boys. After the men have taken the boys outside the village for their period of initiation, the women get together and ask, 'How did I do? Was I believable?' In these cultures, the men and women work together to facilitate this process of transition and initiation.[111]"

As Bly explains, the technique is to create an "artificial wound", that teaches boys how to mend their wounds later on in life.

---

110 'FastStats - Attention Deficit Hyperactivity Disorder'. Accessed 14 Aug. 2014. http://www.cdc.gov/nchs/fastats/adhd.htm
111 Glover, Robert A. *No More Mr Nice Guy!: A Proven Plan for Getting What You Want In Love, Sex and Life.* USA: Barnes & Noble Digital (2001). Ch. 6.

In other, more war-loving tribes, the method they use is rather the opposite. When you want to create aggressive men the key is to take them away from their mothers when they are still young. In Sparta the boys were taken by the State at the tender age of seven. While their sisters continued to enjoy the warmth of the house and their mother's embraces, boys were dressed in the same clothes, winter or summer, and slept without a blanked on straw that they had to cut themselves without a knife, and walked barefoot and bathed in cold rivers, and were underfed and encouraged to steal in order to eat – with harsh punishment if caught. Mothers, instead of giving their blessings to their sons and advise them to be careful and return from war alive, would send them away with the curse to win or die: "With your shield or on it".

Even today, the pressure to separate boys from their mothers at an early age is great. It is a shame to be a "mommy's boy". In contrast, girls can be seen going for a walk at the Mall with their mothers even when they have reached their 30s. A few girls never leave their mothers, and have what psychologists describe a "merging" issue with their mothers.

For boys however, a problematic separation is the norm. Let's see its character with an example. The following post by a Facebook mummy got about 3 million Likes and over half a million Shares:

> "Once a month my 6 year old son takes me out on a dinner date. He opens doors for me, pulls out my chair, talks about his day & asks me how mine was, pays the bill with money he earned by doing chores, and even tips the waiter/waitress. By doing this I am teaching him how to treat a lady & how to take her on a proper date. How to show that he respects the woman he loves (right now that would be mommy). We put our phone and iPad away (except to take this photo) and sit and talk to each other about our days, things we want to do, etc. I'm teaching him proper table manners and that it's rude to sit on your phone on a date with your mom or with anyone else. He learns the value of money and how to manage it. He learns how to do math as we add up what we want and make sure we have 16% of it to leave for a tip. Yes he is young but I believe this is something he should learn now. It's never too early to teach your child how to properly respect others, especially women. As a woman who has been abused & treated like

crap in the past, it's extremely important to me that I teach
my son how to show respect. Too many men these days
have no idea how to treat women or how to take them on a
nice date. It's nice to know my son won't be one of them."

We can observe that separation from the mother does not necessarily
mean physical distancing. The core issue is the blackmail towards the
boy to grow up hastily, the denial of its childhood, its coercion to take up
responsibilities that are not his to take. It is forcing it to accept and
assimilate the role of the *protector* – even while it is still a creature that
needs to *receive*, and not to give protection. In psychological terms, that
kind of separation of the boy from its own needs is equivalent to
abandonment.

The above example with the 6 year old is probably an extreme case,
nevertheless it highlights the general characteristics of the female
manipulation. Although this has emerged as a "spontaneous" and largely
unconscious social practice, it is not a coincidence. It is an *abuse*, aiming
at creating an inextinguishable craving for female affection in the male
psyche, so that throughout their lives they will be forced to beg for it
from women.

The male model

If separation from the mother is one problem for boys, the other is the
lack of a male model. Girls know what they will be like when they grow
up: like their mothers. Boys get to see their fathers very few hours every
week. Overall, they see them very few hours in their lives without the
presence (and policing) of their mothers. This prevents the creation of a
"male bond", like the female bond between mothers and daughters. But,

"there are certain things that boys can only learn from men.
[Men that can] embrace their masculinity, ... can teach their
sons what it means to be male. This includes how to handle
their aggression, how to handle their libido, how to relate to
women, how to bond with a man, and perhaps most
importantly, how to embrace their own masculinity. Men
teach these lessons both by example and by interaction with

young boys"[112].

> "Few men today have experienced a masculine role model with the strong yet open-hearted energy [a strong man] is working to cultivate. In fact, many men today have grown up without a masculine presence in their household. These boys learn about masculinity from the media and from their peers. Unhealthy examples of passive men or overly aggressive men are primarily what he is exposed to. How sad that boys are shown two polar opposites of what it is to be a man..."[113]

A confirmation of the dramatic consequences of this alienation from the father comes from the Harvard Grant Study, which followed the lives of 268 male graduates for 75 years, aiming to "determine what predicts wellbeing".

> "We found that contentment in the late seventies was not even suggestively associated with parental social class or even the man's own income. What it was significantly associated with was warmth of childhood environment, and it was very significantly associated with a man's closeness to his father."[114]

The social expectation to always be pretty

A woman must always be pretty. This is a social expectation that weighs heavily on women rather than men, and is one of the favorite complaints of feminists. If you are a man you don't have to spend an hour every day in make-up, hairstyling, dressing up, etc. (Although recent studies show that for men as well, being good-looking matters: e.g. "'Ugly' men are less likely to attract business investors"[115]).

---

112 Glover, No More Mr Nice Guy!, ch. 6.
113 Brandon, Marianne. *Monogamy: The Untold Story.* USA: Praeger (2010). p.76.
114 "What Harvard's Grant Study Reveals about Happiness and Life - The Daily Beast.". http://www.thedailybeast.com/articles/2012/11/07/what-harvard-s-grant-study-reveals-about-happiness-and-life.html
115 'Judged on your looks, boys? You'd better get used to it - Telegraph'. http://www.telegraph.co.uk/women/womens-business/10695810/Judged-on-your-looks-boys-Youd-better-get-used-to-it.html

Is that a real disadvantage for women? Let's see.

What does a well-groomed woman gain? The attention of the men around her, and at least the praise or perhaps even the jealousy of other women. She may use her beauty to her advantage. In the workplace, this may mean promotion or a pay rise.

In case she is sloppy, she simply has to earn everything like a man: proving herself. So, in the first place, the social expectation to be always pretty is a "positive problem": it can only strengthen her position, not undermine it. For example, a women not getting accepted for a job because she is not beautiful enough cannot be complaining for sexism against women: if female beauty is a criterion for employment, all men are by definition excluded from that job. If her rejection is sexism against women, it is and even greatest sexism against men.

In any case, it is nicer to be attractive, even if you have to pay for it. But what is the corresponding situation for man? For a man to attract similar interest from women, the effort he has to make is much higher. He must be rich, have a position of status, and in any event be successful in some area. These perks, for those that haven't inherited them, i.e. the majority of men, require much more than an hour of vanity care every day.

The harshness(?) of old age for women

Typically, a woman after her mid-30s gradually loses her attractiveness, while a man can be attractive until he reaches a quite old age. Based on this, it is often claimed that old age is harsher on women.

What this view forgets is that not all men are attractive in their old age: only those that are successful. There are not many attractive 50-year-old garbage collectors. As is usually the case, women compare themselves to the men at the top, while the average man, who would correspond to them, is virtually invisible. In practice, the stranglehold on sexuality maintained by women means that in their 40s, 50s or 60s they have more sexual opportunities than men of the same age. A 300 lbs (136 kilos) woman presents her experience in her article entitled "I'm Fat, 40 and

Single – And I've Been Getting Laid Like Crazy."[116] A Swiss prostitute says she worked until she was 66[117], while in South Korea women in their 70s can find men to pay them for sex[118].

An elderly man has gone through the stage of sexual frustration in his youth. He has fought hard to stand out in work, so that he can attract a partner. He has spent a large part of his life having to support a family, an institution that is completely unnatural for him. The satisfaction he has gathered from life is much lower than that afforded to the average woman, that it is not surprising that the suicide rates for older men are overwhelmingly higher than women's, with 32 suicides per 100,000 men compared to only 4 for women[119]. Psychologists know that in order to have a relatively "happy old age", it is essential to have lived a happy life. And life in today's society is much happier for women.

Chapter 6: Happiness

The various studies about the war of the sexes use various criteria to draw their conclusions about the relative position of each sex. These criteria are often chosen based on the social class and the ideology of the researcher.

Thus, a feminist bourgeois who studied in Oxford will conclude that women are more oppressed because they have fewer opportunities to "exploit their talent" in comparison with men[120].

(Socio)biologists, on their end, are not very interested in who wins and who loses. They consider (rightly, from their perspective) that the war of

---

116 'I'm Fat, 40 and Single—And I've Been Getting Laid Like Crazy | Alternet'.
      http://www.alternet.org/im-fat-40-and-single-and-ive-been-getting-laid-crazy
117 Wikipedia, Grisélidis Réal, Accessed Apr. 2, 2020.
      https://en.wikipedia.org/wiki/Gris%C3%A9lidis_R%C3%A9al
118 'BBC News - The Korean grandmothers who sell sex'.
      http://www.bbc.com/news/magazine-27189951
119 https://web.archive.org/web/20150211072214/http://www.cdc.gov/
      violenceprevention/suicide/statistics/rates05.html
120 Seabright, The war of the sexes, Chapter 5.

the sexes is a natural process that occurs in all animals, and what's important for them is that it contributes to the evolution of the species (which is not always true)[121]. The problem is that the evolution of the species is the last thing in the mind of someone struggling for his daily survival, so it is not a suitable criterion to assess the quality of life.

As for Economists, they will examine who has more money. And the list goes on.

Which criterion is the most relevant?

Harvard psychology professor Tal Ben-Shahar, puts it this way: "Happiness, not money or prestige, should be regarded as the ultimate currency – the currency by which we take measure of our lives"[122].

For many it is self-evident that happiness is the most important criterion to compare the lives of people. Indeed, World Happiness Report 2013 of the UN "calls on policy makers to make happiness a key measure and target of development"[123]. The only probable objections have to do with the reliability of the system to measure happiness. Nevertheless, researchers have decided to use "subjective happiness", that is the level of happiness reported by individuals themselves. Subjective happiness has very real benefits in health and longevity. In fact, the above UN report devotes an entire chapter reviewing the "hard evidence".

As we already mentioned in the section on marriage, at least for as long as there have been comparative studies, women have always been happier than men. Let's have a look at the Pew Research Center data from 2003:

---

121 See the discussion about Sexual Selection in the 2nd Part of the book, which examines Biology, p. 77.
122 Ben-Shahar, Tal. *Happier: Learn the Secrets to Daily Joy and Lasting Fulfillment.* USA: Mc Graw Hill (2007). p. xii.
123 UN: World Happiness Report 2013.
   http://unsdsn.org/resources/publications/world-happiness-report-2013

Table 2: Where Women Are Significantly Happier[124]

Country	Men %	Women %
Pakistan	18	34
Japan	31	46
Philippines	25	36
Argentina	40	50
Vietnam	38	48
India	13	21
Peru	33	41
Guatemala	68	76
Indonesia	28	35
Uzbekistan	32	39
Senegal	20	27
Poland	25	32
Turkey	15	21
China	20	26
Lebanon	19	24
Nigeria	34	39
United States	64	68
Mexico	57	61
Venezuela	49	53
Honduras	57	61
South Korea	50	54
% rate their lives on the highest rung of the ladder of life		

124 'Global Gender Gaps | Pew Research Center for the People and the Press'. Accessed 23 Aug. 2014. http://www.people-press.org/2003/10/29/global-gender-gaps

The 6 countries with the largest difference in happiness between women and men are Pakistan, Japan, Philippines, Argentina, Vietnam and India. In the 21 countries in the world with the largest difference there is not even one Western-European country, while the US are included. "Women's greater satisfaction with life is pervasive in many of the less-developed regions of the world: in 7 of the 8 countries surveyed in Asia, 6 of the 8 nations in Latin America and all 5 nations in east and southern Africa."[125]

This means that in countries where the supposed "patriarchy" is stronger, men are more unhappy than women. This finding highlights the true essence of "patriarchy", which is to burden men with greater responsibilities and social expectations, in order to provide women with greater protection and generally better quality of life than they get for themselves.

If the system had really been made up by men, it would be impossible to ultimately favor women. So what's going on here? The answer is that the role of women to the construction of the system has been greatly overlooked. We will have more to say about this later on.

In developed countries, researchers have identified the "paradox" of declining female happiness[126]: while from 1970 onwards

> "by many objective measures the lives of women ... have improved, ... measures of subjective well-being indicate that women's happiness has declined both absolutely and relative to men. The paradox of women's declining relative well-being is found across various datasets, measures of subjective well-being, and is pervasive across demographic groups and industrialized countries."

Of course, it is a "paradox" only if seen from the feminist perspective. But there is nothing paradoxical in that if you endeavor to live the life of a man you will come to know the unhappiness of a man.

---

125 Ibid.
126 Stevenson Betsey, Wolfer Justin. *The paradox of the declining Female Happiness.* American Economic Journal: Economic Policy, American Economic Association, vol. 1(2), pages 190-225, August 2009. http://www.nber.org/papers/w14969

Chapter 7: Life expectancy

Some questions

Before examining the case of life expectancy, consider the following questions:

- Is it ethical that some groups of people live on average more than others?

- Shouldn't all people at birth have the same life expectancy?

- If we consider women and men, and accept that the difference in their life expectancy is based on biology, does that make the difference ethically justified?

- To put it another way: would it be moral, if one sex has a *biological* predilection to longevity, to *socially* assist the other one, on the first's expense, in order to balance them?

- Or more simply: Is it or is it not right to take away years from the sex that lives longer, to give it to the one that is expected to live less?

The importance of life expectancy

First, let's see why life expectancy is important.

Can a prisoner live longer than a free man? Apparently, he can. Does this mean that he is happier? Probably not. The issue should be looked at from the perspective of statistics, in its globality.

In this sense, there is no doubt that *longer life expectancy is correlated with a better life*. Commenting on the results of The Human Genome Project, Steve Jones, professor of Genetics, Evolution and Environment at University College London, says: "The biggest question is: What's your zipcode. The difference in life expectancy between the richest and poorest zipcodes in a city like Glasgow is an astonishing 28 years."[127] The difference between the richest and the poorest countries is of similar dimensions: between Japan and Sierra Leone, for example, it is a whopping 36 years.

Life expectancy today

There is a very amusing or infuriating phenomenon – depending on what perspective you look at it. Evolutionary psychologists have constructed a pile of theories to explain the causes of the biological superiority of the woman. It is supposedly self-evident because women live longer. But they forgot to do historical research and see whether this has always been the case.

Let's have a look at the evidence.

World life expectancy today is 73.5 for women and 68.5 years for men[128]. There is a 5 year difference in favor of women. In Europe, the difference is 7.5 years[129]. There is no longer a country in the world where men live longer than women.

Even in countries where women are said to be particularly oppressed, as in Muslim countries, (e.g. Afghanistan) or developing countries in Africa (Zimbabwe, Sierra Leone), women live at least as long, if not longer, than men. In "patriarchal" Saudi Arabia women have a life expectancy of 80, versus only 74 for men.

History and Prehistory

It is difficult to find historical statistics on life expectancy worldwide. However, since we are not interested in the exact numbers but only in the trends, let's examine a Western society for which data are available, the

---

127 'BBC - Future - Human Social Project: Cracking the real code of life'.
    http://www.bbc.com/future/story/20130417-we-need-a-human-social-project
128 Wikipedia, List of countries by life expectancy. Accessed 19 Jan. 2015.
    https://en.wikipedia.org/wiki/List_of_countries_by_life_expectancy Refers to United
    Nations World Population Prospects: 2012 revision.
129 'BBC News - European men lag behind in life expectancy'.
    http://www.bbc.com/news/health-21760905

US. The following table refers to white men and women[130].

Table 3: Life expectancy for whites in the US, 1850-1970

Year	Men	Women	Difference(years)	Percent %
1850	38.3	40.5	2.2	5.7%
1890	42.5	44.5	2	4.7%
1900	48.2	51.1	2.9	6.0%
1910	50.2	53.5	3.3	6.6%
1920	56.3	58.5	2.2	3.9%
1930	59.1	62.8	3.7	6.3%
1940	62.8	67.3	4.5	7.2%
1950	66.3	72	5.7	8.6%
1960	67.6	74.2	6.6	9.8%
1970	67.9	75.5	7.6	11.0%

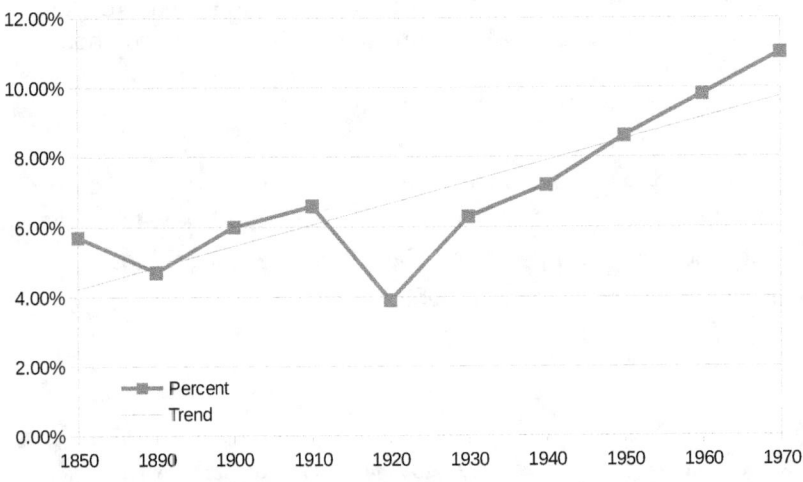

Percentile difference in Life Expectancy USA, up to 1970

130 'Life Expectancy by Age, 1850–2011 | Infoplease.com'.
http://www.infcplease.com/ipa/A0005140.html. There was a rounding to the 1st decimal, and the central year of the time span is referred.

We can see that from 1850 until 1920 the difference was around 2-3 years, a percentage of 5-6%. Since then, the gap has soared, rising steadily every decade, until in the 1970s it reached 7.6 years or 11%. A first conclusion, then, is that the consolidation of the "western way of life", i.e. capitalism and urbanization, not only did not oppress women, but brought them disproportionate profits relatively to men.

What was the case in earlier periods and different countries?

According to feminist B.B. Kalben, the first time a longer life expectancy of women was observed was in 1750[131], in Sweden. What was happening before that?

> "Male life expectancy exceeded female life expectancy during the medieval period... The earliest specific mention the author found of differential mortality between the sexes is from classic Jewish texts. The Jerusalem Talmud, completed about 400 C.E., states that women tend to die sooner than men. The Babylonian Talmud, completed about 100 years later, notes that the death of a wife while the husband is alive is a common occurrence."

The following table shows the median lifespan (that is the age in which 50% of the population is still alive, which is another way to measure longevity) per historical period[132]. The data come from paleopathological research in areas of the Eastern Mediterranean.

---

131 Kalben, Barbara Blatt. *Why Men Die Younger: Causes of Mortality Differences by Sex.* Society of Actuaries, 2002.
   http://www.soa.org/news-and-publications/publications/other-publications/monographs/m-li01-1-toc.aspx

132 It has been adapted from 'Longevity & health in ancient Paleolithic', by Ward Nicholson, http://www.beyondveg.com/nicholson-w/angel-1984/angel-1984-1a.shtml and it is based on Angel, Lawrence J. (1984) "Health as a crucial factor in the changes from hunting to developed farming in the eastern Mediterranean." In: Cohen, Mark N.; Armelagos, George J. (eds.) (1984) *Paleopathology at the Origins of Agriculture* (proceedings of a conference held in 1982). Orlando: Academic Press. (pp. 51-73).

Table 4: Median Lifespan per historical period

Period	Men	Women	Difference	%
1920 – 1800 "Romantic"	40.0	38.4	-1.6	-4.0%
1800 – 1400 "Baroque"	33.9	28.5	-5.4	-15.9%
Byzantine Constantinople	46.2	37.3	-8.9	-19.3%
Medieval Greece	37.7	31.3	-6.4	-17.0%
600 – 120 AD "Imperial Roman"	38.8	34.2	-4.6	-11.9%
120 AD – 300 BC "Hellenistic"	41.9	38.0	-3.9	-9.3%
300 – 650 BC "Classic"	44.1	36.8	-7.3	-16.6%
650 – 1150 BC "Early iron"	39.0	30.9	-8.1	-20.8%
1150 – 1450 BC "Late bronze"	39.6	32.6	-7.0	-17.7%
Circa 1450 BC "Bronze Kings"	35.9	36.1	0.2	0.6%
1450 – 2000 BC "Middle People"	36.5	31.4	-5.1	-14.0%
2000 – 3000 BC "Early Bronze period"	33.6	29.4	-4.2	-12.5%
3000 – 5000 BC "Late Neolithic"	33.1	29.2	-3.9	-11.8%
5000 – 7000 BC "Early Neolithic": agricultural revolution	33.6	29.8	-3.8	-11.3%
7000 – 9000 BC "Mesolithic"	33.5	31.3	-2.2	-6.6%
9000 – 30000 BC "Late Paleolithic"	35.4	30.0	-5.4	-15.3%

As we can see, in practically all historical periods men lived quite longer than women. Therefore, the convenient argument of the feminists and the mainstream biologists that women's longevity is based in their biology, has very shaky legs. The human species started its "career" on earth as hunter-gatherers, and its biology was established in that time and those conditions. So, if some data are indicative of our biological trend, it is much more those of the Paleolithic era, than today's. And at that era, men lived longer than women.

It is important to note that nothing in nature indicates that the male and the female should have equal life expectancy, rather, nature suggests that they can have a different life expectancy. In the Paleolithic era, women lived 5.4 years (or 15.3%) *less* than men. "And that period may have been the most gender-equal time in human history"[133]. If these conditions of equality were maintained today, men in Europe would bury their female peers in their spry 80, and they would have 14.5 years to mourn them, until they turned 94.5, instead of dying at 72.5. Today's inequality against them has cost them 94.5 − 72.5 = 18 years, i.e. a quarter of their lives. This conclusion is perhaps a little early in our analysis for one to digest, since we have not yet presented all the evidence, so please keep on reading.

An unexpected result of the '70s

We stopped the list in Table 3, which shows the life expectancy of whites in the US, in 1970, because from then onwards we have an interesting development[134]. Let's have a look:

---

133 Wikipedia, Palaeolithic. Accessed 18 Jan. 2015.
    https://en.wikipedia.org/wiki/Paleolithic
134 Data for 2011 taken from 'U.S. Life Expectancy Ranks 26th In The World, OECD
    Report Shows'. http://www.huffingtonpost.com/2013/11/21/us-life-expectancy-
    oecd_n_4317367.html.

Table 5: Life expectancy for whites in the US, 1970-2011

Year	Men	Women	Difference	Percent %
1950	66.3	72	5.7	8.6%
1960	67.6	74.2	6.6	9.8%
1970	67.9	75.5	7.6	11.2%
1980	70.8	78.2	7.4	10.5%
1990	72.7	79.4	6.7	9.2%
1995	73.4	79.6	6.2	8.4%
2000	74.8	80	5.2	7.0%
2004	75.7	80.8	5.1	6.7%
2011	76	81	5	6.6%

We can see a clear reversal of the trend: while average life expectancy for both sexes continued to increase, from 1970 onwards there was a dramatic *decrease of the difference* between women and men, instead of a steady increase, as was the case until then.

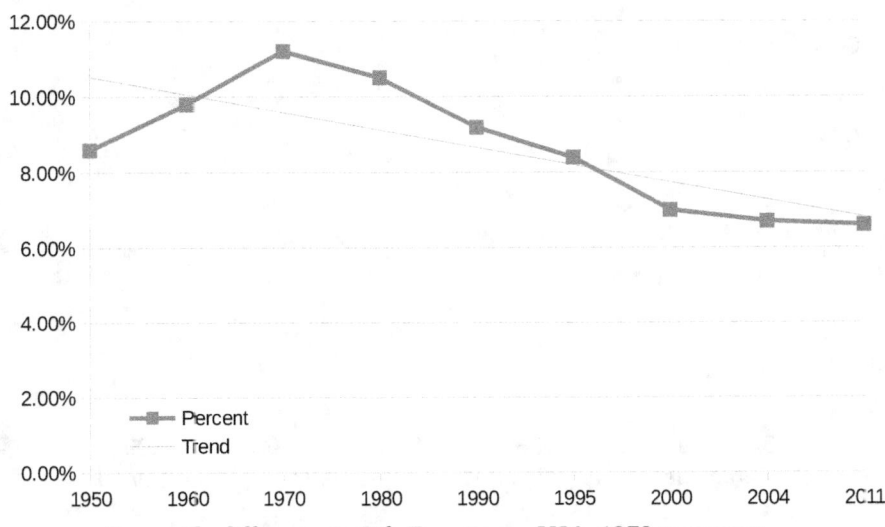

Percentile difference in Life Expectancy USA, 1970 to present

This is a phenomenon which occurred in the US and other Western countries, such as Great Britain and Germany, but not across the world.

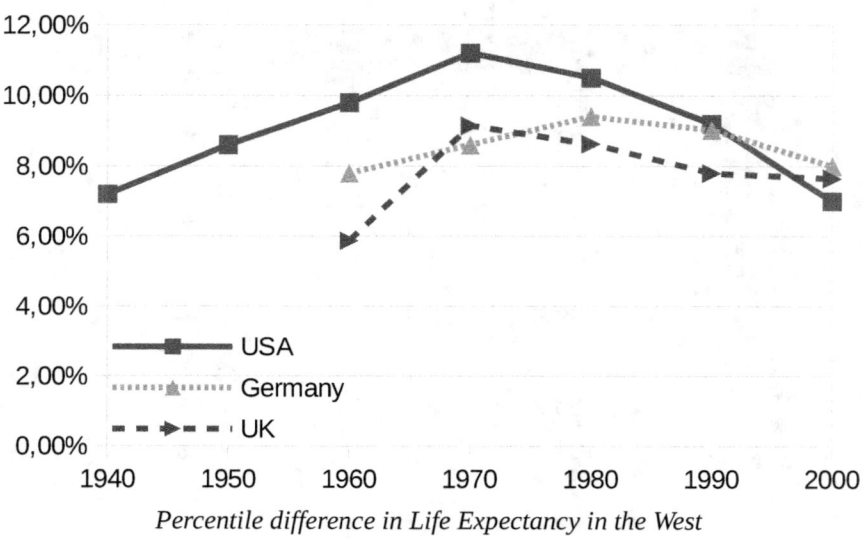

Percentile difference in Life Expectancy in the West

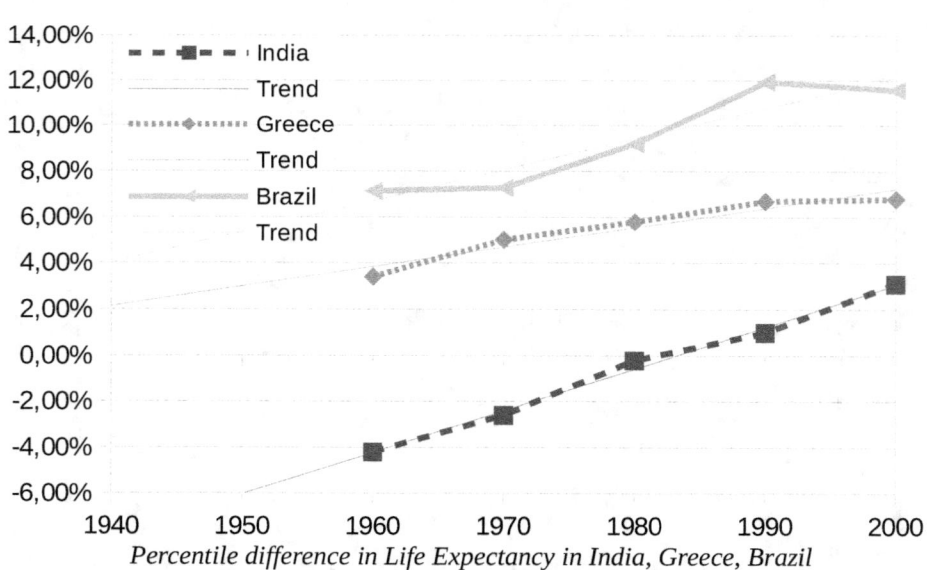

Percentile difference in Life Expectancy in India, Greece, Brazil

In 1974, in China[135], life expectancy was 67 years for women and 64 for men. Today it is 75 vs 72, a steady difference of 3 years (which is a small reduction in the relative difference). In other non-Western countries, like India, Brazil and Greece, the difference between the sexes continues to increase, not decrease[136].

The characteristic downwards trend evidenced in some Western countries in 1970 (1980 for Germany), does not exist in more "traditional" countries.

What happened, then, in the West, in the relations between the sexes, which did not occur in China, India or Greece at that time? The Feminist Revolution, of course, with the exodus of women from the house, their entry the in labor market, and all the consequences we described earlier.

Chapter 8: Conclusion

Suppose that when you are born you get to choose one of two options: (a) a life which is happier and lasts longer, and (b) a life which is more unhappy and which is shorter. Do you really need more variables in order to decide? What if they told you that with option (b), the unhappy life, you had a 10% or 20% greater chance of having a career; would that change your decision? (Let us generously overlook that option (b) would come with a 90% greater chance to end up in prison). Career and status, the two main features considered men's advantages, are simply means to achieve happiness. And these two features are usually elusive, and if you are not born in the upper class, they are so exhausting to achieve, that in most cases it is not worth the trouble.

Maybe the life of a factory worker's wife is harder than the life of a rich male banker. In any case, "by comparison with her husband [...] the factory worker's wife leads a luxurious life."[137] It is therefore normal and

135 'China - Life expectancy at birth'. Accessed 13 Aug. 2014.
    http://www.indexmundi.com/facts/china/life-expectancy-at-birth.
136 See the tables in the Appendix, p. 244.
137 Vilar, The Manipulated Man.

expected that the feminist movement was never popular among the women of the lower classes. Leaders of the "second wave of feminism" in the US, for example, were the bored housewives of middle-class suburbs, who revolted against the "problem that has no name", as Betty Friedan put it[138]. They couldn't really create a movement by claiming to revolt against *idleness,* could they?

An Equal Rights Amendment for the Constitution has been proposed in the US since 1923. It would declare that "Equality of rights under the law shall not be denied or abridged by the United States or by any State on account of sex."[139] Phyllis Schlafly, a leading figure of the movement that led to the defeat of the amendment in the '70s, in her article titled *"What's Wrong with Equal Rights for Women?" (1972),* observes that the American woman is the most privileged person of all the classes of people who ever lived.

> "We have the most rights and rewards, and the fewest duties ... The truth is that American women never had it so good. Why should we lower ourselves to "equal rights" when we already have the status of special privilege?"[140]

---

138 Friedan, Betty. The Feminine Mystique. USA: W.W. Norton and Co. (1963).
139 Wikipedia, Equal Rights Amendment. Accessed 24 Jan. 2014.
    https://en.wikipedia.org/wiki/Equal_Rights_Amendment
140 Schlaflly, Phyllis.*What's Wrong With Equal Rights for Women?* Phyllis Schlafly
    Report, February 1972.

Part 2: Is Biology Responsible for Gender Differences?

Photo by Larry Miller (CC-BY-SA 2.0)

Introduction

The question whether biology plays a role in gender differences is important, and not a trivial one to answer. We have already seen that for the difference in life expectancy, which is perfectly measurable, biology is not yet in position to give a reliable explanation. The issue becomes more complex when we examine a multidimensional phenomenon such as behavior. Does biology influence it depending on whether one is a man or woman? Until very recently, compelling scientific evidence for one or the other opinion did not exist. The answer someone gave depended basically on his political views. Conservatives maintained that biology was crucial, while progressives that it was not a key factor.

The mainstream systemic view has adopted the theory of the "social gender", which originated in feminist circles. That theory fiercely rejects any biological differentiation between the sexes, maintaining that each individual's sex ("gender") is a socially "constructed".

Today, however, it is gradually becoming clear in science that the two sexes have behavioral differences which *are* important, and that these differences are due to biological differences[141]. "[T]hanks to advances in genetics and noninvasive brain imaging technology ... scientists have documented an astonishing array of structural, chemical, genetic, hormonal and functional brain differences between women and men."[142] There are differences that are spotted while in the embryonic stage, before society has a chance to have any effect.

Perhaps the mildest way to argue about the existence of those differences comes from (feminist) scientists that tried "to analyze male-female brain differences for their relationship to gender type as opposed to strict biological sex. Their findings *do not prove* that social learning is the cause of male-female differences in the brain."[143] [emphasis added]. Despite the disproval of their expectations, they do make one crucial observation: "Genes and hormones light the spark for most boy-girl differences, but the flame is strongly fanned by the essentially separate cultures in which boys and girls grow up." That fact, that today's society, despite claims to the contrary, compounds biological differences, is fundamental to understanding the situation in the "war of the sexes". We will discuss this again shortly.

---

141 Del Guidice, Marco, Booth, Tom and Irwing, Paul 'The Distance Between Mars and Venus: Measuring Global Sex Differences in Personality'. PLOS One, 2012. http://www.plosone.org/article/info%3Adoi/10.1371/journal.pone.0029265
142 Brizendine, Louann. The Female Brain. New York: Broadway Books (2006). p.4.
143 The Scientific American Book of Love, Sex and the Brain. Ch. 3.

Chapter 9: Basic knowledge

Before we proceed to examine the biological differences between men and women, let us introduce some basic principles of biology, just to make sure we are on the same page.

Homo Sapiens has not changed in millenia

Mammals appeared 220 million years ago. Primates 75 million years ago. Hominids 15 million years ago. The current species, Homo Sapiens Sapiens, began to separate from Neanderthals 500,000 years ago, and appeared around 200,000 years ago. Since then humans have been practically identical biologically-speaking. If we transferred a man of the stone age to the present, he would be indistinguishable from modern humans. Putting another way: Biologically, the modern human is still programmed for the hunter-gatherer age, for that "combination of time and place" that scientists call "environment of evolutionary adaptedness"[144], even if he has been "teleported" to today's society due to the huge difference in the rate between social and biological changes.

In this sense, for the lives of people and societies, i.e. for politics, any discussion about an "evolution" of the modern man "towards something else" in the future is practically meaningless. When there are people who starve, suffer and die today, there is no sense in waiting for an "evolution" that will occur many thousands of generations later, to solve the problems.

Heritability

"Heritability is the proportion of observed differences on a trait among individuals of a population that are due to genetic differences. Factors including genetics, environment and random chance can all contribute to the variation between individuals in their observable characteristics (in their "phenotypes"). Heritability thus analyzes the relative

---

144 Ridley, The Red Queen, p. 191.

contributions of differences in genetic and non-genetic factors to the total phenotypic variance in a population. For instance, some humans in a population are taller than others; heritability attempts to identify how much genetics play a role in part of the population being taller."[145]

Contrary to the characteristics that are solely attributable to genes and are expressed in all individuals, for instance that all humans have two hands, there are many characteristics that appear with different frequency in a population, and are influenced by both genetic and environmental factors. Regarding behavior, this situation is the norm. This explains why some "masculine" behaviors may not appear in the same degree in all men, or manifest themselves "paradoxically" in women.

What we claim is that there is a biological basis for male behavior and a *different* biological basis of *female* behavior. Men and women have a different starting point, on which there will be societal influences, so that the resulting behavior of each person is manifested. What is not true is that the sexes are a "tabula rasa", and that all behaviors are equally natural for both.

X, Y chromosomes and "if-then" genes

Men and women genetically differ only in their X or Y chromosome. This might lead us to the wrong conclusion that we differ only in our sexual characteristics, not in our behavior. Besides, are not the other chromosomes, which largely define the biological base of behavior, identical between the sexes?

But that's not the case. It is possible to create "if-then clauses" in gene expressions[146]. It is like having a computer program with two games, and an initial menu with two choices. Selecting "1" runs the first game, selecting "2" runs the second one. The same program, but a completely different behavior, based on only a small difference in one parameter. The differentiation mechanism for male and female characteristics and

145 Wikipedia, Heritability. Accessed 18 Jan. 2015.
    https://en.wikipedia.org/wiki/Heritability
146 For more, see http://robertsapolskyrocks.weebly.com/molecular-genetics-ii.html

behavior is similar. Although men and women have much of their genetic material in common, different parts of this common material are active in men and different in women.

Chapter 10: Brain and the unconscious

Over the last couple of decades, with the development of techniques for brain imaging, the notion of the unconscious is slowly becoming a "hard" science. The idea that humans do not have absolute, conscious control of their actions, and have even less control over their desires, can now be corroborated by the brain's structure and functioning.

Psychologist Daniel Kahneman, in work that won him the Nobel prize in Economics, refers to two "modes of thought", which have been named System 1 and System 2[147]. System 1 is fast, instinctive and emotional; System 2 is slower, more deliberative, and more logical. System 1 is "automatic", while System 2 is "effortful".

The brain is the most complex organ, not only in humans but also in other species. We can, however, identify a hierarchical structure in its operation. There are the "lower" functions, such as instincts, the more advanced, such as impulses and emotions, and the "higher" functions of perception and design, which are found mainly in higher mammals. The "lower" are also evolutionarily older. They are absolutely necessary for survival, and are located in the inner parts of the mind. Thus e.g. the hypothalamus, which is associated with the feeling of hunger, thirst and reproductive behavior, and the amygdala, which is responsible for the feeling of fear and aggression, are located almost in the center of the brain. On the contrary, the neocortex, which is responsible for conscious thinking, is the outer part that encloses the rest. What is extremely important is that there are many more synapses that run *from* the amygdala *to* the neocortex than vice versa. This practically means that

---

147 Kahneman, Daniel. *Thinking, Fast and Slow.* New York: Farrar, Straus and Giroux (2013).

when the amygdala is irritated e.g. with the feeling of fear, it sends urgent signals to the neocortex (and other parts) for reaction, and as a result suspends higher brain functions. *The decisions are essentially made by the evolutionary more ancient parts of the brain.* And this does not apply only to what we call "instinctual reactions", those related to urgent situations. Financial investors, neurosurgeons, athletes, musicians, i.e. anyone performing an exceptionally demanding task operates in great part by intuition, "automatically", practically relying on the inner parts of their brains.

What then is the role of the incredibly sophisticated neocortex? Using the words of Robert Sapolsky, a world famous neuroendicronologist, "it massages" the lower synapses pathways. It is useful to *train* them in order to make the right decisions, but *it does not make* those decisions.

What all this comes down to is that our conscious self and what we call conscious decisions are only a thin layer of behaviors over a huge core of unconscious emotions and actions. The easy (System 1) mode is "automatic". This does not mean that we cannot make more conscious decisions (System 2); it means that these are more "effortful", we need to use our willpower, which is a limited resource that can be depleted, much like a muscle that gets tired[148].

What do all the above have to do with out discussion on the sexes?

Emotions and drives related to the reproductive function are ancient. The are located in the lower, unconscious parts of the brain. We cannot consciously choose to like someone. We can choose not to satisfy what our instinct demands, but that requires effort, it burdens and strains us. As Schopenhauer put it, "I can choose what to do, but I cannot choose what to want".

The deep differences between the sexes are rooted in their different reproductive role, and are manifested primarily at the unconscious level. Therefore it is extremely difficult (for some of them) or impossible (for others) to change. And given the magnitude of these differences, they are decisive in the daily life of each sex.

---

148 Baumeister, Roy F. *Ego Depletion and Self-Control Failure: An Energy Model of the Self's Executive Function.* Self and Identity. 1 (2): 129–136, 2002.

Chapter 11: Sexual Selection and Runaway Process

While many are familiar with the Darwinian theory of evolution by Natural Selection, most ignore its second part, Sexual Selection.

The idea of Sexual Selection can be summarized as follows: Almost all species have preferences regarding their sexual partner. A healthy, athletic man is more attractive than a sick, disabled one, so he will be chosen by more women. Individuals who are not selected for reproduction leave no genetic footprint in the future generations, while those that are selected more often leave the largest footprint.

When we compare Sexual Selection with Natural Selection, we see an enormous difference: the former operates at a much faster pace, and is much more decisive in the species' evolution. As a result, it is quite common to find in many species traits that do not enhance survival (natural selection), but fuel only success in reproduction, even at the expense of survival. This occurs through what is termed a "runaway process".

The Runaway Process is fundamental to evolution. This process practically "allows species to evolve in arbitrary directions"[149], i.e. directions that have nothing to do with an advantage in survival. Let's explain this with an example.

Let's suppose that the females of a bird species show a random genetic preference for males with long wings. These males will leave more offspring than those with short wings. In addition, the daughters of the females will inherit the preference for long wings from their mothers. This will result in the population evolving towards having longer wings. But longer wing-length is not necessarily an advantage for survival. In strong storms, birds that have wings that are shorter or longer than average are more likely to get killed. Survival puts the limit to that capricious process, either by limiting the trait that tends to run away, or

---

149 Miller, The Mating Mind, p. 69.

by eliminating the species altogether[150].

However, more often than not, the environmental conditions are not very strict, if seen at a mid-term level with regards to evolution. They allow it the possibility to play these games. The peacock's tail and the nightinggale's song are two of the most impressive products of the Runaway Process seen in nature.

The Runaway Process gives a different evolutionary perspective than the classical one, natural selection: instead of the species evolving by adapting to the environment, by the survival of the fittest, they evolve traits in a random way. These traits can subsequently prove to be useful (if they are useful), and therefore survive in the evolving species. Those two processes, runaway and natural selection, take place simultaneously and give a fuller picture of evolution.

Why are we referring to this process, and what significance does it have for the discussion about the sexes?

One thing is to recognize that sexual preferences are not always compatible with "evolution" or "the good of the species", but that they can have an evolutionary random or indifferent character. Furthermore, once we have identified and studied this process in nature, it is even more important to see that it is not limited to biology, but also extends to social phenomena. Fashion is the obvious example. There is no practical reason for bell bottom pants becoming a fashion in the '70s.

Another, slightly gruesome social runaway example comes from the Far East: foot binding[151]. In China, from the 10th century to the early 20th, "all but the lowest of classes" used to tightly bind the girls' feet to prevent their growth.

> "To enable the size of the feet to be reduced, the toes on each foot were curled under, then pressed with great force downwards and squeezed into the sole of the foot until the toes broke. The broken toes were held tightly against the sole of the foot while the foot was then drawn down straight with the leg and the arch forcibly broken.... At the

---

150 Miller, The Mating Mind, p. 42.
151 Wikipedia, Foot binding. Accessed 19 Jan. 2015.
     https://en.wikipedia.org/wiki/Foot_binding

beginning of the binding, many of the foot bones would remain broken, often for years. However, as the girl grew older, the bones would begin to heal. Even after the foot bones had healed, they were prone to re-breaking repeatedly, especially when the girl was in her teenage years and her feet were still soft."

The preference for small feet probably has an evolutionary basis. It corresponds to the preference for young women, at their fertility peak. The fairytale about Cinderella's tiny slipper comes to mind... But the preference for deformed feet is certainly a (gruesome) runaway result.

A similar example concerns the necks of Kayan women in Burma, which reach incredible lengths with special metal coils that are worn from childhood. Although medically this would probably be classified as a disability, in their society, elongated necks are considered attractive.

Values that are considered normal in today's society, especially the mating system and marriage, are not "normal" for the human species, but the result of a social runaway process. We will identify their beginning in a while, as well as what needs they served in the past; we would only like to note here that these values continue to exist and to propagate following an autonomous inertia which contradicts the interests of humanity.

A Kayan Lahwi woman. Wikimedia Commons.
By Steve Evans. CC BY 2.0

Chapter 12: Why two sexes?

Why sex? Why does every child has to have two parents? Why not three? Or just one? Why do parents need to be of a different sex, and not the same? Why are there two sexes? Are they indeed "equal" or "equivalent"? If yes, in what sense?

We are biological beings, so the above questions are inescapable for whomever wants to approach the gender issues, ever if he is only interested in their political dimension – or rather, *especially* if they want to discuss their political dimension.

Why two parents?

The first interesting question is why every child is the result of sex between two parents. Most microorganisms reproduce by splitting the initial individual in two. Many plants reproduce by suckers. Parthenogenesis initially seems to have a huge biological advantage: you reproduce 100% of your genes, compared to only 50% when reproduction involves sex. Why has this been practically eliminated in the higher species? Which biological disadvantage has proven even more formidable?

The answer is parasites. Viruses, bacteria and other microorganisms with a much shorter reproduction cycle need several generations to break the genetic code of an organism's cells and infect it. The recombination of genes that occurs during the sexual reproduction of higher species makes every new generation a new challenge for those microorganisms. If higher species reproduced asexually, parasites, having solved the problem in the previous generation, would party with the new ones, like the European diseases did with the populations of America when the New World was discovered.

A second question arises: why do we not have three or more parents? To answer that question we need to look at a few more things about the biology of males and females. The answer, as we will shortly see, has to do with the polarization that happens between the sexes, resulting in each in-between, different sex being "punished" biologically.

Why two sexes?

We have understood why the species needs two parents. But, we have yet to see proof that excludes them being of the same sex. Why not make everyone hermaphrodite? Why must there be a male and female? Why should it be exactly two sexes and not more? This is the issue that has the greatest social implications.

What defines males and females?

What characterizes an individual as male or female?

> "There is one fundamental feature of the sexes which can be used to label males as males, and females as females, throughout animals and plants. This is that the sex cells or 'gametes' of males are much smaller and more numerous than the gametes of females. This is true whether we are dealing with animals or plants. One group of individuals has large sex cells, and it is convenient to use the word female for them. The other group, which it is convenient to call male, has small sex cells."[152]

In biological terms, females must invest much more heavily to the production of their gametes, than males. The hen's egg, the female gamete, is way bigger and more costly to make than the sperm of the rooster which is invisible to the naked eye. In mammals the mother must use incomparably more resources, not only to build the larger gamete (oocyte), but also to gestate. This is the fundamental biological difference, from which all other sex differences result.

Let us now return to our question, why two sexes? The first thing to note is that the universal[153] occurrence of two sexes emerged through the evolution of simpler asexual systems. That is, in the beginning there was

---

152 Dawkins, Richard. *The Selfish Gene.* UK: Oxford University Press (2006). p. 141. By Permission of Oxford University Press.
153 In higher organisms the existence of two sexes is universal. For a more complete discussion, see The Red Queen.

hermaphrodite reproduction, where two individuals exchanged genetic material with "isogametes". The male and female sex emerged as "specializations" thereon.

Let's follow this process through The Selfish Gene[154]:

> "Parker and others showed how this asymmetry *[in gametes]* might have evolved from an originally isogamous state of affairs. In the days when all sex cells were interchangeable and of roughly the same size, there would have been some that just happened to be slightly bigger than others. In some respects a big isogamete would have an advantage over an average-sized one, because it would get its embryo off to a good start by giving it a large initial food supply. There might therefore have been an evolutionary trend towards larger gametes. But there was a catch. The evolution of isogametes that were larger than was strictly necessary would have opened the door to selfish exploitation. Individuals who produced smaller than average gametes could cash in, provided they could ensure that their small gametes fused with extra-big ones. This could be achieved by making the small ones more mobile, and able to seek out large ones actively. The advantage to an individual of producing small, rapidly moving gametes would be that he could afford to make a larger number of gametes, and therefore could potentially have more children. Natural selection favoured the production of sex cells that were small and that actively sought out big ones to fuse with. So we can think of two divergent sexual 'strategies' evolving. There was the large-investment or 'honest' strategy. This automatically opened the way for a small-investment exploitative strategy. Once the divergence between the two strategies had started, it would have continued in runaway fashion. Medium-sized intermediates would have been penalized, because they did not enjoy the advantages of either of the two more extreme strategies. *[This is the answer why we have two, and not three or more sexes]*. The exploiters would have evolved smaller and smaller size, and faster mobility. The honest ones would have evolved larger and larger size, to compensate for the ever-smaller investment contributed by the exploiters, and they became immobile because they would always be actively chased by the exploiters anyway. Each

154 Dawkins, The Selfish Gene, p. 142.

> honest one would 'prefer' to fuse with another honest one.
> But the selection pressure to lock out exploiters would have
> been weaker than the pressure on exploiters to duck under
> the barrier: the exploiters had more to lose, and they there-
> fore won the evolutionary battle. The honest ones became
> eggs, and the exploiters became sperms."

Therefore, if the defining characteristic of the female is the larger investment in the gametes (and later on in gestation), what characterizes the male is his tendency to spread his sperm far and wide.

Note that in the excerpt above the female reproductive function is marked as "honest" and the male as "exploiting". This discrepancy is what the males will later on in evolution be required to compensate for, by becoming providers or by other means, such as evolving greater risk taking behaviors, i.e. by making detrimental psychological adaptations.

Chapter 13: Male and Female Sexual Strategies

The biological war of the sexes

Each sex's different role in reproduction entails different reproductive strategies. Those strategies might sometimes comprise elements of cooperation between the sexes, however they are essentially competitive.

Let's suppose that each sex could follow the strategy that benefits it more, independently of the other. Since the female makes a much greater reproductive investment and has a *de facto* limited number of offspring, she "wants" (that is, it is evolutionary beneficial for her) to be fertilized only by the best possible male – let's call him the alpha-male. The male's "pure" strategy is the complete opposite: his spermatozoa cost almost no effort to make, therefore his "score" in the number of offspring has no upper limit. So it is advantageous for him to fertilize the largest possible number of healthy females.

Let us now introduce the factor of parental care: in many species, particularly birds, males contribute to the upbringing of their offspring, increasing their chance of survival. How does that modify the optimum strategy for the two sexes?

For the female, it still is optimal to be fertilized by the best male, and receive his care in return for her reproductive availability. However, since the male's sperm is practically infinite while the care he can provide is limited, the following variation arises as optimal: utilize his sperm, while utilizing another, lower male's paternal investment. Indeed, research in colonies of "monogamous" birds has found that the percentage of "bastards" in each nest is about 40%[155].

For the male, the optimum strategy is basically the same, viz. to fertilize all females. For the alpha-male this is an easy strategy to follow, since the females are naturally attracted to him and come to him in drives. For almost all the other males, from whom the females demand an investment in paternal care, there are two options: to provide or to rape. If they choose to provide, they still remain open to free offers from females who mated with even lower-ranked males.

We observe that in nature there is no place for human morality: infidelity exists because it has a huge evolutionary advantage, in terms of quality for the females, and in terms of quantity, i.e. the number of offspring, for males.

The system described above is even more complex in practice. The female is in danger of losing her mate's providing, so until she finds a better provider she must guard him in other not to lose him to someone better than her. On the other hand, the male does not "want" to be raising someone else's offspring, so he must guard his mate so that she does not become pregnant with someone else's child. However, it is not our purpose to examine thoroughly all the possible combinations and compromises that may arise as a result of these strategies. What we want to emphasize is that the female and the male reproductive strategies are fundamentally different.

---

155 Ridley, *The Red Queen*, p. 222.

Males court, females choose: Flirting

Females choose. To the males falls the heavy duty of courting. And that consists in displaying their higher genetic qualities. How do they display them?

Consider, as an example, that women are attracted solely to wealth. A man claiming "I am rich", performs quite a meaningless display. He can easily be lying, because it costs him nothing. But driving an expensive car, wearing expensive clothes and paying expensive restaurants is a much more reliable indication of his wealth. The difference is in the *cost*.

In biology the example that illustrates this principle is the peacock's tail. The vivid colors and the symmetrical designs are just one of the quality indicators. The most important is that, ironically, carrying such a huge tail is a hindrance to survival when tigers chase after you. It has a huge biological cost; it is a handicap. Therefore, only the qualitatively best males can cope with it. "Oh! Look what a huge tail he has! He must be really fast and strong, to have managed to survive with it!" - say the females. "The handicap principle suggests that prodigious waste is a necessary feature of sexual courtship."[156] This principle is well established in what is called "signal theory" in economics: signals that have a big cost are more reliable indicators. Those that cost nothing are characteristically termed "cheap talk".

In "tournament species", like with wild horses or gorillas, the "alpha-males" get all the females. Their superior quality is advertised by way of battles, which can be fierce and have a high cost for the loser, but also for the winner. The females are not extorted to mate with the winner: they are simply only receptive to him. He is also responsible of guarding them against the annoying, inferior males. Male "jealousy" in this case is more a service to the female, than a reproductive tactic.

Each species as a whole would be better off if its males were not forced to pay the colossal cost of flirting. "Peacocks as a species would be much better off if they did not have to waste so much energy growing big tails."[157] We could therefore say that flirting is a "luxury good". The

156 Miller, The Mating Mind, p. 125.
157 Ibid.

human species has expanded this biological principle to the field of economics. As early as 1899 economist Thorstein Veblen had recognized what he termed "conspicuous consumption", i.e. the consumption of luxury goods as a way to display status. Even the origin of trade, the economic core of historical societies, is related to the procurement of luxury goods like gold and gems, which are practically useless beyond their use to signal status and ensure the provision of sex.

We begin to see now why females are able to define the terms of the sexual game, and why these terms do not benefit humanity.

Chapter 14: The Dominant Narrative and its Criticism

The dominant narrative about human sexuality, as Ryan & Jetha describe it[158], is the following:

> "1. Boy meets girl.
>
> 2. Boy and girl assess one another's mate value from perspectives based upon their differing reproductive agendas/ capacities:
>
> • He looks for signs of youth, fertility, health, absence of previous sexual experience, and likelihood of future sexual fidelity. In other words, his assessment is skewed toward finding a fertile, healthy young mate with many childbearing years ahead and no current children to drain his resources.
>
> • She looks for signs of wealth (or at least prospects of future wealth), social status, physical health, and likelihood that he will stick around to protect and provide for their children. Her guy must be willing and able to provide

---

158 Ryan, Christopher and Jetha, Cacilda. *Sex at Dawn: The prehistoric origins of modern sexuality*. USA: Harper Perennial (2011). Introduction. By permission of the authors.

materially for her (especially during pregnancy and breastfeeding) and their children (known as male parental investment).

3. Boy gets girl: assuming they meet one another's criteria, they "mate," forming a long-term pair bond—the "fundamental condition of the human species," as famed author Desmond Morris put it. Once the pair bond is formed:

• She will be sensitive to indications that he is considering leaving (vigilant toward signs of infidelity involving intimacy with other women that would threaten her access to his resources and protection) – while keeping an eye out (around ovulation, especially) for a quick fling with a man genetically superior to her husband.

• He will be sensitive to signs of her sexual infidelities (which would reduce his all-important paternity certainty)— while taking advantage of short-term sexual opportunities with other women (as his sperm are easily produced and plentiful)."

The authors emphasize that

"While we don't dispute that these patterns play out in many parts of the modern world, we don't see them as elements of human nature so much as adaptations to social conditions— many of which were introduced with the advent of agriculture no more than ten thousand years ago. These behaviors and predilections are not biologically programmed traits of our species; they are evidence of the human brain's flexibility and the creative potential of community."

They propose instead a model of free sexuality as being a "natural" condition for humans.

However, the two models, the "dominant" of monogamy-plus-cheating and that of sexual freedom, are not mutually exclusive. Humankind did evolve with a sexuality much freer than that described in the dominant model, but under the pressures it prescribes. The factors of sexual attraction are largely those described in the dominant model, and since attraction happens "automagically", without us having any control over it, there is a strong biological, not social basis to it.

Free sexuality is at odds with the way attraction works – especially for women, who "possess" sex. It performed a broader function than reproduction: it was the cohesive element of human society, and was the framework within which the truly different male and female sexual strategies were forced to operate. In other words, free sex did not mean that the special preferences of each sex were eliminated. More particularly, it did not mean that women had different attraction circuits: they always preferred the most dominant men. As we will see, free sex was a "concession" from women, or rather, in a greater degree, an aggressive conquest of men.

Chapter 15: What is Sexy?

There is a slogan than one can see in feminist fiestas printed on XXL T-shirts: "All bodies are beautiful". Not true. Some are more beautiful, and some are uglier.

Many progressives, reacting against the "imposed standards of beauty" argue that attractiveness is "socially determined". Their typical example is the plump beauty models of past centuries, who today some might consider even repulsive. And it is indeed true that some of the factors defining attractiveness are social. But not all of them.

There are three classes of attraction factors: universal, social and personal.

Universal factors

The physical characteristics that make a woman attractive are those indicating health and fertility. "Features that have universal sex appeal include clear, smooth skin, plump lips, clear, large eyes, good muscle tone, sprightly gait, symmetrical features, and a low waist-to-hip ratio – all of which are associated with fertility."[159] Particularly, low waist-to-hip ratio is an attractive characteristic independently of how thin or plump the woman is. Plump models of the past had relatively thin waist, despite their weight.

On a man, physical characteristics that are attractive are the height, a strong, muscular V-shaped body with high shoulder-to-hip ratio, a deep voice, a symmetric face.

Both sexes, then, are attracted by specific physical characteristics. Beauty is largely objective. "The components of beauty are quite definable and consistent around the world – although the components differ depending on whether men or women are the judges."[160]

But there is a factor that is decidedly different for the sexes. The most important feature for a woman to consider a man attractive is not physical. It is his social status. "Dominance and the traits associated with it predict men's mating success, but [physical] attractiveness and the traits associated with it do not."[161] Women habitually use wealth as a proxy for status, so that a rich man is by definition attractive.

The costume experiment leaves no doubt: Men and women looked at pictures of people of the opposite sex and of various levels of physical attractiveness. The models wore three different types of dress: high status (white shirt for men or silk blouse for women, blazer, rolex), medium status (off-white shirt, khaki slacks), low status (uniform of a hamburger chain). The interviewees then reported how willing they would be to engage into different types of relationships with the models. Men were very willing to meet the prettiest model, completely indifferent to how she was dressed, while they were not willing to date the homely model in either costume. "Women, however, were affected by how the men were dressed... In fact, for women, the blazer and Rolex made the homely model more acceptable than the best looking model in the fast-food

159 Buss, Why women have sex, ch.9.
160 Townsend, What Women Want – What Men Want, p. 7.
161 Hill, Alexander K, et al. *Quantifying the strength and form of sexual selection on men's traits.* Evolution And Human Behavior, 2013.
     http://www.wellingresearchlab.com/uploads/1/3/5/7/13572010/hill_et_al._2013.pdf

uniform for all types of relationships."[162]

An important observation is that while the physical characteristics are objective in nature, status is relative. In a group of pretty women, everyone is attractive for a man. In a group of men, only he who has the greater status is attractive. That is exactly what pushes men, willing or not, to be competitive and to form hierarchical structures. Moreover, a woman's attractiveness remains relatively stable, while a man's depends on the circumstances and has a great variation, even from second to second. This is a reality difficult and taxing for a man to handle in his social interactions.

Social factors

Socially-defined attraction factors are e.g. preference for slenderness or plumpness. Another such factor is white or tanned skin. In the US for example, in the beginning of the last century, white skin was considered attractive. The invention of the airplane and transatlantic trips made it possible to have summer vacations in the French Riviera, so the higher class were tanned from sunbathing. As a result, tans became attractive. Socially determined factors, then, are often those that associate an attribute with the upper classes.

Another, somewhat grotesque example comes from the Elizabethan era. At that time, only the rich could afford to buy sweets, and in the absence of basic dental hygiene, only they had blackened teeth. Black teeth became a status symbol, and women that had white teeth used to color them black with a special paint.

Personal factors

Finally, our personal history may strongly influence our preferences. For instance, a blue-eyed first girlfriend might give us a preference for blue-eyed women from then on. Sexologist John Money proposed that we all have a "love map", a unique template of what we find attractive. Love maps are formed starting in childhood, based on our positive or negative

---

162 Townsend, What Women Want – What Men Want, p. 63.

experiences with people. "The nice blond grocery store clerk who always gave you candy – check in the blond hair column." The bald priest who was very strict and oppressive during confession – dislike balds and maybe even priests. "These childhood experiences condition us to find certain features attractive or unattractive."[163] Psychologists have countless examples of people seeking the behavioral style of their parents in subsequent sexual partners. By adolescence, all this information "is imprinted in the brain's circuitry... [W]hen a sufficient number of "hits" line up with your love map, then attraction blooms."[164]

Personal factors are responsible for the variation in attractiveness, and hence the confusion it creates over the existence or lack of objective attractiveness. That is, if we try to measure someone's attractiveness based on people's opinions, we will see that those opinions are not identical. Nevertheless, they range in a zone around one's "average" attractiveness.

In other words, every person might be special regarding his/her tastes, and the way s/he gets attracted by others might be determined much more by his/her personal history than the universal or social factors. However, individual differences are eliminated when talking about society as a whole, so it is quite clear that some people are generally more or less attractive.

We will see bellow[165] that while in men there is a normal distribution in their preferences, classifying for example 50% of women above average, women have a very elitist one, classifying most men below average.

Chapter 16: Human Sexual Characteristics

In today's world one can find many different sexualities. Straight, gay, bi,

---

163 Buss, Why women have sex, ch.1.
164 Buss, Why women have sex, ch.1.
165 See Part 3, The difficulty to find a mate, p. 122.

monogamous, polygamous, polyamorous, free relationships, sex only in marriage, etc. Obviously everyone has the right to one's own sexuality. Nevertheless, it is important to ask whether there is such a thing as a "natural" form of sexuality for humans. This question tries to identify not inescapable constants, but rather natural tendencies in human sexuality. Moreover, it tries to define the degree to which these can be identified in any type of society.

The main issue before us is to examine the extent to which men and women (separately) are monogamous or polygamous.

An answer to this question requires us to start by examining men and women's sexual characteristics.

Cryptic ovulation and constant sexual appetite

Man is one of the few species on the planet in which ovulation is hidden[166]. In chimpanzees for instance, there is the distinctive swelling of the female genitalia. Dogs secrete hormones that signal estrus. Man, however, has no way to consciously determine if a woman is ovulating.

Hidden ovulation constitutes strong evidence that humans are polygamous. All other mammals that have it, like dolphins and gray langurs, are polygamous.

What is the purpose of hidden ovulation? It probably serves many purposes together.

In a polygamous system, it obscures paternity. In chimpanzees and lions that do not have it, males will kill the offspring of females that haven't mated with them during their estrus, in order for her to ovulate again and mate with them. But when you are not certain about a woman's fertile period and you had sex with her, it is possible that you are the father, so it is evolutionary risky to kill the offspring.

In hunter-gatherer communities, even modern ones, women exchange sex for meat. The same thing happens in all primates that have meat in

---

166 This section is based on the article in Wikipedia, Concealed Ovulation,
     http://en.wikipedia.org/wiki/Concealed_ovulation

their diet. Obviously a female has a greater chance to be given meat when she is ovulating. In this respect, women's constant sexual receptivity, as well as their sexual characteristics such as breasts full of fat that mimic estrus, have evolved by being evolutionary advantageous. That is, "human female anatomy evolved to mimic permanent signaling of fertility"[167].

Even those who consider pair bonding the "fundamental condition of the human species" recognizes that "cheating" is inevitable: the relevant theory, the "cuckoldry hypothesis", argues, as we have seen, that cheating gives women the freedom to mate with her (biologically superior) lover, while ensuring the continuous providing of her (stable) partner. Her regular mate cannot know the time of ovulation and be extra vigilant. Research has indeed shown that during their fertile days women are more likely to have sex with their lover[168].

However, the explanation for cryptic ovulation that suits all the other sexual characteristics of both sexes (which we will discuss shortly), is that of *social bonding*.

The number one reason for aggression, not only in humans but in every species, is male-to-male aggression over reproductive access to females[169]. The second reason is males attacking females over denial of sexual access.

The abundance of female sexual availability served social cohesion in the first human communities by eliminating the causes of competition and violence among men – as well as violence against women.

A pregnancy has a huge biological cost for a woman, and in the evolutionary era it was even more costly. Certainly social peace is valuable to the whole community, but is it worth so much, that women need to pay for it so dearly? Mainstream biologists largely reject that hypothesis, given that a woman's reproductive capacity is her more valuable asset. But they overlook a critical and, if one gives it some

167 Szalay, Frederick S., Costello, Robert K. *Evolution of permanent estrus displays in hominids.* Journal of Human Evolution, Vol. 20, issue 6, June 1991, pp. 439-464 http://www.sciencedirect.com/science/article/pii/004724849190019R
168 Baker, Sperm Wars, p. 42.
169 Sapolsky, Human Behavioral Biology, available at https://youtu.be/NNnIGh9g6fA

thought, obvious point: not all copulations result in pregnancies. The human species has an average of 1000 copulations per pregnancy, as compared with 20 in lions. In any case, women in prehistory spent all their fertile years either pregnant or unovulating due to breastfeeding. While they were unable to conceive, they could still satisfy men's sexual hunger in order to eliminate frustration and subsequent aggression.

Female orgasm

Female orgasm is still a vast mystery, and object of intense debate among scientists. There is no universally accepted theory for its evolutionary role. We will limit ourselves to describing only a few of its characteristics.

While it is not necessary to conceive, female orgasm increases chances of conception. This fits with our hypothesis of a poly-sexual society. It is the way by which, while sex was "free for all", the "best" men, i.e. those that could give an orgasm, had more chances and a greater reproductive success.

Modern research, for example, has found that the probability of female orgasm increases when the man is rich[170]. Wealth might not have been a factor in the hunter-gatherers of the past, but in today's society, as we have seen, it is used by women as an indication of high status, and by unconscious implication, genetic quality.

Female orgasm, therefore, seems to be an unconscious mechanism of sexual choice. It is the center of every woman's fantasy. Indicative of its great importance in the sexual game is that man too, in his sexual fantasies, envisions the female orgasm and not his own.

Sperm competition.

> "Sperm competition is a term used to refer to the competitive process between spermatozoa of two or more

---

170 "females proved to be more orgasmic with the socially dominant males, especially when a low-ranked female copulated with a high-ranking male". The Evolution of Desire, p. 232.

different males to fertilize an egg of a lone female."[171]

Sperm competition exists in all species that are not monogamous – notably humans. The female reproductive tract has developed a biologically hostile environment for the spermatozoa. Most of them die relatively soon, but enough survive, so that fertilization may happen up to four days later, if you are lucky (or unlucky) and the ovum descends at that time. Within that time frame, in a non-monogamous environment, sperm from several men will be present in the female reproductive tract. Those that are more plenty have a statistically higher probability to fertilize the egg. As a result of this evolutionary pressure, a human ejaculation contains about 250 million spermatozoa. In gorillas, where females are monogamous, an ejaculation contains one fifth of that number, 50 million.

Sperms from two males engage in a real war inside the female reproductive tract[172]. They use toxins that kill rival sperm. In experiments with flies, males that had been exposed to conditions of intense reproductive competition, produced a sperm after a few dozens generations which was so toxic that it could kill not only the rival sperm, but even females that had not been exposed in the same conditions and had not developed resistance to it[173].

In gorillas, on the other hand, spermatozoa from different males, rather than fighting, cooperate as if they were from the same male: they "swim" together, creating something like a "super sperm" which makes it easier for the sperm to advance towards the ovum. The occasional rape from a lower status gorilla was not enough evolutionary pressure for the species to develop a toxic sperm[174].

The need for numerous spermatozoa led polygamous species to develop one more adaptation: large testes and penises. "So, although an adult silverback gorilla weighs in at around four hundred pounds, his penis is just over an inch long, at full mast, and his testicles are the size of kidney

171 Wikipedia, Sperm Competition. Accessed 19 Jan. 2015.
     http://en.wikipedia.org/wiki/Sperm_competition
172 See Baker, Sperm Wars.
173 Sapolsky, Human Behavioral Biology.
174 Sapolsky, Human Behavioral Biology.

beans, though you'd have trouble finding them, as they're safely tucked up inside his body. A one-hundred-pound bonobo has a penis three times as long as the gorilla's and testicles the size of chicken eggs."[175] Man is somewhere in the middle, in the size of the testes. It seems he was not programmed to have the impressive intercourse frequency of bonobos, that have sex every two hours.

Another adaptation due to sperm competition the shape of the human penis. It is specifically designed so that when thrusting outwards it pulls out the pre-existing sperm of the competitor[176]. Scientists experimenting with plastic phalluses and artificial vaginas found that a single thrust was sufficient to remove 90% of the seminal fluid[177]. This explains the intense back-and-forth... action, which is characteristic of the human sexual act, as well as its longer duration compared to other species[178]. It also explains why the penis shrinks immediately after ejaculation: so that it does not pull out its own sperm.

> *I'm ready for love, oh baby I'm ready for love*
> *– Bad Company*

Have you been kicked in the balls? Deliberately or accidentally? Chances are that if you happen to feature balls, you have. It hurts, doesn't it? Why then is such a sensitive organ not better protected? Why can't it be inside the body, as happens in most mammals, e.g. in gorillas? The answer is that sperm is better preserved at lower temperatures. Males in polygamous species need every possible advantage in sperm competition, so nature made them risk the aforementioned kick in the groin so that the testes are better ventilated. Ryan & Jetha make a witty comparison:

> "A scrotum is like a spare refrigerator in the garage just for beer. If you've got a spare beer fridge, you're probably the type who expects a party to break out at any moment. You want to be prepared. A scrotum fulfills the same function. By keeping the testicles a few degrees cooler than they

---

175 Ryan, Sex at Dawn, ch.15.
176 Baker, Sperm Wars, p. 178.
177 'BBC NEWS | Health | Penis is a competitive beast'.
    http://news.bbc co.uk/2/hi/health/3128753.stm
178 Ryan, Sex at Dawn, ch.17.

would be inside the body, a scrotum allows chilled spermatozoa to accumulate and remain viable longer, available if needed."[179]

A double strategy for women

The exceptional importance of Sperm Competition is that it dramatically changes the terms of the sexual game. In a sexually promiscuous environment the *biologically* best male is not necessarily the *reproductively* best one. It is possible for a biologically inferior, weak and ugly man to have highly competitive sperm, thus giving a woman's male children an evolutionary advantage.

As a result, the optimal strategy for women, in such a setting, is drastically modified. It becomes two-dimensional. On the one hand, the standard attraction towards the "best" men ensures genetic quality. On the other, maintaining a pool of sexual partners, as opposed to having only one, promotes sperm competition, i.e. helps select quality sperm. In "complex multi-male, multi-female" groups, as those "our hominid ancestors probably lived in", "sometimes, females ... appear to use sperm-production ability as the main fitness indicator. A chimpanzee female might mate with every male in the group every time she becomes fertile. She lets their sperm fight it out in her reproductive tract, and the strongest swimmers with the best endurance will probably fertilize her egg."[180]

The consequences for men

In a society like our ancestors', where sexual life was dictated by sperm competition and was... orgiastic in character, it made no sense for men to exercise self-restraint. The "party guys" of the past seized all the reproductive opportunities, genetically defining man's sexuality thereafter. Today's men, although society no longer permits it, are still programmed to desire plenty and varied sex. Their happiness largely depends on getting it, since positive emotions correspond to what promoted their reproduction (and survival). Colors are brighter, food is

---

179 Ryan, Sex at Dawn, ch.17.
180 Miller, The Mating Mind, p. 183.

tastier, and life is beautiful for a man who has an adequate sex life. Life is drab, colorless and meaningless, when his sexual life is limited.

Sex drive

A completely different dynamic emerges from the different reproductive position of each sex. This dynamic is encapsulated in the sex drive[181]. In other words, *men and women's different sex drive is what determines the differences in the behavior of men and women in the psychosomatic level.*

The male sex drive is much stronger than the female one. Baumeuster and Twenge's review on the issue states:

> "Across many different studies and measures, men have been shown to have more frequent and more intense sexual desires than women, as reflected in spontaneous thoughts about sex, frequency and variety of sexual fantasies, desired frequency of intercourse, desired number of partners, masturbation, liking for various sexual practices, willingness to forego sex, initiating versus refusing sex, making sacrifices for sex, and other measures. No contrary findings (indicating stronger sexual motivation among women) were found. Hence we conclude that the male sex drive is stronger than the female sex drive."[182]

Since there are still many who dispute this[183], and this dispute is particularly prevalent in "progressives", it is critical to distinguish between the sex drive and other aspects of sexuality. As the above authors point out, "the gender difference in sex drive should not be generalized to other constructs such as sexual or orgasmic capacity, enjoyment of sex, or extrinsically motivated sex." Some maintain that women enjoy sex more

---

181 Drives are instinctive tendencies that push individuals towards behaviors that reduce excitation or satisfy psychosomatic human needs.
182 Baumeister, Roy F. Catanese, Kathleen R. Vohs, Kathleen D. "Is There a Gender Difference in Strength of Sex Drive? Theoretical Views, Conceptual Distinctions, and a Review of Relevant Evidence". Personality and Social Psychology Review August 2001, vol. 5, no. 3, 242-273. http://citeseerx.ist.psu.edu/viewdoc/summary?doi=10.1.1.186.5369.
183 An article with this prejudice is e.g. http://www.psychologytoday.com/blog/dollars-and-sex/201307/response-the-economics-slut-shaming

than men. Maybe they do. Maybe they don't. What is certain is that they have a weaker sex drive. Sex for men is like food, and their sex drive actually shares common brain pathways with hunger. For women, sex is more like cake. You need to eat food, even if it's not that great, and you will do anything to get it if you are really hungry. But eating a cake is a different business. You might really enjoy a good one, but you don't really need it, and wouldn't make many sacrifices to get it.

In *Why Women Have Sex,* the authors report: "Studies consistently show that men report higher levels of sex drive than women. This holds true for college students, middle-aged people, and even eighty- and ninety-year-olds."[184] Additionally, "gender differences in how women and men are sexually aroused ... give women extra leverage in sexual economics... Simply the sight of an attractive woman can lead a heterosexual man to become aroused, and this gives women, who tend to be less keyed to visual attractions, an edge."[185]

The word "stronger" usually has positive connotations, so maybe the expression "stronger sex drive" fails to adequately describe how huge a disadvantage that is for men.

Nora Vincent is a lesbian feminist who, using expert guidance, disguised and lived as a man for almost a year. She expected to enjoy "male privilege", but her experience turned out to be different. In her book, she characteristically writes:

> "If you have never been sexually attracted to women, you will never quite understand the monumental power of female sexuality, except by proxy or in theory, nor will you quite know the immense advantage it gives us over men. Dating women as a man was a lesson in female power, and it made me, of all things, into a momentary misogynist..."[186]

Since drives are *unconscious impulses* that define our actions beyond our will, we could alternatively say that women have a much stronger *control* over their sex drive than men.

---

184 Buss, Why Women Have Sex, ch. 6.
185 Buss, Why Women Have Sex, ch. 6.
186 Vincent, Norah. *Self-Made Man: One Woman's Year Disguised as a Man.* USA: Penguin Books (2006). Ch. 4.

The better overall position of women in society can be explained on the basis of this difference alone.

Biological differences

The first observation is that it is a biological and not a socially determined difference. In *The Female Brain*, we read:

> "The sex-related centers in the male brain are actually about two times larger than parallel structures in the female brain.... Males have double the brain space and processing power devoted to sex as females. Just as women have an eight-lane superhighway for processing emotion while men have a small country road, men have [Chicago's busy] O'Hare Airport as a hub for processing thoughts about sex whereas women have the airfield nearby that lands small and private planes.... These structural changes in the brain start as early as eight weeks after conception, when testosterone in the male fetus fertilizes the sex-related brain center – called the "area for sexual pursuit" in the hypothalamus – to grow larger. A second massive surge of testosterone at puberty then strengthens and enlarges other brain connections in the male that feed information to these sex centers, including the visual, smell, touch, and cognitive systems. The twenty-five-fold increase in testosterone between ages nine and fifteen fuels these larger sex connections in a male's brain for the rest of his youth."[187]

Apart from brain wiring, behavior is influenced by hormones. In both sexes, the hormone related to the sex drive is testosterone. People with problems in the production of testosterone, either men or women, have no appetite for sex. The difference is that the daily production is about 20 times greater in men".

The next example from the same book shows the importance of testosterone: 42 year old female teacher Jill complained about having "no libido", so she was given testosterone supplement.

> "During the time between appointments, Jill mistakenly doubled her dose of testosterone. Her face was blushing bright red when she came into the clinic. She sheepishly

---

187 Brizendine, The Female Brain, p.91.

told me of her mistake and said her sexual urges were now so strong that she was running into the bathroom between classes to masturbate. She said, 'This is becoming a real bother, but now I know what it must feel like to be a nineteen-year-old boy!'"[188]

Consequences

The difference in sex drive does not mean that at every moment every single man is more willing to have sex than any woman. It is a mood, the magnitude of which varies over time. It is not uncommon for a woman to be in a mood where she seeks a lot of sex. The difference is that a healthy man is almost permanently in this mood. A woman may spend days, weeks or even months without thinking about or looking for sex[189], and that can be normal. But sex is always on the minds of men.

Baumeister summarizes this difference by saying that women have a greater *"erotic plasticity"*[190]: their sex drive can much more easily adapt to consequences, since it is "milder than men's"[191], while it exerts a much more constant pressure in men.

The relative weakness of the female sex drive is highlighted by lesbian couples, where no man is present to take the sexual initiative. Perhaps contrary to some popular fantasies, these couples have such low frequency of sexual intercourse (47% have sex less than once a month) that female sociologist Pepper Schwarz coined the term "lesbian bed death"[192] to describe it.

It is easy to understand the evolutionary origin of this discrepancy. It is beneficial females to be able to control their urges, since it puts them in a better place to negotiate rewards for themselves and their offspring. Males, with their millions of spermatozoa, have a greater reproductive

188 Brizendine, The Female Brain, p. 90.
189 Townsend, What Women Want – What Men Want, p. 13.
190 Baumeister, Roy F. "Gender and erotic plasticity: sociocultural influences on the sex drive". Sexual and Relationship Therapy, Vol. 19, No. 2, May 2004
http://www.hawaii.edu/hivandaids/Gender_and_Erotic_Plasticity__Sociocultural_Inf
luences_on_the_Sex_Drive.pdf
191 Townsend, What Women Want – What Men Want, p. 13.
192 Blumstein, Phillip and Schwartz, Pepper. *American Couples: Money, Work, Sex*. USA: William Morrow (1983).

success when they are always ready for sex, even willing to make sacrifices for it.

However, in modern daily life that has not been built around sex but around work, school, family and other commitments, having such constant pressure is a huge handicap for men. It is the reason for which girls have a greater ability to concentrate in the classroom, and diachronically have outperformed boys in all courses[193]. This is also the reason why men spend an incredible amount of time and money hunting after sex. Money which women enjoy in the form of luxuries, and time which they spend in grooming and their very important social-networking – including nurturing their relationships with their children.

An extra gift of nature

Women are thus endowed by nature with control over their sex drive to a degree which is inconceivable for men, as a weapon to use in the sex war. But nature has also given women another powerful gift: bisexuality.

In his book on the Pick Up Scene titled *The Game*, Neil Strauss describes how he discovered a tactic for having threesomes. He first had girls massage him. Then he started kissing the first girl, and gently pulled the second into the kiss. "Once Hea and Isabel's lips met, the spark of sexual tension that had hung in the room during the massage exploded. They were all over each other, as if they'd been wanting to do this all along. But they hadn't. They'd been bitter rivals less than an hour earlier. I didn't understand it – but then again I didn't need to." After this chance discovery, he gradually perfected the technique: "It was all just a routine now... And it worked ... consistently. Once the girls' lips touched, they transformed from strangers to lovers. It shocked me every time to see two women get intimate so quickly in such an unusual situation."[194]

Bisexuality is more widespread in women than in men. Studies[195]

193 Voyer, D. et al, *Gender differences in scholastic achievement: A meta-analysis.* Psychological Bulletin, Vol 140(4), Jul 2014, 1174-1204.
194 Strauss, Neil. *The Game: Penetrating the Secret Society of Pickup Artists.* USA: ReganBooks (2005).
195 'Why Are So Many Girls Lesbian or Bisexual? | Psychology Today'. http://www.psychologytoday.com/blog/sax-sex/201004/why-are-so-many-girls-

estimate the percentage of "not strictly heterosexual" women in the US at 14.4%, compared with 5.6% of men, in New Zealand this figure is 16.4% vs 5.6%, while in Sweden the female percentage is even higher, at 20%.

It is significant that the stronger the sex drive is in a woman, the more bisexual she tends to be. Researchers have found that "the higher women's sex drives, the more they desire both sexes. Conversely, the higher men's sex drive, the more they desire either one sex or the other, depending on their sexual orientation. For most men, a higher sex drive simply intensifies their existing sexual orientation."[196] In other words, women are either not much interested in sex, or, if they are, they have an extra outlet with other women. In both cases, men emerge as the losers. Nature's wisdom is really admirable...

It seems then that exists a reliable answer to the eternal question: are all women bisexual? No, not all. Only those that care enough about sex to bother. But as far as typical man is concerned, the above answer can be shortened to "Yes. All of them."

Apart from women that have an explicit homo- or bi-sexual orientation, there is an aura of keen sexuality in female groups, that is not present in male ones. The touching, kissing, body language which one can observe in girl groups, would undoubtedly constitute a flirting environment if we saw them in mixed companies of girls and boys. Women's greater "erotic plasticity" allows them to derive sexually-charged pleasure from their in-between interactions. They don't much need men to hug: they can do that without them.

It is fascinating to note that what nature has given to women as an unconscious tendency, has been turned into a conscious tactic by the feminist movement of the '70s. It was typical for feminist conferences to include "lesbianism seminars", so that women didn't have to "sleep with the enemy"... A similar proposal in today's men's Movement would be simply unthinkable (even though the movement is not hostile against gay men). Men cannot do without women. Women *can* do without men. A male counterpart to the myth of the Amazons is nowhere to be found...

---

lesbian-or-bisexual
196 'BBC - Science & Nature - Sex ID - Study Results'.
    http://www.bbc.co.uk/science/humanbody/sex/articles/results/sexdrive.shtml

The Coolidge effect

The following anecdote can be found in every book on evolutionary psychology:

> "The President of the US Calvin Coolidge and Mrs. Coolidge were being separately shown around an experimental government farm. When Mrs. Coolidge came to the chicken yard she noticed that a rooster was mating very frequently. She asked the attendant how often that happened and was told, 'Dozens of times each day.' Mrs. Coolidge said, 'Tell that to the President when he comes by.' Upon being told, President asked, 'Same hen every time?' The reply was, 'Oh, no, Mr. President, a different hen every time.' President: 'Tell that to Mrs. Coolidge.'"[197]

"In biology and psychology, the Coolidge effect is a phenomenon seen in mammalian species whereby males (and to a lesser extent females) exhibit renewed sexual interest if introduced to new receptive sexual partners, even after refusing sex from prior but still available sexual partners."[198]

Initially observed by chance in laboratory mice, this phenomenon has been confirmed in other mammals. "Males continue to become aroused to the point of ejaculation in response to novel females, and the response to the eighth, the tenth, or the twelfth female is nearly as strong as the response to the first."[199] Shepherds have known this for millennia: rams that are shown the same ewe again ...in disguise, with a canvas thrown over her, are not so easily fooled, and shun her.

men's interest for sexual variety is a phenomenon observed in every culture. The rich and powerful men of history, whenever they could, had harems, not just one woman. That possibility alone was enough motivation for men to make efforts to climb up the power ladder.

The difference between men and women in how much importance they give to sexual variety is highlighted by the existence of prostitution. Not

197 Wikipedia, Coolidge Effect. Accessed 19 Jan. 2015.
    https://en.wikipedia.org/wiki/Coolidge_effect
198 Wikipedia, Coolidge Effect..
199 Buss, The Evolution of Desire, p.80.

only are the vast majority of prostitutes women, but the few who are men are most commonly for gay men clients. Male prostitution for women is a marginal phenomenon catering to wealthy older women, and most men prostitutes are in developing countries, with the exception of the occasional expensive gigolo. In Nevada, the first legal "prostidude" for women soon abandoned the trade: in two months, fewer than 10 women were willing to pay him for sex[200]. On the other hand, the arrest of well-known actor and sex symbol Hugh Grant for going with a prostitute underlines men's continued need for sexual variety: the street prostitute he picked up was incredibly less attractive than his girlfriend of the time, Elizabeth Hurley. She was just a different woman...

Even more enlightening is the sexual behavior of gay men as opposed to lesbians. The first thing we must note is that gay men have male preferences as to what they find attractive and what they seek from their partner; it's only the object of their desire that changes. Similarly, homosexual women have female preferences. In homosexual circles, every sex may play out its sexual strategy autonomously, unhindered by the strategy of the opposite party. Hence, each sex's characteristics are better contrasted. Quoting Donald Symons, "homosexual men behave in many ways like heterosexual men, only more so, and lesbians behave like heterosexual women, only more so"[201].

What does this mean? "A Kinsey Institute study of gay men in the San Francisco Bay area found that 75 percent had had more than one hundred partners; 25 percent had had more than one thousand.... Most lesbians have fewer than ten partners in their lifetimes."[202] Donald Symons explains it this way:

> "Although homosexual men, like most people, usually want to have intimate relationships, such relationships are difficult to maintain, largely owing to the male desire for sexual variety; the unprecedented opportunity to satisfy this desire in a world of men; and the male tendency toward sexual jealousy... I am suggesting that heterosexual men

---

200 'Nation & World | Legal gigolo leaves brothel; few customers | Seattle Times Newspaper'. http://seattletimes.com/html/nationworld/2011453672_gigolo27.html
201 Symons, Donald. *The evolution of human sexuality*. New York: Oxford University Press (1981). p. 304.
202 Ridley, The Red Queen, p. 182.

would be as likely as homosexual men to have sex most often with strangers, to participate in anonymous orgies in public baths, and to stop off in public restrooms for five minutes of fellatio on the way home from work if women were interested in these activities"[203].

As Kinsey summarized it,

"There seems to be no question but that the human male would be promiscuous in his choice of sexual partners throughout the whole of his life if there were no social restrictions.... The human female is much less interested in a variety of partners."[204]

Female accommodation of male sexual strategy

We have already seen how women's continuous sexual receptivity served a social purpose, one of social cohesion. The long-standing evolutionary balance between the two sexes resulted in the emergence of strategies in women, which accommodate men's sexual strategy, obviously skewing the results in favor of women.

Women's capacity for successive sex, as many as 10 or (in the case of prostitutes) 50 times per night, is another such evolution.

Another interesting evolutionary phenomenon in this regard is the existence of *anovulary cycles*. In today's society, the effect is not so pronounced, probably due to changes in diet. But in women in past generations, for about 5 years after menarche and while presenting all the symptoms of fertility, their ovaries failed to release an ovum[205]. Practically, women could indulge in abundant sex without the risk of getting pregnant. Imagine men's delight! This feature was certainly advantageous to women, because they could benefit from the meat that sex entailed from an early age, waiting until later when they would have physically matured to bear children. But if seen from the perspective of

---

203 Symons, The evolution of human sexuality, p. 297-300.

204 Kinsey, A. C., Pomeroy, W. B., & Martin, C. E. *Sexual behavior in the human male.* Philadelphia: Saunders (1948).

205 Shlain, Leonard. *Sex, Time and Power: How Women's Sexuality Shaped Human Evolution.* USA: Viking Penguin (2003). p. 138.

society, it was a period during which women contributed sex in the communal sexual economy.

> "Aware of the quirk of anovulatory cycles, many ancient cultures held a very liberal attitude toward sex among their young people. Accounts from Mesopotamia, ancient Egypt, and classical Greece record young people indulging in unbridled sexuality during fertility rites and certain religious holidays. Herodotus tells of young girls serving as sexual temple priestesses. After several years of duty, they would leave to marry and begin families. There apparently was no social stigma attached to this service."[206]

Conclusion

No scientist today would argue that humans are a monogamous species. The debate is whether the pair bond as we understand it today, namely the exclusive relationship with occasional infidelity, is the "natural state". Matt Ridley in *The Red Queen* argues that a human is "an ape in which monogamous pair bonds are the rule but many males have affairs and occasional males achieve polygamy; an ape in which females mated to low-ranking males often cuckold their husbands in order to gain access to the genes of higher-ranking males"[207]. From this perspective marriage is not so much an institution that serves a specific social status quo, but a direct analogue at the institutional level of the naturalness of the exclusive pair bond. All the physical traits we described above and which do not fit with monogamy, (i.e. cryptic ovulation, sperm competition), are ascribed to "lapses".

Another position put forth by some scientists, one which is more consistent with the biology of sexual characteristics, is that man is "slightly polygynous". This position acknowledges the naturalness of multiple relationships, at least for the man. But it supposes that at least half of the men in primitive societies would accept relatively calmly to spend their lives without mates, while some had all the women. Neither the economy of the era, nor biology befit this conclusion.

---

206 Shlain,Sex, Time and Power, p. 141.
207 Ridley, The Red Queen, p. 348.

The natural mating system of the human species, then, is a form of many-to-many relationship.

However, today's mating system is undoubtedly one of *social* monogamy to which one must add *sexual* infidelity. Which sex does this situation suit more? As a male writer puts it, "Society doesn't like our biological strategy any more. They feel it's corrupt and have instituted something called marriage to put a stop to it.... Society admires and honors the female reproductive strategy. They feel it's righteous and have instituted something called marriage to promote it."[208]

Women can enjoy the material benefits of marriage, living in their normal state of a lower sex drive, and when they are in the mood for something extra they just have to reach out into the sea of sex-hungry men, and grab the best they can find. They can easily maintain a small court of "admirers" waiting in the wings, for easy sexual access if needed. And they can "yield" to exceptionally attractive men when they get the chance, without feeling any particular guilt, since "it was an accident". Having defined a relationship framework that suits them, being the real dominant sex, they have the "legality" of relationships on their side: their sexual "crimes" are rarely premeditated, exactly because they have so many chances to make them in hot blood.

Contrariwise, men have to bear the additional guilt that they "go looking for it", in order to have even one hundredth of the opportunities of a typical woman...

"She had established beyond doubt that her husband Anthony was betraying her. What had particularly enraged her was the revelation that he had met this other woman, not through some chance, unplanned encounter, but by placing an advertisement in the "lonely hearts" column of the magazine Private Eye – a well-known method of arranging adulterous liaisons among the London middle classes."

- Jonathan Coe, House of Sleep

---

208 Pilinski, Michael. *Without Embarrassment*, USA: Kipling Kat Publishing Company (2002). p.22.

Chapter 17: Love, Eros, Lust: What's Love got to do with it?

Bio-anthropologist Helen Fisher, in order to identify the brain structures that are associated with love, examined people in love with an MRI. She concluded that

> "there are three basically different brain systems that evolved from mating and reproduction. One is the sex drive: the craving for sexual gratification. W.H. Auden called it an "intolerable neural itch," and indeed, that's what it is. It keeps bothering you a little bit, like being hungry. The second of these three brain systems is romantic love: that elation, obsession of early love. And the third brain system is attachment: that sense of calm and security you can feel for a long-term partner....
>
> In these three brain systems: lust, romantic love and attachment – don't always go together. They can go together, by the way. That's why casual sex isn't so casual. With orgasm you get a spike of dopamine. Dopamine's associated with romantic love, and you can just fall in love with somebody who you're just having casual sex with. With orgasm, then you get a real rush of oxytocin and vasopressin – those are associated with attachment. This is why you can feel such a sense of cosmic union with somebody after you've made love to them.
>
> But these three brain systems, lust, romantic love and attachment, aren't always connected to each other. You can feel deep attachment to a long-term partner while you feel intense romantic love for somebody else, while you feel the sex drive for people unrelated to these other partners. In short, *we're capable of loving more than one person at a time.* In fact, you can lie in bed at night and swing from deep feelings of attachment for one person to deep feelings of romantic love for somebody else. It's as if there's a committee meeting going on in your head as you are trying to decide what to do."[209]

---

209 Fisher, Helen. *Why we love, why we cheat.* TED talk.

A first conclusion we can draw from these findings is that marriage which is supposed to last for a lifetime corresponds, in the best case, only to attachment, and not to the other kinds of "love" we might feel. The most interesting conclusion, however, concerns the differences of the two sexes. Men have more dopamine receptors in the brain's pleasure centres, while women have more oxytocin receptors. This hints that for men, sex drive, as well as romantic love ("eros") are more potent feelings, perhaps contrary to common prejudice. And it also means that women may derive more satisfaction than men from long-term intimate relationships – the ideal marriage. In this sense, marriage serves women's emotional needs much more than men's.

If this is the case, and men feel romantic love more intensely, why are they not the ones who are the most fervent readers of romance novels? Why don't they indulge in romance in their daily lives, as women do?

The answer is that men are much less allowed to connect with their emotions. Louann Brizendine observed it at a neurobiological level: "The typical male brain reaction to an emotion is to avoid it at all costs."[210] However, as we will see[211], this is the result of a very strict socialization against male sexuality.

Chapter 18: The Flintstonization of Prehistory and System's Apologists

Systemic sociobiologists have a working hypothesis: that the current system is the only natural state of human society, so all their work is done "backwards", trying to support that belief by tracking a supposed continuity between prehistoric and contemporary behaviors. A central pillar of their views is that marriage, basically today's monogamy, has always existed; this is why they call "marriage" all prehistoric social forms of pair bonding. In the same manner, they consider that the degree

---

http://www.ted.com/talks/helen_fisher_tells_us_why_we_love_cheat.html
210 Brizendine, The Female Brain, p. 123.
211 See Part 5, Rage, p. 203.

of violence and aggression that characterizes historical societies is "natural" for the human species, and that is has always existed.

Ryan and Jetha call this "the flintstonization of prehistory"[212], likening it to the famous cartoon featuring a modern prehistoric man.

Same biology, different "society"

An interesting insight on the "naturalness" of our society comes from game theory: in complex games there are usually more than one optimal strategies ("nash equilibria").

Similarly, with the same biological foundation we can have more than one "society" in biological species, and especially in humans. A society of peace and sexual freedom is a possibility, as well as a society where sex is not free and violence prevails. And as we will see in Part 4 of this book, a single external (environmental) "push" can be all that is needed to switch humanity from one type of society to the other, just as a lever is enough for a train to change rails.

Class society seems to "work". Proof of concept: it has existed for a few thousand years – although that could be called just a drop in the ocean compared to the millions of years of existence of the human species. But if some can accept injustice and exploitation as an "inevitable" feature of human society, they have more trouble accepting environmental disaster.

The current state of "equilibrium" that humanity has been pushed to, that is the set of moral rules and the expected and acceptable social behaviors, is leading to a frantic and unsustainable exploitation of natural resources. We have reached a point where environmental destruction is probably irreversible. The environmental crisis is the most important argument for the more apolitical citizens, for the fact is that the system is problematic, and that no, it is not a "natural" system which is the only one which is compatible with our biology. Cancer cells may be an existing biological possibility, but they eventually lead the organism to death.

---

212 Ryan, Sex at Dawn, Ch. 2.

Part 3: The War of the Sexes

A weaker sex drive is at the basis of female superiority

Introduction

In Part 1 we examined woman's privileged position without making many references to biology. The purpose was if not to convince the reader, at least to suggest a different take on the supposedly "oppressed woman".

In progressive circles, the word "biology" is anathema. Reacting to the biologistic arguments of reactionaries, progressives take cover under the "tabula rasa"[213]: "humans are malleable, so biology's role is 0%". Part 2 of this book showed that this is not true. There is a whole generation of progressive scientists, psychologists[214], neurobiologists[215] and others, who grew up in the '60s and '70s and who had as a starting point the progressive view about the sexes at that time, viz. that differences were purely a product of socialization. But their research led them to reconsider this doxa and to acknowledge that biology is responsible for many of the differences between the sexes, and this, in turn, prompted them to eventually conduct many of the studies that document these differences.

For the most complex human behaviors, it is currently difficult to determine the extent to which society or biology are responsible. But as we have seen, there is no doubt that biology pushes us towards a specific direction. Not all behaviors are equally probable.

Today, enough research exists to validate the argument that women hold a privileged position in society. For some thinkers and activists, this is now an undeniable fact[216]. However, many of these researchers do not share a common conception about why this is the case. Feminist Hanna Rosin rejoices for instance, because supposedly "the economics of the new era are better suited to women"[217]. Historian Martin Van Creveld in

---

213 "The Blank Slate: The Modern Denial of Human Nature" by Steven Pinker is a
    famous book opposing the theories about tabula rasa, if from a conservative
    viewpoint.
214 Townsend, What Women Want – What Men Want, p. 1.
215 Brizendine, The Female Brain, p. 2.
216 Subreddit "men's Rights" is the internet place where the relative discussion takes
    place. https://www.reddit.com/r/MensRights
217 'The End of Men - Hanna Rosin - The Atlantic'.

The Privileged Sex has a different reaction, one probably closer to the truth: after making groundbreaking work establishing the timeless superiority of women in history, he states: "Our need of, and love for, women being as strong as it is, most of the time we do not really mind the fact that they are privileged in so many ways"[218].

However, as we argued in previous chapters, the clearest way to understand this fact is to focus on women's comparative advantage in their sex drive, i.e. their lesser need for sex. That is something one should constantly bear in mind. It is the basic fact which is at the foundation of this section in which we examine the several dimensions of the war of the sexes.

Chapter 19: Is There a "War of the Sexes"?

Everyone fights with their spouse. Big time. And everyone knows many couples, friends, relatives, that also fight. And yes, some still dispute that there is such a thing as a war of the sexes.

Biological dispute

An objection comes, perhaps surprisingly, from biology. We have already seen that the optimal reproductive strategies for men and women are not complementary, but antagonistic. The man's biological benefit, i.e. to mate with many women for free, contrasts with the female's, who wants to mate only with the best, and secure paternal care from the best possible provider – and the mate and the provider are not necessarily the one and the same man.

However, some biologists believe each sex's independent efforts to

_____

http://www.theatlantic.com/magazine/archive/2010/07/the-end-of-men/308135
218 Van Creveld, Martin. *The Privileged Sex*. USA: CreateSpace Independent Publishing Platform (2013).

exercise their optimal strategy can help the "evolution of the species", and since the species as a whole benefits from this process, these biologists argue that both sexes benefit in the long run. Therefore, they claim, there is no such thing as a "war" of the sexes.

If one agrees with this view, then one should believe that the male mantis is happy and benefits from being decapitated and eaten by the female during copulation, even before completing ejaculation, because it is supposedly for the benefit of its offspring and its species. "Remarkably, this is not the culmination of the sex war but its ultimate, harmonious resolution"[219], says Paul Seabright.

In humans, however, self-consciousness and the perception of death complicates things. If you offer a man the possibility to donate his sperm so that 10,000 women are fertilized, maximizing his "reproductive success", provided that you take off his head afterward, it is doubtful that it would make him very happy.

Furthermore, as we mentioned earlier, the ability of man to create civilizations more rapidly than natural selection can follow, is likely to lead to societies which are less compatible with his "nature". While positive emotions have been programmed to correspond to situations increasing the chances of survival and reproduction, this has happened in a particular natural period, which does not correspond to today's circumstances. When the environment changes, the evolutionary adaptations may become "out of tune" with the new environment. Downplaying or semi-deliberately ignoring this fact has led systemic scientists to conclude that we are not "an animal that was built to be happy; we are an animal that was built to reproduce"[220].

If humans are able to culturally depart from their biological origins, and reduce (or increase) their happiness, there is nothing to guarantee it will happen equally for the two sexes. Some social arrangements might be more or less beneficial for one or the other sex.

---

219 Seabright, The War of the Sexes, Ch. 1.
220 Fisher, Helen. *Why We Love, Why We Cheat.* TED Talk.

Left-wing disputes

Another challenge to the notion of the war of the sexes comes from some groups on the left. Their view is that there are no substantial grounds for war between the sexes, but that it is the system which makes the sexes fight each other, following the logic of divide and rule[221]. This notion borrows arguments regarding immigrants: just as all workers, be they native or immigrant, have a common interest against capitalists, so both sexes should have a common interest against the system.

This view has some truth in it. But if you do not pursue your analysis, leaving untouched the question of which sex is more oppressed, it is not only useless but also harmful to the cause which seeks to overthrow the system. True, both sexes share the same interest in fighting against the system. But someone could say the same thing about capitalists, who are themselves oppressed by their system, and who need to constantly fight each other and the workers.

The truth is that the system is more complex than some textbook "marxists" might perceive. The contrast of capital vs labor, although it is fundamental, relies on the creation of intermediate layers, such as the petty bourgeoisie. These are given privileges, so that under normal circumstances the petty bourgeois accept the system, and when they see that their position has improved when compared with the proletarians, they start to believe that the system is beneficial and they ultimately support it. When these mid-layers disappear, as happens in economic crises, the whole system is destabilized. In this sense, women's preferential treatment from the system is a precondition for its stabilization.

This support by the system does not happen by chance, neither is it done without consideration. Phyllis Schlafly is fully aware of the transaction that is taking place. She argues that by having children, who will eventually be paying "decades upon decades of taxes into the Social Security system", a woman contributes to the system much more "than any worker who pays taxes … all his or her life"[222].

---

221 This is for example what Ryan & Jetha claim, Sex at Dawn, Ch.2.
222 Schlafly, Feminist Fantasies.

We give you children, i.e. future workers, and you cut us some slack. That's the deal.

The best example for female preferential treatment is what happens in imperialistic wars, such as Hitler's or Hirohito's. Even when Germany recruited boys and old men for war, it never enlisted women. That would have led to the collapse of the system: women may "fatalistically" resign themselves to the idea that their sons and husbands be sent to war, but they would never accept being recruited themselves. As Schlafly "indignantly" writes against those that propose female enlistment, "Of the thousands of books written about World War II, no one ever wrote that Hitler or the Japanese should have solved their manpower shortage problem by using women in combat."[223]The system knows that it is dangerous to break its unholy alliance with women.

Chapter 20: Common Misconceptions

Let us consider some common misconceptions in the debate on the war of the sexes.

Why don't you admit it?

If men are the oppressed sex, why don't they get out and fight? Why wasn't there ever a massive movement in favor of male liberation? Why are there not one or two famous people who support it, like famous feminists who fight on the other side?

The answer leads us back to sex. For a woman, to argue that she is unprotected and wronged does not make her less attractive. If anything, a submissive position is in line with primal patterns of female sexuality[224], and often makes her more attractive.

---

223 Schlafly, Feminist Fantasies.
224 "submissive fantasies appear to be representative of feminine sexual instinct".
    Brandon,, Monogamy, p. 63.

For men, however, things are different. The most attractive feature of a man is, as we've seen, status. A man who complains is a poor bugger, a complete turn off. If he claims that he is oppressed he is by definition a loser, and is dismissed as such. "It's your personal issue, not a social problem".

A man cannot even complain to the woman with whom he has a relationship and supposedly mutual support. Especially her. Social worker Tom Golden writes:

> "In my years of working with couples in therapy I have very rarely seen a woman who routinely listened to the emotional pain of her male partner. Think purple polar bear. Very rare. Women do often claim that they want a man who is in touch with his feelings but if you scratch and sniff you find that this means that he should be in touch with HER feelings. It is a rare woman who can regularly sit with the man she loves and non-judgmentally hear him out on a feeling level. Yes, women will claim that men give them no chance to do this, that they are cold and unfeeling, but give her a chance in therapy to listen to his pain and what I have seen repeatedly is that she has a very hard time with this and often recoils."[225]

Men's Rights Activists are systematically the object of derogatory and vulgar attacks. "Usually stuff like virgin (impotent), neckbeard (stereotypically unattractive), fedora wearing (pseudo-intellectual), misogynistic (doesn't have a point just hates women), or fragile (not stoic enough) are used..."[226] It's so insulting when others laugh at you that not many have the stomach to take it.

Roy Baumeister, in his acknowledgments to his book *Is There Anything Good About Men?*, writes that "many [people] have helped, although, to be honest, quite a few advised me not to write this book. They thought that saying anything favorable about men is taboo and could seriously

---

225 'The Invisible Blue Taboo — The Burden of Boys and Men | Men Are Good'.
http://menaregood.com/wordpress/the-invisible-blue-taboo-the-burden-of-boys-and-men
226 https://www.reddit.com/r/MensRights/comments/2lv14c/
22_years_on_the_failings_of_feminism_the_book

damage my career. I hope they are wrong"[227].

Esther Vilar in the reissue of her book *The Manipulated Man* 35 years after its first edition, reports: "I hadn't imagined broadly enough the isolation I would find myself in after writing this book. Nor had I envisaged the consequences which it would have for my subsequent writing and even for my private life – violent threats have not ceased to this date."[228]

In crisis periods, the problem of male silence becomes particularly obvious because it has serious effects on men's health. The expectation of success is inscribed so deep in the male psyche, that they are ashamed to ask for help for both their physical and mental health. "[They are] dying of embarrassment and ignorance"[229], while the standard (feminist) approach is to add insult to injury, giving them full blame for not asking help, while ignoring that this attitude has been imposed on them since childhood by the system itself.

Is oppression so deeply ingrained?

An argument that is dear to feminists is that women have integrated oppression, and that is why they often support "patriarchal" structures. Left Feminism compares that with the integration of the workers, who support parties who favor the system: if workers support the parties of the capitalists who exploit them, why should it be surprising that women support patriarchy?

The problem with this argument is that women support "patriarchy" more than men. Slut shaming is done by women, who have undertaken the role of social policing against those who "give it up cheaply" and drive the price of sex down. Marriage, the most "patriarchal" institution of all, is a basic pursuit for women, not for men. And so is childbearing. The creepy custom of female genital mutilation, as we will see shortly, is

227 Baumeister, Roy F. *Is there anything good about men?: How Cultures Flourish by Exploiting Men.* USA: Oxford University Press (2010). p. vii.
By permission of Oxford University Press, USA.
228 Vilar, Esther. *The Manipulated Man.* USA: Pinter and Martin Ltd. (2009).
229 'BBC News | Health | Crisis in men 's health targeted'.
http://news.bbc.co.uk/2/hi/health/458758.stm

mostly opposed by men while it is supported by women.

Let us make an analogy: many workers may support bourgeois parties, but capitalists support them even more, they don't oppose them. In US elections in 2012, for instance, up to 35% low-income voters voted Republican, but there were even more high-income voters who supported them, 55%. And undoubtedly, capitalists are the clear winners with this system so it makes sense that they should support it. The majority of men, however, do not benefit from "patriarchy". Women do, and that is why they support it more.

Is it not as difficult for women?

The human mind has trouble intuitively understanding probabilities and statistics[230]. "Even statisticians [are] not good intuitive statisticians."[231] For women, this may be because they function more by "intuition", – meaning that the world is built to suit them more, so they can allow themselves to be guided by their "gut feeling" – so it is often more difficult for them to see the facts objectively.

Try to present a typical feminist evidence of men's hardships. For instance, that 95% of prisoners are male. These feminists will always have a "counterexample" at hand: "Yes, but the women are imprisoned as well". Men are four times as likely to commit suicide than women. "Yes, but yesterday a cleaning-lady killed herself jumping off the roof of her building". Roy Baumeister "strongly suspect[s] there is no point in debating with feminists"[232].

Of course, many of men's difficulties we have been describing also apply to some women. But the scientific way to draw conclusions about the relative position of the two sexes is to examine the scope and extent to which the findings apply to each sex. A "counter-example" such as: "my second aunt was divorced by her husband and he took the children with him" does not prove that men initiate more divorces or are more often

230 'Why Our Brains Do Not Intuitively Grasp Probabilities - Scientific American'.
    http://www.scientificamerican.com/article/why-our-brains-do-not-intuitively-grasp-
    probabilities
231 Kahneman, Daniel. *Thinking, Fast and Slow.* Introduction.
232 Baumeister, Is there anything good about men? p. 9.

granted custody of the children. One needs to examine the statistical data for each social phenomenon.

The difficulty to find a mate

A frequent complaint of women has to do with the difficulty of finding appropriate mates, a difficulty which is supposedly greater than men's. What they don't seem to understand is that their difficulty is due to their elevated expectations. Anyone, man or woman, can find a mate provided they lower their standards enough. Men are forced to lower them more than women – even despite having more "democratic" standards to begin with. "Research has ... found that most men find most women at least somewhat sexually attractive, whereas most women do not find most men sexually attractive at all."[233] For example, research in the most popular dating site, OKCupid, found that men have a normal distribution in their preferences, classifying 5% of women as most attractive, 5% as least attractive, and the other 90% in between. Women on the other hand, rate 25% of men as least attractive, while 80% of the men are rated below average[234]. Let us compare these findings graphically, see next page.

> Empirically, [men] are willing to have sex with partners who meet just minimal thresholds on traits they themselves rank as desirable, such as intelligence and kindness. In contrast, women typically maintain high standards."[235]

---

233 Buss, Why women have sex, Ch. 8.
234 'Your Looks and Your Inbox « OkTrends'. Accessed 31 Oct. 2014.
    http://blog.okcupid.com/index.php/your-looks-and-online-dating
235 Buss, Why women have sex, Ch. 8.

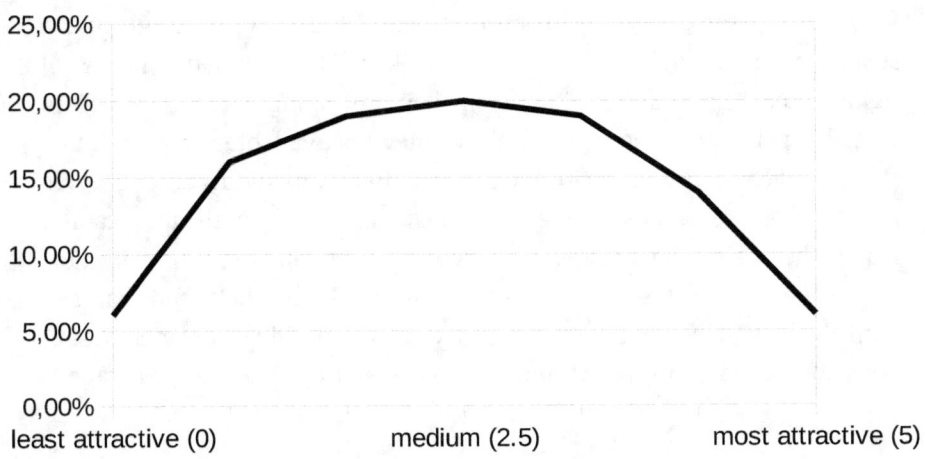

The normal distribution of men's preferences...

Male Appraisals of Female Attractiveness:
Female population distribution, as rated by men

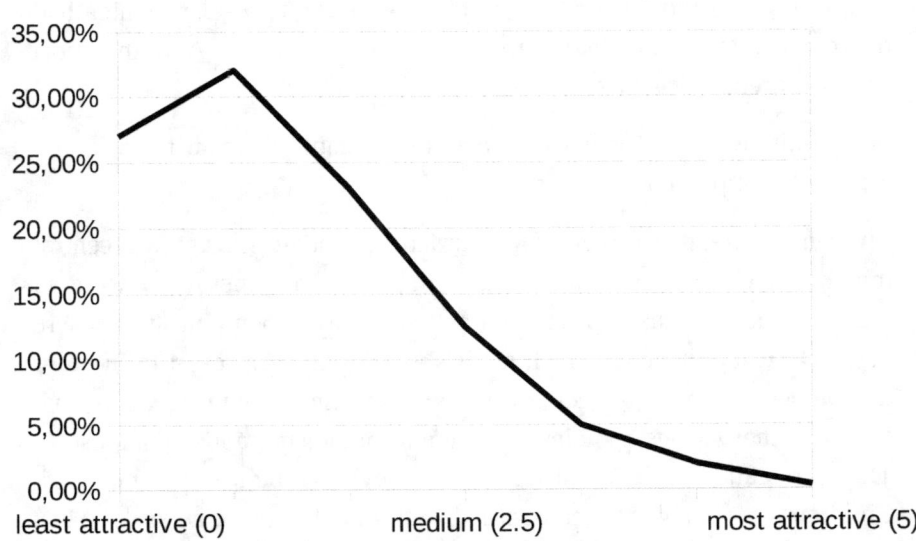

... and the elitist preferences of women

Female Appraisals of Male Attractiveness:
Male attractiveness distribution, as rated by women

"Men lower their attraction standards for casual encounters.

Women who cannot find a man for a long-term relationship and marriage have not understood that their tactic for casual sex does not work as well for a relationship. Keeping disproportionally high standards, given the sexual asphyxiation of men, *does* work in the women's phase of lighthearted "exploration", i.e. when they are young and more open to sexual experiences. The most attractive men are available for sex with no strings attached. But in "marriage mode", after women turn 25 or 30, this tactic backfires, because while these men can bed them all, they cannot marry them all. The most unwise women then mistakenly "calibrate" their expectations: the fact that the captain of the football team had sex with them at one point (even if Bill Clinton wouldn't consider it sex) does not mean that they will find a similar man to marry at a later stage.

Chapter 21: Meat for Sex

Class society led to the excessive escalation of the sex war by overturning the prehistoric "contract" between the two sexes, which had the fairly direct and clear form of "sex for returns". And the most important return was meat.

For primitive humans, meat was the most valuable and nutritious food – especially for pregnant women.

The current trend in favor of vegetarianism underestimates the central importance of meat in the human diet. In prehistoric times, there were no diary products to make up for meat as a source of protein, nor were there any dietary supplements which today's vegetarians can resort to in order to compensate for the lack of protein. Of the 20 amino acids that compose the various proteins, the human organism cannot compose 8. These are called basic amino acids, and they must be taken from foods. Children are unable to compose 2 additional amino acids[236]. Meat contains all basic amino acids, while plants contain only a few. As a consequence, vegetarians need an exceptional variety of plant foods to

---

236 Shlain, Sex, Time and Power, p. 123.

avoid protein deficiency.

Apart from being an invaluable source of protein, meat is the most invaluable source of iron, which is not easily absorbed from plant foods. Blood uses iron to transport oxygen which is necessary for the functioning of the energy-consuming human brain.

And it is quite interesting that meat is *even more essential* to the woman-gatherer than to the man-hunter. "A man adopting a vegan diet is at low risk for developing a serious anemia. A woman in her reproductive years without access to modern nutritional knowledge who makes the same choice *cannot avoid* anemia."[237] [emphasis in original].

Our related primates, while feeding primarily on fruits and various plants, supplement their diet with insects and small rodents. The first European settlers in Australia were perplexed when they saw Aborigines living a lazy life, eating insects and mice[238]. They thought they did so because they were hungry, while in fact they were just taking advantage of an easily obtainable source of iron.

What pushed our male ancestors to hunt big animals was (partly) the value of meat. Not only its nutritional value, but also its exchange value: prehistoric men exchanged meat for sex. Helen Fisher argued that this was the first human "contract" in her book characteristically entitled *The Sex Contract (1982)*[239].

Buying sex with meat is actually a widespread practice in many species. Its extreme expression is, of course, the praying mantis and some arachnids that eat the male after copulation. In other species of insects, the male prepares a ball from a nutritious substance, similar to a spider's web, and offers it to the female in exchange for sex. In primates, males offer small rodents to their potential mates. In many human tribes, exchange of meat for sex is a standard custom.

The huge value of meat, which men supplied, counter-balanced the huge value of sex which women "supplied", and was the basis of a prehistoric

237 Shlain, Sex, Time and Power, p. 41.
238 Ryan, Sex at Dawn, ch.1.
239 Fisher, Helen E. *The Sex Contract: The evolution of Human Behavior*. USA: William Morrow & Co (1982).

equality of the sexes. "The anthropologist Ernestine Friedl does accept that in the few societies, for instance among Australian aborigines, in which meat was the central component of the diet, men were more highly ranked than women."[240] Prehistoric society was a society of "enough": (under normal circumstances) it was neither a society of deprivation, nor a society of abundance. If men limited the provision of meat, this was a real problem for women – maybe as serious as when women limited the provision of sex to men. Without meat women could not survive – and without sex men could not reproduce. Women's control over sex was balanced by men's control over meat. This dynamic equilibrium between the sexes was crucial for mankind. It was hard-wired in the basic psychology of each sex. Man could never do without sex – and woman, perhaps using looser terms, without man supplying her with meat.

What happens now in the "affluent society"? When women have guaranteed access to food, the value of the man-as-provider plummets. But his biology has not had time to catch up with the new (social and economic) circumstances. He still needs sex in the same degree. As a result, we have the tilting of the balance in favor of women, which has characterized the more recent period of humanity.

Chapter 22: The Sexual "Double Standard"

It is socially acceptable, and even somewhat of a selling point, for a man to sleep with many women, but a woman who sleeps with many men is a "slut". Feminists claim that this "double standard" is sexist, and that it is degrading for women. Recent studies, however, leave no room for doubt: *the double standard is imposed by women themselves, as a method to increase the profits they derive from sex. Let's see how this is works.*

In previous chapters we showed that women have a weaker sex drive,

---

240 Harman, Chris. *"Engels and the Origins of Human Society"*. International Socialism, No. 65, Winter 1994. https://www.marxists.org/archive/harman/1994/xx/engels.htm

which means that they are less interested in sex. In sociology, one speaks of the "principle of less interest": power lies in the hands of the person who cares the least.[241] Limiting supply, by "slut shaming", allows women to demand more in return for their sexual favors. "This echoes the traditional grandmotherly advice against premarital sex, colloquially expressed in the metaphoric terms that a man who can get free milk will not buy the cow".[242] (Quotes in this chapter are from the extensive review by Baumeister and Twenge, *"Cultural Suppression of Female Sexuality" (2002)).*

Researchers studying sexuality in society in relation to the proportion of men and women in a given population found that every time social phenomena (wars, etc.) limited the availability of men, making them a sought after commodity, men were able to impose their terms more effectively. "There is more sexual activity when men (as opposed to women) are in the minority.... In other words, when men have the edge, sex is cheap and abundant. When women hold the advantage, sex is rare and expensive. Men prefer sex to be free and easy; women are better off when it is precious." For example, a large scale survey of 42 societies found teen pregnancy rates to be correlated with the sex ratio. "Specifically, teenage girls are ironically *more* likely to get pregnant when there is a shortage of men." [emphasis added]

Related studies have clearly shown that "suppression of female sexuality during the formative adolescent years comes directly and primarily from female sources." To begin with, "mothers are the main source of anti-sexual messages for daughters". After mothers, the most crucial factor in inhibiting sexual activity are the female peer groups, who gossip and shun girls who "dispens[e] sexual favors too liberally". Boys follow behind, condemning "easy" girls, although many don't seem to mind it if a girl is "sexually wild". "Thus, the widespread pressure to maintain a good reputation for sexual restraint and propriety appears to have been enforced primarily among the female peer groups."

Pick Up Artist (PUA) guru Mystery describes how in a company of

---

241 Wikipedia, Principle of less interest. Accessed 19 Jan. 2015.
   https://en.wikipedia.org/wiki/Principle_of_least_interest
242 Baumeister, Roy F. and Twenge, Jean M. *"Cultural Suppression of Female Sexuality"*. Review of General Psychology 2002, Vol. 6, No. 2, 166-203.

women, your "target's" friends will "protect" her from making a spontaneous act that she might later regret[243]. In truth they "protect" her from themselves, just as the mafia provides "protection" to shops. They make sure that she will sell sex expensively, otherwise she will be called a slut and will be ostracized from the group. Lawrence Shannon describes this situation in his characteristic style:

> "Predatory females rely heavily on the consensus of the pack and thereby encounter difficulty in making individual decisions. The pack includes their mothers and girlfriends and constitutes the sole governing body in the life of a predatory female. The blessing or cursing of the pack (a committee decision), is largely determinate in the rise and fall of lovers, husbands, and gynaecologists."[244]

In 1965, when the double standard was at its strongest, "Women who engaged in premarital sex were condemned as immoral by 91% of the women ... as compared with condemnation by only 42% of the men." If the double standard were really in favor of men and detrimental to women, we would have here a double deception. Women have been deceived by 91% to support this system, and men have been tricked by 58% to not support it...

The most interesting picture, though, comes from later work seeking to determine

> "whether the double standard was still active in the late 1990s, long after the sexual revolution. The women who took part in their survey strongly asserted that the double standard was still powerful and pervasive, even though they themselves did not endorse it (and in fact showed evidence of a reverse double standard that judged promiscuous men more harshly than women). One may infer from these findings that the women perceived continued societal pressure on women to restrain their sexual behavior, but this pressure seemed external to them insofar as they did not endorse the double standard themselves. The researchers reported that women cited external pressures of gossip and

---

243 Mystery, with Chris Odom. *The Mystery Method: How to Get Beautiful Women Into Bed.* New York: St Martin's Press (2007).
244 Shannon, Lawrence. *The Predatory Female: A Field Guide to Dating and the Marriage-Divorce Industry.* USA: Banner Books (1985). p. 20.

reputation as forces that pushed women to hold back sexually."

When questioned "Who judges women who have had sex with many partners more harshly?", women are shown to have a clearer perception of reality: only 12% answered that men are harsher judges, while 42% pointed to women themselves.

Ways of restricting female sexuality

John Marshal Townsend, in *What Women Want – What Men Want: Why the Sexes Still See Love and Commitment so Differently*[245], presents research results showing that women feel intense negative feelings of remorse when they are "easy", which gradually lead them to reject casual sex. Given that emotions are created unconsciously, i.e. automatically, he concludes that women's predisposition to withhold sex and not give it away "easily" must have a genetic, rather than a social explanation. However, if things were so, there would be no need for social institutions to impose this restraint.

A look at traditional societies, where things are simpler and less covert, is enlightening. The restriction of female sexuality is so deeply rooted in tradition that there are elaborate rituals for this purpose, performed when the menarche appears.

> "Though these rituals varied from place to place, two features remained constant. Elder women isolated the initiate and instilled in her that she was not to dispense future sexual favors easily, because they were extremely valuable. The key purpose of the menarche ritual was to impress upon the girl that she was now in possession of both a great power and an enormous responsibility. While many menarche rituals are celebratory and loving, the ethnographic record drawn from a wide variety of cultures is replete with numerous examples of draconian ones. Among the Loango of East Africa, menstruants are confined to isolated dark huts and are prohibited from setting their foot on the ground or looking at the sun for two years. Far

---

245 Townsend, What Women Want – What Men Want, p. 50-51.

away in New Ireland, in the South Pacific, girls are similarly confined for four years in small darkened cages and also not allowed to touch the ground. When the symptoms of a girl's first bleed occur among the Guaranis of South America, she is sewn into a cocoon hammock strung between two trees, with only a small slit through which she can breathe. Shrouded as if she were a corpse, the girl has to maintain a vigorous fast until her bleeding is over."[246]

In Western societies, women use other, more subtle techniques to discourage sex. A typical one is frigidity. Esther Vilar argues that this phenomenon originates from a quite conscious process: in order to obtain the high profit in material benefits that is typical of the 70's American woman, "the demands of her art of seduction are minimal.... All she really needs are a few good curves and the nerve to say no long enough.... The logical result of such business tactics, steadily perfected through the generations, is frigidity..."[247] Even Simone de Beauvoir herself seems to agree: "the boundary between frigidity and the will to frigidity is an uncertain one"[248]. Being anorgasmic herself up to her 40s, and after overcoming her problem with the help of a man, she was able to describe it in her book.

> "Resentment is the most common cause of feminine frigidity; in bed the woman punishes the man for all the wrongs she feels she has endured, by offering him an insulting coldness. There is often an aggressive inferiority complex apparent in her attitudes. [Frigidity] would appear to be a punishment that the woman imposes as much upon herself as upon her partner; wounded in her vanity, she feels resentment against him and herself, and she denies herself pleasure."

Female Genital Mutilation

We have shown that women can use rather grotesque methods to teach sexual restraint to girls, even limiting their own pleasure in their war of the sexes. Up to what point are they willing to go?

---

246 Shlain, Sex, Time and Power, p. 137-138.
247 Vilar, The Manipulated Man, p. 171.
248 De Beauvoir, Simon. *The Second Sex*. UK: Jonathan Cape (1956). p. 452.

The disturbing culmination of this tendency is the practice of Female genital mutilation (FGM).

In the West, feminist and mainstream rhetoric depicts this practice as another heinous crime of patriarchy performed by men on women so that they can keep them under control and ensure paternity. Egyptian (female) anthropologist Fadwa El Guindi argues, however, "that FGM is not a matter of male control, and is not intended to appeal to men... Removing the clitoris is chosen by women for women, she maintains, to reduce sexuality before marriage and enhance it afterwards; she argues that the reduction in sexual desire is usually temporary"[249]. Feminist G. Greer, who traveled to areas that practice FGM and did her own research, explicitly rejected the idea that FGM is male driven: "This is indeed a curious explanation of something that women do to women".[250]

The fact that it is practiced by "elder women", like the menarche rituals described earlier, is neither the only nor the most serious indication that this is a female issue. In their paper, Baumeister and Twenge cite numerous studies and evidence that suggest so. "The decision about whether and when a particular girl will receive the operation is made by her mother or grandmother". Men in Islamic African countries not only accept to marry uncircumcised women, but in fact they prefer it. They consider European women very desirable for wives, "because the men found the European women (who had not had genital surgery) enjoyed sex more. These findings are directly contrary to the theory that African men prefer women whose sexuality has been stifled by surgical methods." An interesting study in Sudan questioned 300 men who had two or more wives, one of whom had had the operation while the other had not. "Nearly all of the men reported that they preferred the wife who had not had the genital surgery."

There is a social dynamic developing around FGM in African countries, that parallels that of slut shaming in the West: women that have been subjected to it, (and whose attractiveness has as a result waned), denigrate and shame those that have not been subjected to it. They want

249 Wikipedia, Female Genital Mutilation. Accessed 31 Oct. 2014.
    https://en.wikipedia.org/wiki/Female_genital_mutilation.
250 Baumeister, Cultural Suppression of Female Sexuality.

to believe that "very few men would marry a girl who has not been excised and infibulated" – an argument which fortunately is contradicted by men's preferences.

> "Sure enough, most observers conclude that the practices are most zealously defended by women. Men seem generally indifferent (consistent with Greer's impression that the men often do not even know). Some fathers object to having their daughters subincised or infibulated, but the men's objections are overruled by the women in the family, who insist on having the operations performed. [Researchers] also reported several findings indicating that men argued for less severe surgical practices but were thwarted by the women's determined support for the practices".

The authors conclude that "the evidence regarding subincision and infibulation indicates that women control and maintain the practice. This too supports the female control theory *[of female sexuality]* and contradicts the male control theory".

How did this practice come about? Scientists do not know. Its origins are lost in time, and the practice predates the advent of Islam. We can nevertheless make some observations. The areas which practice FGM have often been afflicted with extreme poverty and hunger. Extreme circumstances demand extreme measures. If your hand is caught in the chain and the ship is sinking, the only way to survive is to cut it off. In today's affluent West, women sacrifice their orgasmic capability in order to gain leverage in their demanding material safety from their husband. It is, then, not inconceivable to imagine a more extreme corresponding practice in the relentless past of the rise of class society.

It is quite probable that female competition played a trigger role in establishing this practice: FGM is something that older women do to younger ones, not something that women do to themselves. The antagonism between mother and daughter appears mainly in puberty. The mother grows older and gradually leaves the sexual game, exactly at the time that the daughter enters it. Confusing correlation with cause, she feels resentment and becomes aggressive towards her daughter, who is "stealing her youth". The evil "step mother" in the Snow White fairy tale depicts exactly this shift in the behavior of the mother.

Female genital mutilation, then, is the extreme expression of the voluntary self-restraint of female sexuality.

Conclusion

The sexual double standard arises naturally, in a sense, due to different sexual dynamics. Men want sex more, and are more available. "Consider the famous psychology experiment in which female research assistants were sent out across campus to approach attractive males and ask if they wanted to have sex that night. Seventy-five per cent of the men said yes (and those who couldn't make it that night asked about the next night). When the experiment was repeated with the genders reversed, all the women said no."[251] Women hold the key to sex and are therefore in position to choose "up", i.e. to pick someone with relatively greater "mate value". Men who have had many sexual encounters have been selected by many women, so they are "better" than most men, and this, for females, signifies their superior quality. In biology this is called "mate copying" and has been observed in many hen species: when researchers put some stuffed females around a male, preference for that male rises. Exactly the same phenomenon has been observed in the human female: in studies, women were found to give a man higher mark if shown in a photograph next to attractive women, rather than if he were shown alone. This behavior is not observed in men[252]. On the other hand, for a woman to have been with many men shows that she has found many "betters" than her, thus suggesting her "low quality".

Moreover, since sex can offer more to women than just pleasure, i.e. money, safety, a provider for her and her children etc., women benefit from keeping it expensive, so they can demand more from the men they select.

It is thus clear that women voluntarily suppress their own, already

---

251 'Why won't guys grow up? Sexual economics - The Globe and Mail'. http://www.theglobeandmail.com/globe-debate/why-wont-guys-grow-up-sexual-economics/article5172942
252 Buss, Why Women Have Sex, Ch. 1.

naturally subdued, sexuality, in order to fortify their position in the war of the sexes. In the words of Baumeister and Twenge, "women have worked to stifle each other's sexuality because sex is a limited resource that women use to negotiate with men, and scarcity gives women an advantage." This is the most central expression of the phenomenon mentioned earlier, viz. that society intensifies the differences between the sexes, rather than equalize them.

We can now explain the fear of being raped, that we discussed in Part 2. Knowing, consciously or unconsciously, their silent conspiracy around sex, it is natural for women to fear punishment. And since sex is the issue, they imagine this punishment to be sexual.

This said, the general picture in today's feminist era is not one of female sexual repression. Women can have their cake and eat it, having a strict "moral" judgment when it comes to other women's or men's sexual behavior, while being much more lenient when it concerns themselves.

Chapter 23: Games People Play

In this section we will see why women are in a better position to satisfy their social needs. But first let's define a frame of reference for these needs. To do this, we will use *Games People Play*, a book by eminent psychologist Eric Berne[253].

Berne describes the interactions between people as exchanges of what he calls "strokes". The baby needs his mother's caress in order to feel intimacy and safety. This need for positive stimuli, the "infantile stimulus-hunger", is transformed in adults, due to social and other difficulties, resulting "into something which may be termed recognition-hunger".

> "A movie actor may require hundreds of strokes each week
> from anonymous and undifferentiated admirers to keep his

---

253 Berne, Eric. *Games People Play: The Psychology of Human Relationships.* USA: Penguin Books (1964).

> spinal cord from shrivelling, while a scientist may keep physically and mentally healthy on one stroke a year from a respected master... 'Stroking' may be employed colloquially to denote any act implying recognition of another's presence. Hence a stroke may be used as the fundamental unit of social action. An exchange of strokes constitutes a transaction, which is the unit of social intercourse..."

Stimulus-hunger and recognition hunger are two fundamental aspects of human psychology. A third one is "structure-hunger". To many people "unstructured time", when there is no framework set for an interaction, makes them feel at a loss, awkward, uncomfortable. They dread the specter of silence, these moments when no one can think of something interesting to say. "The eternal problem of the human being is how to structure his waking hours. In this existential sense, the function of all social living is to lend mutual assistance for this project."

One of the activities that structure time is work, but "it is of interest here only insofar as [it] offer[s] a matrix for 'stroking'". Conventional social interactions offer another way to structure time.

Beyond these, "as people become better acquainted", interactions in the sphere of personal relationship begin to take place. And this is where things start to get interesting:

> "These incidents superficially appear to be adventitious, and may be so described by the parties concerned, but careful scrutiny reveals that they tend to follow definite patterns which are amenable to sorting and classification, and that the sequence is circumscribed by unspoken rules and regulations. These regulations remain latent as long as the amities or hostilities proceed according to Hoyle, but they become manifest if an illegal move is made, giving rise to a symbolic, verbal or legal cry of 'Foul!'"

Berne calls these kind of interactions Games. Indeed, "the bulk of social activity consists of playing games".

So what is the problem with Games? "Games are substitutes for real living and real intimacy". They have "ulterior quality" and have profit as their goal. "Every game ... is basically dishonest".

Female Games

Using the above terminology, we can posit the following: Society has been configured so that it is easier for women to get the "strokes" they need, as attested by measurements of happiness and the dramatic reversal of life expectancy in their favor. Due to their more controllable sex drive, they are in position to play dishonest games with men, so that the strokes they receive are obtained at men's expense. "Good" women do it completely unconsciously, just because they can and it pays – i.e. it is pleasant. "Bad" women do it on purpose, calculating their profit in advance.

The Flirting Game

A woman's life, from the end of childhood up to decrepit old age, are spent playing the flirting game. Women set its rules and derive pleasure from it. The great majority of men play this game at a negative psychological cost. The game, in its milder form, goes as follows: "[She] signals that she is available and gets her pleasure from the man's pursuit. As soon as he has committed himself, the game is over." In a more "advanced" level, "[She] gets only secondary satisfaction from [his] advances. Her primary gratification comes from rejecting him, so that this game is also colloquially known as 'Buzz Off, Buster'. She leads [him] into a much more serious commitment than the mild flirtation ... and enjoys watching his discomfiture when she repulses him."

As in all Games, in flirting, the female motivations are unconscious. At the conscious level, she has put on make-up, a nice dress, highlighted secondary sexual characteristic (her legs, chest, butt) supposedly because "she just feels like doing that", not because she likes men to look at her of flirt with her. In other cases, a bit more consciously, she *does* want men to flirt her, but only the "alpha males", not every second-class loser in town. The Average Frustrated Chumps who are attracted to her are summarily shot down "collateral damage".

Social scientists have called this "social flirting". The game is virtually free, with no cost for women, and, as mentioned earlier, with a negative cost for men. It is like playing craps, with men winning only with double sixes, while women win with all other outcomes. If we wanted to balance it from the perspective of game theory, we should introduce a cost factor for women, a punishment, i.e. some form of violence, verbal or physical, from the conned man. However, as this is forbidden, socially or legally, the average man is left completely unprotected.

One result of the flirting game is that since the great majority of approaches are rejected, many men decide to stop playing the game altogether. The situation has reached such a point that a (female) columnist in The Telegraph is calling for "perhaps government intervention" similar to "Do It for Mom" that took place in Denmark, so that men can "do their job and flirt". A very important task, as "women's self-confidence can rise significantly with all the glory that comes from a man talking you up."[254]

The "benefit" for women, especially the most insecure ones, from this collapse, is that they can derive extra pleasure from whining "what has happened to real men?"

> "Nora Vincent ... said she thought dating women would be one of the most pleasant parts of her undercover life. As a lesbian, she had already dated women, but now there would be many more available to her, and she looked forward to the experience. She found it sobering and discouraging. As a man, she would approach women at the bar to try to chat them up, and more often than not she got a quick and unkind (sometimes downright humiliating) rejection. She soon lost her nerve and, were it not for the demands of her experiment, she says she would have given up. She wondered how men manage to do it, to persevere, to summon up their courage to approach women despite the expectation of being rejected most of the time and despite the accumulating history of bad outcomes. She said she did not know which was worse, the women who rejected you at a glance without giving you a chance to prove yourself, or the ones who rejected you after a couple of dates and some degree of getting to know you."[255]

---

254 "Lads! Britain needs you to do your duty and get flirting" - The Telegraph, Aug. 24, 2015 https://www.telegraph.co.uk/news/2016/08/24/lads-britain-needs-you-to-do-your-duty-and-get-flirting
255 Baumeister, Is There Anything Good About Men, p. 211.

While the game has only immediate profits for women, it does nevertheless have an indirect cost. It produces a disappointment in men that might turn into rage. This is why women can fall victim to "sexist" teasing on the street, especially if they are dressed provocatively. However, women who are teased are not necessarily those that "play" the most. This statistical deviation is perhaps the reason cat-calling is generally presented as a problem for women, while it is only a minimal cost that the female sex pays, in relation to the psychological benefits they derive from the Game. And let us keep in mind that only a very small number of these "teasings" is really annoying. Most are good-natured and welcomed by women. If you are feeling down and want to fix your mood, you can wear something nice and go out for a walk at a street market, where you can enjoy the sellers' humorous cat-calling...

The Raping Game

Revealingly, Berne does not consider the Raping Game as being separate from the Flirting Game. Berne argues it's just one of its variations, in the "3rd degree". The description of the game is as follows:

> "[She] leads [him] into compromising physical contact and then claims that he has made a criminal assault or has done her irreparable damage. In its most cynical form [she] may actually allow him to complete the sexual act so that she gets that enjoyment before confronting him. The confrontation may be immediate, as in the illegitimate cry of rape, or it may be long delayed, as in suicide or homicide following a prolonged love affair. If she chooses to play it as a criminal assault, she may have no difficulty in finding mercenary or morbidly interested allies, such as the press, the police, counselors and relatives."

Rape fantasy is one of the most common fantasies for women. Studies in the past 30 years have indeed found that "between 31% and 57% of women have rape fantasies, and these fantasies are frequent or preferred in 9% to 17% of women. Considering that many people are ashamed to report rape fantasies, these stats are most likely lowball figures."[256]

---

256 'Why Do Women Have Erotic Rape Fantasies? | Psychology Today'.
    http://www.psychologytoday.com/blog/psyched/200805/why-do-women-have-

Certainly, not all rapes are caused by women. To go from a fantasy to provoking a real rape you need to be at least a bit disturbed. But then, "Mental disorders are common. World wide more than one in three people in most countries report sufficient criteria for at least one at some point in their life."[257] Given this, it is not unreasonable to suspect that many rapes are actually female-initiated.

Chapter 24: What Does a Woman Want?

"The great question that has never been answered, and which I have not yet been able to answer, despite my thirty years of research into the feminine soul, is 'What does a woman want?'" – Sigmund Freud, in a letter to a friend

The question "What does a woman want", which can be more clearly stated as "what must I do to get her in bed", is a timeless question. The majority of men, be it today or in every other historical era, has no clue, and Freud's admission is a revealing example. But an answer exists. And it has obvious importance for the war of the sexes: if all men knew it, their problem with sex could be solved.

Since Freud himself admitted he did not know the answer, perhaps we would do well to hear what those that have made it have to say. The Pick-Up Scene (PU, or Seduction Community, or Pick-Up Artist community – PUA), which took its first steps in the '70s, picked up steam in the internet era. The net "facilitated a global consortium of men comparing experiences, relating observations and testing theories"[258], allowing them to circumvent "the public social stigma, ridicule and outright hostility attached to men attempting to understand the psychologies of women". Many of the techniques proposed by PUA's "are in fact grounded in solid empirical findings from social,

---

erotic-rape-fantasies
257 Wikipedia, Mental Disoder. Accessed 19 Jan. 2015.
    https://en.wikipedia.org/wiki/Mental_disorder
258 Tomassi, Rolo. *The Rational Male.* Nevada: Counterflow Media LLC(2013).

physiological and evolutionary psychology."[259]

For many years, women were so successful in obscuring the truth about female libido that its very existence was questioned. Victorian ethics is characteristically indicative of this. For most men, female libido continues to be a mystery. Some, few, know that it exists and know how to bring it to the surface. But the blackout on the part of women towards the majority of men continues.

So what did the PUAs find? In their own words[260]: There is a secret society of sex, and you are either in or out. About 52% of the people on earth are its members. 50% are women, and 2% men. Its members hide the truth behind a smokescreen: if you are a member of the community, no one will ever deny you anything. If you are not, you will beg and scrap for any small favor.

PUAs were not the first to speak about this "secret society". Compare it with the following excerpt from *Love in the Time of Cholera*, by Gabriel Garcia Marquez (1985).

> *"The world is divided into those who screw and those who do not. He distrusted those who did not: when they strayed from the straight and narrow, it was something so unusual for them that they bragged about love as if they had just invented it. Those who did it often, on the other hand, lived for that alone. They felt so good that their lips were sealed as if they were tombs, because they knew that their lives depended on their discretion. They never spoke of their exploits, they confided in no one, they feigned indifference to the point where they earned the reputation of being impotent, or frigid, or above all timid fairies, as in the case of Florentino Ariza. But they took pleasure in the error because the error protected them. They formed a secret society, whose members recognized each other all over the world without need of a common language, which is why Florentino Ariza was not surprised by the girl's reply: she was one of them, and therefore she knew that he knew that she knew."*

---

259 Oesch, Nathan and Miklousic, Igor. "The Dating Mind: Evolutionary Psychology and the Emerging Science of Human Courtship", Evolutionary Psychology, 2012. 10(5): 899-909 http://www.epjournal.net/wp-content/uploads/EP10899909.pdf
260 See PUA Tyler Durden's text *"Secret Society"* on the Internet.

Chapter 25: So, What Does a Woman Want?

Although a man's status is his more attractive feature, being rich does not mean that you can have any woman you want. It's more complicated than that. There are men who, without being rich or particularly successful in society, still manage to be successful with women.

Is there some common factor that characterizes those that make it? The answer is yes. It is *vitality*[261]. It is something that women measure continuously in a man, second by second, and do so completely unconsciously, that is, very effectively. High status "just" helps a man preserve his vitality.

Let's say, for example, that you are the most successful businessman in a party, the Bill Gates type. Everyone is conscious of your presence, everyone looks at you from the corner of their eyes and laugh at your jokes. All this deference makes you irresistibly attractive to women. However, back in your own living-room, where you don't have all this attention focused on you and you are not getting the "strokes" you need, your vitality subsides, and your attractiveness with it.

Many men can't understand why women find self-important "fakes" attractive. It is precisely because, although "fakes" are vain and hollow, they manage to maintain their vitality by tapping in their status. In many cases, this is an imaginary status, it's just inside their heads, but that is enough to serve as a pillar for their inflated sense of self. That's why, for instance, narcissists are naturally attractive.

A young working-class man has no status on which he can rely. He has his 8- or 12-hour job wearing down his vitality. His attempt to rise in the hierarchy to increase his status is likely to backfire, since he might find that his struggle depletes all his vitality, and as a result, he will forever remain unattractive. He therefore sets off with a great handicap against men of the upper classes. That is why working-class guys who have made it in "the Game" have depended on some other trait. They might be

---

261 See for instance Townsend, What Women Want – What Men Want, p. 17.

very attractive physically. The might have a really strong character. Or they might have the character of a seducer.

The character of the seducer

> "Professional seducers ... are able to capture their partners without becoming involved themselves. This they do by encouraging the other person to look at them directly and to talk freely, while the male or female seducer makes only a well-guarded pretence of reciprocating."[262]

Seducers rely on what psychologists call "one-sided intimacy". It is the Holy Grail of the PU community. Women are trained throughout their life to recognize emotions, in themselves and in others, so it is extremely difficult to trick them. Some men, very few of them, can do the same spontaneously. These are the ones the PUAs call "naturals". PU boils down to the question of knowing how a non-natural can train to achieve one-sided intimacy effectively.

The problem for the average man is that sometimes during the flirting process his own (real) need for intimacy surfaces. Women sense this "neediness". They feel that they cover his need, and conclude that they are supporting his vitality. As a consequence, its value is diminished, and women are turned off. The PU solution is for the man to kill his need for intimacy so that it doesn't interfere with the seduction process.

One great theater actor once wrote that in order to appear true on scene, the actor must have his attention focused on the little toe of his right foot. This anecdote emphasizes the importance of *diversions* to hide our intentions (in the case of the actor, his "intention" to deceive the audience), and achieve contact in an emotional level. Most of those who manage to be successful seducers have a very specific *diversion* hiding their need for intimacy – not only from women, by also from themselves: it is their need for power.

Since approaching a woman is one of the most embarrassing things for a man, let's use the embarrassing example of flatulence in an elevator to show how a *force majeure* can have a liberating effect. Suppose you are

---

262 Berne, Games People Play. Ch. 16.

in an elevator with someone (of the same or opposite sex, it doesn't matter). There is no reason or occasion to engage in easy chatter. Suddenly, unexpectedly or because you miscalculated things, a silent exit of flatus escapes through your anus. You are instantly seized by panic, thinking that the other person will smell your perfidious smell. The result is that while up to now you felt you had nothing to say to them, a whole bunch of interesting things come spontaneously to your mind. You acquire an energy that magnetizes, with the expectation of course that it will magnetize their attention away from the foul smell. As is the case in this (silly) example, a higher-level need and a deep sense of inferiority, such things which characterize those who seek power, can under certain conditions give the impression of genuine vitality. *It is often a deeper wound and a deeper terror that makes someone withstand the fear of rejection.*

Seducers present themselves as independent men, men who do not need women – because they really don't need them as human beings, only as a means to their ends. Beyond that, it's a matter of strategy to lure them to bed. But

> "You cannot have a close relationship with strategies. With them we cannot feel. We can reach our goals, live the joy of conquest and power over the other, make them look at us. But this has nothing to do with real getting together, intimacy, love. In our relationship we should leave space for the pain and confusion that appear when we disarm our strategies. This is the way home, the way to unite with another human being. The way of love."[263]

It is important to note that, in hetero land, *all* men try to seduce women. The difference with seducers is that they *manage* to do so. And this is because women are really attracted by the traits they exhibit. Nowadays, where women are free to satisfy their sexuality, they often find themselves uncovering the seducer's (counter-)game and realizing that intimacy was "one-sided" *after* they have had sex. As a result, they feel betrayed. The need for power of those that they gave themselves to is often a serious pathological situation. The pathology might start to reveal

---

263 Bucay, Jorge and Salinas, Silvia. *Amarse con los ojos abiertos.* (2009).

itself through abuse, abandonment, or the revelation that he is sleeping with other women as well, that she was not as "special" as he was claiming... These kind of experiences lead some women, especially those who are in their hunting phase looking for a husband, to conclude that "all men are jerks". But not all are. Only those to whom they give it easily.

The perversion of the mating scene, as a consequence of the predominance of female strategies, results in men being unable to secure the sex they need, unless they have one perversion of their own to compensate. Of course, there is always an occasional non-rich and average looking man who is capable, smart, sensitive, honest and full of life, and who can get enough sex with his true value. More commonly, however, it is the outrageously handsome, outrageously rich, and outrageously disordered who make it.

We need to make an important distinction at this point. Due to the prevalence of chivalry, women have the expectation that their own wishes have absolute priority over the others' – having an entitlement typical of a proper blue-blooded princess. The dub "jerks" men who put their own desires over the other's (i.e. women's). But putting your needs first is normal and healthy – in fact, it is the *only* normal and healthy thing to do. In this sense, not all men thus labeled are "jerks". If you have no choice than to play the game, and the game is dishonest, using dishonest means is fair game. When you cannot untie the Gordian Knot, you have to cut it. The question is whether you will use these means for the rest of your life. Real "jerks" are those who treat men (i.e. situations outside of flirting) like women need to be treated in flirting. Because these types have a greater familiarity with manipulative tactics, they are more successful with women.

The battle for vitality

The battle for vitality plays a central role in the war of the sexes. This critical battle has largely been won by women who defend their benefits mercilessly, while men are in confusion and, at best, offer only passive resistance.

Vitality is the ability to feel the joy of life. It is what 3-year-old children radiate, what makes them lovable[264]. It is what charming men have managed to maintain. And it is what charming women have managed to maintain. The problem is that women manage to maintain their own vitality by demanding that men protect it, destroying their own in the process.

The description of this process by Warren Farrell is mind-blowing:

> "The process of protecting comes by coping with the shadow side of the world. And with that coping comes a loss of innocence. When the man who has mastered protecting meets the innocent woman, he 'falls in love' because her innocence allows a reunion with the self that got lost in the process of coping with complexity. Although he appears to have fallen in love with her, he really falls in love with his own lost innocence...
>
> The more innocent—or traditional—the woman, the more she seeks the man who can handle complexity. It is exactly his ability to handle complexity that allows her to retain her innocence. (The protector literally protects her innocence.) But in the process of dealing with the shadow side of life, he distances himself from his own spirituality, thus decreasing her love for him even as she increases her dependence on him.
>
> Conversely he becomes spiritually dependent on her and loves her more even as he respects her less. He respects the part of himself that can master complexity but hates the part of himself that had to compromise."[265]

As a female writer, staunch advocate of the traditional role for the woman – and therefore also for the man – summarized it "The man must know the ways of the world for you to continue to live carefree."

Women's preference for easier and more enjoyable jobs can be seen from

---

264 Youngian psychologists have a very descriptive way to talk about these. The part of human that can enjoy life is the archetype of the Child inside him, that has been kept alive and in the adult has evolved to the Lover. "King, Warrior, Magician, Lover" by Robert Moore and Doug Gillete (HarperSanFrancisco, 1990) is a fascinating description, from that perspective, of the healthy process of maturation for the man.

265 Farrell, The Myth Of Male Power, p.143.

this perspective. Work is fine to the extent that it can offer women independence, but they are not willing to sacrifice their vitality for it. Why give away the joy of life working in a well-paid but soul-wrecking job, when a man can do that for their sake? In return, women are prepared to "love" him – and give him access to the female body he needs. If Dorian Gray was willing to sell his soul to the devil for eternal youth, women can achieve this by paying a much lower price.

"We call it love. But she has not really 'fallen in love,' she has 'fallen in respect.'" writes Warren Farrell.[266] Although even this "respect" is more often a thin veil of hypocrisy covering their selfishness and their interest, as revealed by the modern rates of divorce initiated by women and infidelity on the part of women. Female innocence is actually not that innocent at all... All the above are at the basis of that uncomfortable feeling which men have, viz. that women do not fall in love with them but with the life they can offer them.

To understand the female condition, the key idea is that women try to remain children, keeping all children's benefits and lack of responsibility, all the while claiming all the rights of adults as well. "I want you to take care of me like a child" is the requirement of an average woman. Women who have acquired a human degree of responsibility are right to complain that men are attracted by immature and irresponsible women. But men don't really have a choice. Nature has made humans naturally protective of children, and female seduction piggy-backs on this tendency by presenting men with a childish profile. It is not something women do consciously. Everyone just follows the easy road, one which maximizes their pleasure and minimizes unpleasant situations. If men could, they would do it themselves. In fact, those that can, do. What could balance the situation would be a set of social expectations that relieved men from responsibilities and suffering, thus protecting their vitality, and assigning those responsibilities and suffering to women. Why should it be considered a good thing that women can avoid hardship through their sexuality? "There is much to be said for the constructive contribution of suffering to creative and spiritual life; suffering can temper the soul."[267]

---

266 Farrell, The Myth of Male Power, p.143
267 Goleman, Daniel. *Emotional Intelligence: Why it can matter more than IQ*. UK: Bloomsbury (1996). ch.5.

Indeed, there is such a thing as protecting one's innocence too much. Psychological maturation has been likened to body building. Body builders work their muscles to the point when they provoke a small rupture. The organism heals the wound, making the muscle stronger in the process. Two things can go wrong: either the rupture is too serious, and the wound won't mend, or no rupture occurs, and then there is no growth. The same happens with psychic traumas. Well-meaning but unwise parents who overprotect their children, not letting them have their own experiences and be subjected to the consequences of their actions, turn them into adults who cannot handle even minor difficulties. This is what the children of the bourgeoisie usually suffer from. They've had it too easy. And that is also what makes women fill the offices of psychologists. Generally speaking, the problem of boys and men is that the wounds they accumulate in life are too big, while the problem with girls and women is that their problems are too small.

Given that the sexual balance is tilted so much in favor of women, they have no reason not to take the easy road. Irvin Yalom describes this in one of his novels: "the truly beautiful woman is so often feted and rewarded solely for her appearance that she neglects developing other parts of herself. Her confidence and feelings of success are only skin-deep, and once her beauty fades she realizes she has little to offer: she has developed neither the art of being an interesting person nor that of taking an interest in others."[268]And what is true for "the truly beautiful woman", is made true for every woman, through women's control of the sexual economy.

Winning the flirting game

> *He who fights with monsters should be careful not to become a monster himself. - Friedrich Nietzsche*

Can a man win the flirting game? How?

There is a basic principle in poker, which all good players know: Don't play if you don't have an edge. This is also in Sun Tzu's classic book *The*

---

268 Yalom, Irvin. *The Schopenhauer Cure: A Novel (P.S.)*. USA: Harper Perennial (2006).

Art of War, written thousands of years ago: "One mark of a great soldier is that he fight on his own terms or not at all."[269] (The irony of having to quote from a book on war to talk about human relationships is not lost on the author).

In order to win you must want to play the game, despite it being unfair and rigged. You must respect it. Since women get their strokes from playing the game, not only do they love it and demand that you play it, but what's more they have a huge ego-investment in it. The man who will try to skip it in order to reach the point of intimacy that he craves, gravely insults them.

To be a consistent winner you necessarily need at least one of the following three advantages: a) money/status, b) exceptional physical attractiveness, or c) the "psychological advantage", i.e. a set of psychological adaptations (or disorders) which women find attractive. And attraction is only the first prerequisite for sex. You then need to create a "connection", reach intimacy, overcome any inhibitions... The average man can get lucky enough only due to exceptionally good circumstances.

At this point we need to comment on "well-intentioned" exhortations such as "why bother with that kind of woman, look at other ones". The first observation is that the flirting culture is so universal that if there are other kind of women you need too much good luck to meet them. You need extra good luck for them to be attractive. And even more luck for them to be available so that they end up in your bed. And after all this good luck, you have managed to accomplish only a small fraction of your sexual potential, and you need to go through the same ordeal again.

A second observation is that even playing these ritualized and dishonest games, a beautiful woman remains attractive. Having sex with her has inherent value. Of course, admonitions to avoid her are meaningful if sex will lead you to emotional commitment / marriage / emotional and financial destruction. For those kind of women (some say, practically all) Rev. Lawrence Shannon's advice is a real treasure:

---

269 Sun Tzu, Sun Pin, D.E. Tarver *The Art of War: Sun Tzu's Classic in Plain English with Sun Pin's: The Art of Warfare.* USA: iUniverse Star(2002).

"The man on a date must carefully approach the wicker basket containing the snake (predatory female). He must then gently unlatch the lid and softly woo the creature while lowering his scrotum into the basket. The trick is to seduce the snake and get the lid back down before she strikes."[270]

Self-sabotage

Men can feel the risk involved in emotionally committing to a woman. The illustrative example is male anxiety before a marriage ceremony. men's gut ring the bell telling them that they are stepping into something dangerous. It markedly contrasts with the female's triumph which results from achieving a long-lasting profitable agreement.

In order to avoid danger many men resort to self-sabotage. They might dress inelegantly, say inappropriate things, behave in unattractive ways. In the PU literature such behaviors are attributed to the fear of rejection, and are undesirable. You "reject" her unconsciously, before she gets the chance to reject you. In fact, the greatest part of PU deals with overcoming that "non productive" fear. And this is where PU fails, for two reasons: (a) the fear corresponds to a real danger, and (b) training in failure does not lead to success.

Let's see an example for (a), taken from *The Game*[271]. Neil Strauss describes the case of a well-to-do man who, went from being a total failure with women, to managing to find a beautiful woman and leaving the "PU community", all of this because he had learned the PU techniques. His later reappearance, with a night call to Neil, is compelling.

"I tried to kill myself today," he said.

"What happened?"

"My wife is expecting our first baby in ten days, and I'm miserable. I do everything for her, but it's not enough. She's driven me away from my friends. My business partner is leaving me. She spends all my money and all she does is

---

270 Shannon, The Predatory Female, p. 48.
271 Strauss, The Game, ch.6.

complain." He paused to choke back his tears. "And now that she's having this baby, I'm trapped."...

"When I first got in the community, I wrote down everything I wanted," he said. "And now I'm living the life I imagined. I have the money, the big house, and the beautiful girl. But I wasn't specific enough about the beautiful girl. I never wrote that she had to treat me with respect and kindness."

Neil Strauss comments that "He had pretended to be someone he wasn't just to seduce a woman, and now he was suffering the consequences." As Rollo Tomassi puts it, "The problem with just employing PUA skills to get any woman is that sometimes it actually gets you *any* woman."[272]

> *"Never try to impress a woman or she'll always hold you to that standard." -W.C. Fields*

Men's unconscious self-sabotage aims to prevent such situations. Whether it is a 35-year-old man trying to avoid "gold diggers", or a teenager needing a girl to love him "for what he really is" and not for his expensive shoes, the background is the same. Self-sabotage, revealing less than your "best self", or even showing parts of your "worst self", is a defense against danger. The danger of entrapment, in the case of the 35-year-old, and of emotional abuse, in the case of the teenager. Of course, self-sabotage is not a satisfactory solution, since it drives women away and leaves men sexually deprived.

The second reason PU fails is that training in failure does not lead to success. PUAs encourage men to be bold, and approach women even if it is a certain crash and burn. The rationale is that gradually, after several failures, men will be a desensitized to the fear of rejection. This is a big mistake. Continuous failure under stressful conditions typically trains one to keep on failing, and consolidates fear rather than alleviating it.

The solution (?)

The truth is that for some problems there is no true solution. Quoting Sun

---

272 Tomassi, The Rational Male.

Tzu again, "To secure ourselves against defeat lies in our own hands, but the opportunity of defeating the enemy is provided by the enemy himself. Thus the good fighter is able to secure himself against defeat, but cannot make certain of defeating the enemy."[273]

The issue with PU is not that it doesn't work at *all*. It's that it doesn't work *enough*. It can make someone better with women. It can help him become accepted in women's company, to become their "entertainer". But it cannot make him get enough sex.

Even in the rare cases when someone manages to consistently prevail in the flirting game and reach sexual intercourse, he then discovers that his problems have not been solved. Former Guru Pick-Up Artist RooshV, who traveled the world bedding women and writing specialized pickup guides for each country, wrote in his blog:

> "In spite of being in the game as long as I have, I sometimes feel weird urges to turn the mini-relationship into a serious one, especially if I like the girl. I want to contact her more, see her more, and with the girl I mentioned above, I imagined how it would be like to actually live with her – not for having sex on demand but just pair bonding and growing old with someone. These beta commitment fantasies of mine always turn negative as I consider the loss of freedom and privacy with no strong advantage that makes the deal profitable for me. Mini-relationships and harem maintenance are nothing more than entertainment and serious relationships are drudgery, one step away from slavery. Both are unsatisfactory.
>
> So what's the answer? Is it eternal bachelorhood, of banging a handful of new girls each season, hopping from one new mini-relationship to the next, but achieving no depth or novelty in what you haven't achieved before, or is it making what could be the biggest mistake of your life by knocking a girl up and riding the fatherhood roller coaster for the next 20 years? I could go out this weekend and hit it hard, maybe getting laid, but my intensive pursuit of sex in the past decade has sated me where I wouldn't be upset if I failed. Or maybe the answer is that the happiness I have sought in women can't be achieved at all, and whether I ride the slut

273 Sun Tzu, The Art of War.

carousel or settle down with one girl, I'll still end up asking myself, 'Is this it?'"[274]

Women, being the stronger sex, have solved the dilemma of "sex or intimacy" very simply: have sex with the few and most attractive men during your party years, and settle down after you turn 30 with one of the many guys girls disparagingly call "marriage material", and then gain intimacy with your children. If, in the meantime, there is an "accidental" pregnancy, and you won't abort, the system will force the unlucky man to cover a great part of the expenses for the upbringing of the child, either by marriage or by alimony. For men, on the other hand, there is no safe and viable solution apart from turning to prostitutes.

Chapter 26: Prostitutes

Not all prostitutes are the same.

There are luxury prostitutes who get paid thousands of dollars a night. Others just find it to be a profession which pays a decent wage. Many prostitutes enjoy it: in a classic study carried out in New York, one in four prostitutes reported "inclination" as a reason for selecting this profession[275]. Arianna, a prostitute from Calgary, Canada, who had been working as a prostitute for 5 years, said "It's my body, what I choose to do with it is what I choose to do.... It is a very empowering industry. I'm the happiest I've ever been."[276]

Others, who come from very poor backgrounds, see it as their only way out of poverty. And of course, there are those who are forced into prostitution (trafficking).

There is no doubt that forced prostitution is a heinous crime. However,

---

274 'Maybe It Doesn't Really Get Better Than This'. Accessed 23 Dec. 2014.
    http://www.rooshv.com/maybe-it-doesnt-really-get-better-than-this
275 Sanger, W. W. History of Prostitution (1858).
276 'Calgary sex workers on Canada's prostitution bill: 'It's so backwards' | Calgary
    Herald'. http://blogs.calgaryherald.com/2014/06/05/calgary-sex-workers-on-
    prostitution-bill-its-so-backwards

violent coercion occurs in only a tiny minority of the cases[277]. Arriana says that she's "never, ever come across an underage person or somebody being forced to work." What happens, then, with the overwhelming majority of cases where prostitution is the woman's choice?

The debate has been rekindled by recent attempts in France, Canada and elsewhere to criminalize *clients*. This hypocritical practice is supposedly in favor of prostitutes, as the penalty is imposed on the customers and not the sex provider. Sure enough, such proposed measures are strongly opposed by prostitutes' unions, as they argue the obvious, i.e. it will push sex workers to go further underground, ending up in illegal and dangerous situations.

In every totalitarian regime, as well as in the biggest economies of the planet, be it the USA, Japan, Russia or China, prostitution is illegal. The penalization aims to deprive men of that sexual outlet, so that they are forced to work and become "successful" within the system in order to have access to a woman. This aim is, of course, never spelled out; instead, various "moral" arguments are invoked. It is supposedly unethical for a woman to lease her vagina for 10 minutes for money, while it is ethical to give away all her time, all her being, her own life, what Marx called her "working power"; it is ethical to become alienated in a soul-crushing job in a super market with unpaid overtime, zero advancement or promotions, unhealthy working conditions leading to musculoskeletal problems, precariousness, and to suffer from the degrading behavior of a manager, for 8, 10 or 12 hours a day, in order to earn the same amount of money which those 10 minutes of sex would have obtained. This kind of petty-bourgeois morality has *de facto* been thrown in the bin in countries where survival is not taken for granted. In countries like Thailand, not only it is not a shame, but is an honor for a daughter to be a prostitute. That way she can support her old parents financially. Luxury prostitutes have also overcome the negative prejudices clouding their profession, and do not consider it as wholly shameful. It is time for society to overcome the social stigma and consider prostitution like another profession. The view that "prostitution is not a job", a mantra often mentioned by

---

277 Weizer, Roland. *Sex Trafficking and the Sex Industry: The Need for Evidence-Based Theory and Legislation.* 101 J. Crim. L. & Criminology 1337 (2013). http://scholarlycommons.law.northwestern.edu/jclc/vol101/iss4/4

feminists, is a hard-core systemic view which actually argues that "work (in capitalism) is not prostitution". The simple truth is that, as Charles Bukowski put it, women (including feminists) hate whores, because they drive the price of vagina down.

Opposition to prostitution is the point in which the supposedly progressive feminists converge with the most conservative, traditional women and the most reactionary regimes.

It is spectacularly hypocritical that such war is waged against explicit prostitution, while in fact all women might be prostitutes, to a certain extend. Scientists have immense difficulties defining what indisputably constitutes prostitution.

> "There may be no crisp demarcation between prostitution and gift giving. 'Gift giving or even cash payment for sexual intercourse,' one scholar writes, 'cannot be used as criteria to define prostitution, for these occur in courtship or even in marital situations.' As the prominent evolutionary biologist Nancy Burley notes, 'Since prostitution and courtship exist as a continuum, the vast majority of copulatory opportunities involve costs to males in terms of time and/or material goods.'"[278]

Chapter 27: Life Expectancy, again

We have presented enough evidence by now to make the issue of men's reduced life expectancy quite clear.

The title of a BBC article reporting on a scientific experiment, says it all: "Sex-starved flies live shorter, more stressful lives."[279]

"Sexual frustration impairs the health of fruit flies and causes premature death", scientists discovered. Their method was to genetically modify

---

278 Buss, Why women have sex, Ch. 8.
279 'BBC News - Sex-starved fruit flies live shorter, more stressful lives'.
       http://www.bbc.com/news/science-environment-25120980

male flies so that they excreted female pheromones, attracting the sexual interest of males but (obviously) refusing to engage in sexual intercourse. "Male flies who were stimulated to mate but prevented from doing so, had their lives cut short by up to 40%. Those allowed to copulate not only lived longer but suffered less stress."

The exact same experiment would probably be a bit difficult to conduct with humans, but one can find analogies between this experiment and men's situation today. "The starkest difference between male and female health can be seen by comparing socio-economic classes. Women living in the *least favourable* circumstances are healthier by far than men living in the *most favourable* conditions. Long-term illness is 40% higher among unemployed men than in unemployed women."[280] [emphasis added]. *Stress* is what makes men have such bad health, and what intensifies men's stress, especially in the lower social classes, is their difficulty to satiate their sex drive.

Feminism, despite its scorn and hostility for men, has ultimately been good for them. Better, in any case, than the previous system, the so-called "traditional society". Its greatest service to men has been the idea of abolishing virginity. Although the "sexual revolution" was a flare that came to pass, women since then have been negotiating their sexual availability on looser terms. You no longer need to marry a women to have sex with her. This was the main reason why, as we have seen, men's life expectancy increased in relative terms from an all-time low in the '70s. Less sex-starvation means having a longer, healthier life.

Chapter 28: Why Do People Have Children?

Procreation is obviously necessary for the perpetuation of the system. Therefore it is easy to answer the question: why does every social system

---

280 'BBC News | Health | Crisis in men 's health targeted'.
    http://news.bbc.co.uk/2/hi/health/458758.stm

need children? The interesting part of the answer, however, is to see how the system's need is transformed into a need of its members, of each individual. Or, if we look at things from another standpoint, how small, "individual" decisions to procreate are linked to the reproduction of the system as a whole.

The first thing to observe is that humans are the only beings who can consciously decide whether to have children or not. This was not always the case. Before mankind understood the mechanism of reproduction, things were simple; there was no option. Women became pregnant every 4-5 years, from when they were approximately 18 to the age of 32; they had on average 3-4 children of which 2 would survive and reach their reproductive age. The hunter-gatherer social organization required a steady number of clan members which was maintained even, if needed, with infanticide. "Foraging societies limited the number of infants so they wouldn't become a burden to the group or allow overly rapid population growth to strain food supplies."[281]

With the Agricultural Revolution and the possibility to produce surplus and accumulate food, every additional member of society not only didn't burden the whole, but brought more wealth. It was the era when the sacred books forbid men from spending their semen in vain: it had to be used to produce more servants for the system. Within the extended family and the household economy children were economically beneficial as future producers, carers for the elders – in short, they represented a primitive form of social security. The material benefits of procreation for society met those of the parents.

This utilitarian use of children survives to this day. In China, for instance, where the Welfare State is inefficient or lacking, society has a strong preference for boys who will take care of their elderly parents. It is mandated by law that a son must see his parents once a week; daughters are not under a similar obligation.

In the Western world, the elderly can survive based with the Welfare System, with their pensions and health insurance. In such a system, children are not financially advantageous; on the contrary they are a huge

---

281 Ryan, Sex at Dawn, ch.14.

economic burden. For example, the upbringing of an average child in Australia costs cne million Australian dollars (about $780,000).

Children are therefore costly. Are they worthwhile because they may "bring happiness"? According to several studies, not at all.

> "Children do not bring happiness. In fact more often they seem to bring unhappiness. That is the conclusion of one academic study after the next – and there are so many that it makes one wonder if researchers kept trying, hoping for a different result... Using data sets from Europe and America, numerous scholars have found some evidence that, on aggregate, parents often report statistically significantly lower levels of happiness, life satisfaction, marital satisfaction and mental well-being compared with non-parents.... There is also evidence that the strains associated with parenthood are not only limited to the period during which children are physically and economically dependent. For example, [researchers found that] older parents whose children have left home report the same or slightly less happiness than non-parents of similar age and status. Thus, what these results are suggesting is something very controversial – that having children does not bring joy to our lives."[282]

It we take a more detailed look at these studies we will realize that the effect of procreation on the happiness of parents is not the same for both sexes. The study "The effects of offspring on the psychological well-being of older adults"[283] found that "the average effects of offspring were distinctly more negative for men than for women". Indeed, "among well-educated white men, there is a rather strong evidence that childless persons have been happier than others". The same is true for all black men, independently of education and income level. Another study found that "childless elderly women were both lonelier and more depressed than mothers while no differences between childless elderly men and fathers were found."[284]

282 'Does Having Children Make You Unhappy? - NYTimes.com'.
    http://parenting.blogs.nytimes.com/2009/04/01/why-does-anyone-have-children
283 Glenn, Norval D and McLanahan, Sara. "The effects of offspring on the psychological well-being of older adults", Journal of Marriage and Family, Vol. 42, No. 2, May 1981. http://www.jstor.org/discover/10.2307/351391
284 Vikstrom, Josefin el at. "The influences of childlessness on the psychological well-being and social network of the oldest old", BMC Geriatrics 2011, 11:78.

If we summarize the findings, we see that procreation today is a burden for men, and that it has a relatively neutral or marginally positive effect for women. So why do so many people have children?

The answer lies in what Eric Berne identifies as children's "usual function of structuring time for their parents"[285]. They solve the "eternal problem of the human being [which] is how to structure his waking hours"[286]. It is what common people refer to as "give a meaning to your life". These are people, the majority, who throughout their lives cannot find another meaning than converting their unstructured time into structured, so they can handle it and bear it. They remind one of the tactic of "nerds", who like role-playing or other table games which create a structured environment in which they can interact safely. In this sense, procreation is what "life-nerds" do to keep themselves busy.

This description is schematic and leaves many factors unaccounted for. Between existential angst and structured parental time, the second is obviously preferable. In this regard the above analysis is not intended to blame people for choosing to have children. (The life-nerds). It only aims to highlight the tragedy of contemporary social life, where children are used by their parents as an outlet to unfreedom and lack of meaning.

For women, however, there are also biological reasons to have children, contrary to assurances from older Feminists that it is all about social expectations. "I was desperate for a baby and I have the medical bills to prove it. I still have pregnancy dreams, waiting for something that will never happen", wrote Germaine Greer herself, the same Feminist who emphasized the precedence of "independence" and career over procreation. Women's strong bond with their babies gives them intense pleasure, due to their neuroanatomy and their hormonal functions. Oxytocin, also called the "bonding hormone", which regulates the maternal behavior, is strongly associated with the centers of pleasure and reward in women's brains.

> "Many women experience the first "mommy brain" symptoms long before they actually conceive a child...

---

http://www.biomedcentral.com/1471-2318/11/78
285 Berne, Games People Play, Ch.5.
286 Berne, Games People Play, Ch.5.

> 'Baby lust' – the deep-felt hunger to have a child – can hit a woman soon after she's cradled someone else's warm, soft newborn... The sweet smell of an infant's head carries pheromones that stimulate the female brain to produce the potent love potion oxytocin – creating a chemical reaction that induces baby lust."[287]

"Baby lust", thus, is not a social construct but a biological reality, intensified by our society. It is what pushes women to have a child at all costs, like a drug addict who will do anything to get her daily fix. It is one of the strongest roots of the alliance between women and the system.

This said, raising a child is not necessarily a bad thing. It is like having a Ferrari. It is actually nice, but if you don't have the money to support it and the time to enjoy it, it will become a burden and make you miserable. You also need to know how to drive, and to be good at it, otherwise it makes no sense. Herb Goldberg writes that

> "There is, I believe, in this day and age where children do not necessarily enhance the survival potential of the family, only one 'right' reason for a man to father children, and that is that the process of being a father excites him and is seen as enriching, fulfilling and joyful, and the realities of his life allow him to participate fully."[288]

Family more often than not does not help a man mature. It stunts him. Men who marry and have children expecting it to make them more mature are like the student who not knowing the answer to a question writes whatever comes to his mind, hoping that by chance he will score some points. "Having children should be saved for last, for the time when the man has played out his fantasies, has had relationships with many women, explored and given himself the gift of finding out who he is."[289] *Maturity, money, free time*: if all these three conditions are not met, a father turns into a tragic figure. From this perspective, the fact that working-class men have children at all is one of the greatest tragedies of our times. In the Middle Ages, there were already revolutionary

---

287 Brizendine, The Female Brain, p. 97.
288 Goldberg, Herb. *The Hazards of being Male: Surviving the Myth of Masculine Privilege.* USA: Signet (1987). p. 155.
289 Goldberg, The Hazards of Being Male, p. 155.

movements of the poor, expressed in the medieval form of heresy, that rejected reproduction and refused to have children, "not to bring new slaves into this 'land of tribulations'"[290] – a precious vein of thought that is now unfortunately lost.

The children of the working class have parents who have no time for them. Due to their egocentrism, which is a normal psychological stage in their development, these children come to believe that they don't deserve their parents' love and time. Amazing intuition. It is exactly what their parents think, considering that it is their personal right to bring children in the world, even if they don't have the preconditions to take care of them, even if they can't offer them the quality parental time children need in order to have a dependable psychological basis for a life worth living.

The man bears the greater part of the financial responsibility of the family, even though he has much less time to spend with his children than his wife, who works less and enjoys the company of her children more. This "transfer of happiness" from the man to the woman makes the man more unhappy. It is notable that it does not make the woman much happier than if she didn't have children. Despite the intense maternal pleasure, and despite the protection her man offers her, the system's assurance that "children bring happiness" is a deceitful lie, even for women. It is just not such an egregious lie as it is for men.

Chapter 29: Turning Down the Marriage Deal

Most men are still willing or unwilling victims of marriage (i.e. of procreation). Love – idealization – marriage – divorce – alienation from the children – loneliness: this downwards spiral is common nowadays. "Among college-educated couples, the percentage of divorces initiated by wives is a whopping 90 percent."[291] Even in marriages that last, the

---

290 Federici, Caliban and the Witch, p. 35.
291 'Who initiates the divorce more often, the wife or the husband?'. Accessed 14 Sep. 2014. http://www.divorce-lawyer-source.com/faq/emotional/who-initiates-divorce-

man cannot usually avoid alienation, since he is trying to do the impossible: to balance being a competitive, successful, trustworthy provider as well as a sensitive husband and father. Spending his day as a go-getter focused on efficiency and his afternoon patiently spending half an hour feeding the baby a freaking banana is an absurdity. The result of the pressure to do both is to exhaust all his energy and to eventually feel the burn-out.

The good news is that there are signs that men are reacting. The PU scene is one example. The men's Rights Movement is another, more politically advanced attempt at fighting back. But until recently it was marginalized – although in the last few years the possibility that this movement could make an explosive entry into the political scene is in the offing. A movement with a greater impact is what in the US is called "MGTOW, Men Going Their Own Way", or in Japan "herbivore men". In Japan for example, more than a quarter of men 16-24 years old "were not interested in or despised sexual contact"[292], which is a rational and expected response if you consider that the corresponding percentage in women is 45%. And obviously, in the absence of sex, these men have no interest in relationships or marriage.

> "Satoru Kishino, 31, belongs to a large tribe of men under 40 who are engaging in a kind of passive rebellion against traditional Japanese masculinity. Amid the recession and unsteady wages, men like Kishino feel that the pressure on them to be breadwinning economic warriors for a wife and family is unrealistic. They are rejecting the pursuit of both career and romantic success. 'It's too troublesome,' says Kishino, when I ask why he's not interested in having a girlfriend. 'I don't earn a huge salary to go on dates and I don't want the responsibility of a woman hoping it might lead to marriage.'"[293]

It is the phenomenon described by American psychologist Hellen Smith in *Men On Strike: Why Men Are Boycotting Marriage, Fatherhood and*

---

men-or-women.html

292 'Why have young people in Japan stopped having sex? | World news | The Observer'. http://www.theguardian.com/world/2013/oct/20/young-people-japan-stopped-having-sex

293 Ibid.

the American Dream – and Why It Matters:

> "Men slowly discover that the effort to win women's attention via employment is not rewarding them the way it did for their dads and granddads, and that now only herculean efforts to make considerably more than women will give them an edge in the mating market. — Blogger Chateau Heartiste, on why men are opting out
>
> Men are now opting out of work and marriage altogether or are just not trying as hard in many cases."

Smith is politically conservative, so she claims that "While this may be good for individual men, it is not good for society as a whole." Nevertheless, putting the interest of the human beings before that of the system, as a proper psychologist should do, she advises men who don't want to enter the game that they have the right to stay out. She even advises them that they can resort to pornography and masturbation as a more viable solution. Between working 60 hours a week in a soul-destroying job in order to acquire a wife and children with whom 67%[294] of men will eventually be separated and will probably have to pay alimony, and the other option, i.e. remaining unemployed, living in one's parents' basement with a little pocket money and a couple of equally hippyish friends, pornography, and so on, the second option is simply a more rational choice.

> "It seems that the task of living up to women's expectations is so high that many men just don't measure up. They simply give up and find a life that brings them some reasonable amount of comfort. Yes, the basement, video games and porn might be a poor second (or not), but at least it's attainable and doesn't sit around trying to shame them for not performing up to par."[295]

Revealingly, the USA and Japan are two countries that have adopted a "hard line" against prostitution, which is officially illegal in both

---

294 "One study from the University of Michigan predicts that among first-time marriages, the rate of divorce may be as high as 67 percent." In *Raising an Emotionally Intelligent Child*.

295 Smith, Helen. *Men On Strike: Why Men are Boycotting Marriage, Fatherhood and the American Dream – and Why It Matters.* USA: Encounter Books (2013). p. 134.

countries. In other parts of the planet, pornography and masturbation is not the only alternative: prostitution is better. If men overcome the guilt syndrome and their insecurities, they can cover their sexual needs in this way.

We must stress that for the rest of their needs, especially the need for intimacy, i.e. the need to escape loneliness, women are not the most appropriate solution anyway. If anything, a "needy" man is an unattractive man, and his neediness must be taken care of before he can become an "eligible" party. If a man tries to cover his neediness with women while not having met the prerequisites, he falls into a vicious circle.

The way out of loneliness, in the long term, is only through friends – whether or not a man is in a relationship with a woman. This truth is one which men forget or never discover in their struggle for the daily vagina. The conclusion reached by anthropologist Robin Dunbar is that "men's well-being depends on meeting up with friends and 'doing stuff'"[296]. Four friends, two times a week. Epicurus had said this centuries ago: "Of all the goods offered by Wisdom for a happy life, the most important by far is friendship". Epicurus also compared friendship with sex. "The sexual act itself has nothing reprehensible, but much more important than sex is friendship, that dances around the world calling us to wake up for the sake of happiness".

Unfortunately, "As adult males in our culture the phenomenon of being without even a single buddy or good friend is a common one – so widespread in fact, that it is not seen as unusual nor is it even spoken about."[297] This overintensifies the man's dependence on women.

It is of sociological interest that an exhortation in favor of prostitutes is insulting only for the petty bourgeois. The rich are well aware that you ultimately buy women with money, so they learn to use the services provided by luxury prostitutes. The poor, early in their lives, see the most beautiful women of their class ascending using their sexuality, and soon

---

296 'Men's wellbeing depends on meeting up with friends | Daily Mail Online'.
   http://www.dailymail.co.uk/health/article-2469485/Mens-wellbeing-depends-meeting-friends.html
297 Goldberg, The Hazards of Being Male, p. 127.

lose all their romantic illusions. At best, their father will teach them, at the right time (neither too late, nor too early) that the only realistic way to have the attractive women they desire is to visit a brothel. Given the "strong evidence that commercial sex is safer than non-commercial sex"[298] regarding STDs, only naive puritans remain opposed to prostitution.

Prostitutes for sex, friends for intimacy. That is the best and most dependable model to ensure men's happiness in today's era. It is the best the average non-rich man can do.

What about Love?

Up to now we have focused on sex. But if sex was men's real problem, brothels would be a sufficient solution. men's real problem is that they want love too. And safety, and respect, and to find themselves... Warren Farrell in *The Myth Of Male Power* uses men's need for love as the backbone around which he analyzes the male predicament. This said, sex remains one of the most basic human needs (especially for men), along with air, food and sleep. This is illustrated in A. Maslow's "hierarchy of needs"[299].

---

298 Ward, Helen & Robinson, Angela (2004) *Response to Paying the Price, Home Office consultation on prostitution.* British Associationfor Sexual Health and HIV. http://www.bashh.org/documents/1118/1118.pdf
299 The illustration is from Wikipedia, Maslow's hierarchy of needs, Accessed 2 Nov. 2014. https://en.wikipedia.org/wiki/Maslow%27s_hierarchy_of_needs

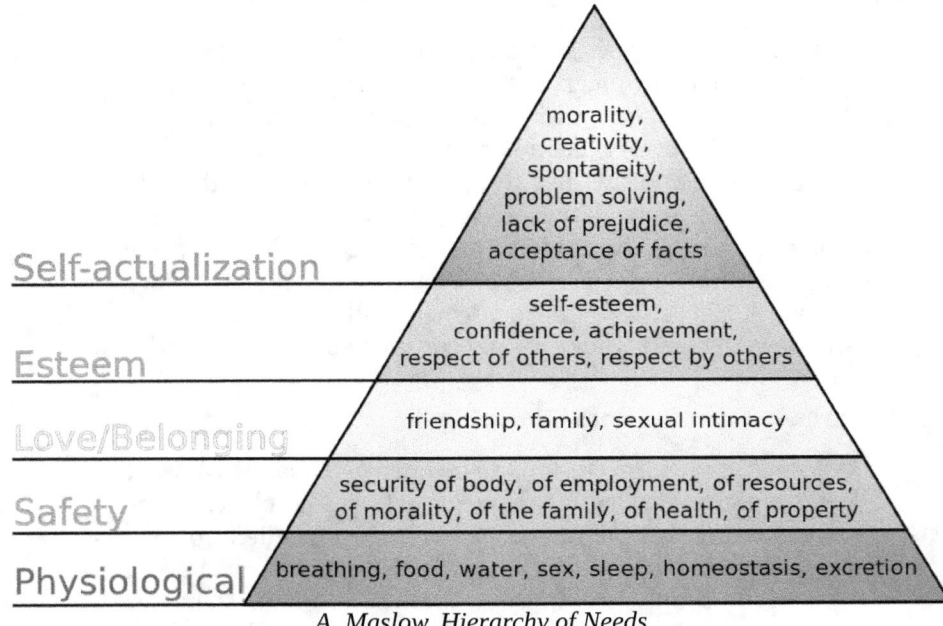

A. Maslow, Hierarchy of Needs

We can locate sex in the lowest, most basic level of needs. The pyramidal shape emphasizes the principle that the non-satisfaction of a level of needs makes it difficult or impossible to satisfy a higher one. Men typically realize their unmet need for love *after* they satisfy their need for sex – which usually means never. On the other hand, a man married with a woman who gives him "love", lives in a contradictory situation: the female expectation that accompanies this "love" is that he stops fully satisfying his need for sex – which for men, as we've seen, requires a variety in sexual partners.

Men are victims of a grave misunderstanding. They believe that female love is worth the trouble, because they imagine it like the love they themselves are capable of giving. However, female "love" is so different from the male one that it should have a different word. While the man's love is associated with feelings of protectiveness towards the woman, the woman's love is calculating (albeit unconsciously), wholly oriented to satisfying her interests. "Women are fundamentally incapable of loving a man in the way that a man expects to be loved by a woman. Men believe that love matters for the sake of it. Women love opportunistically."[300]

> "One of the biggest stumbling blocks for men, especially those reared by women, is the understanding that no woman will ever love them, particularly in the manner they desire.... A woman's love is like a hand powered grinding wheel. If you pump furiously and wind it up, she will do the job, make noise, even throw off sparks. She will respond, but only respond. The minute you release the handle... she begins winding down. She can only respond in a temporary manner. That's why an adult female will rarely call you or initiate anything. They are only constructed to respond."[301]

Here is how a man describes his need for love:

> "We want to relax. We want to be open and honest. We want to have a safe haven in which struggle has no place, where we gain strength and rest instead of having it pulled from us. We want to stop being on guard all the time, and have a chance to simply be with someone who can understand our basic humanity without begrudging it. To stop fighting, to stop playing the game, just for a while.

> We want to, so badly.

> If we do, we soon are no longer able to."[302]

To feel loved, you need to feel fully accepted as you are. With your strong points, and your weak ones. *Especially the weak ones*. Only women loath weakness in a man. What good is a vulnerable guy? The only exception they are prepared to make is this: "I want a strong man with one weak spot – me and our family, and we're so dear to him he'll do anything for us. But with everyone outside the family he'll be able to walk over them if he has to."[303]

The female libido is in direct line with male dominance. A man who washes the dishes might be a good girlfriend with a woman, but will never rouse her sexually. Man is like a zebra: free in the wild, it's a

300 Tomassi, The Rational Male, p. 273.
301 Shannon, The Predatory Female, p. 29.
302 Tomassi, The Rational Male, p. 311.
303 Townsend, What Women Want – What Men Want, p. 67.

beautiful wild animal; when tamed and domesticated, it's just a donkey with pajamas. Someone with a visible need to be emotionally covered by a woman, and who has no other options, loses all attractiveness – even within marriage, and indeed *especially* in it. "If a man is so sensitive or timid he can't stand up to you, you begin to look at him as a child – someone you protect under your wing. For me that kind of feeling is almost incestuous. It's not good sexually."[304]

Female "love" is in a sense schizophrenic. Women love men who radiate vitality and aggressive energy, but trying to divert all these exclusively towards themselves they castrate them and deprive them of that energy. But it is exactly this energy that makes a man creative and successful in anything he does, especially his work. The result is that for men, "There is no rest, there is no respite or reprieve from performing"[305]. (Feminist) psychologist Marianne Brandon recognizes this situation:

> "It is not enough that he is strong and accomplished in the world. That is, sometimes men are strong in the workplace, but they become more lazy and passive at home. Knowing that her man has the capacity for strength is not enough for her to surrender. She must feel it at home, and particularly in her bedroom, for her to let go sexually. This can be its own challenge for men who engage their alpha energy at work and want to come home and relax. But in terms of instinct, home is still a den, and he is still a member of the pack. His partner still needs to feel his instinctual energy for her to more naturally engage her own instinctual feminine side.... Sometimes my male patients believe that this is too much work, and their lives are already filled. Cultivating their alpha energy at home requires more effort than they feel they can give to a relationship. I sympathize."[306]

It's quite telling that this woman psychologist, who considers monogamy unnatural albeit socially necessary, can offer nothing more to this dead end of men except her "sympathy".

---

304 Townsend, What Women Want – What Men Want, p. 154.
305 Tomassi, The Rational Male, p. 312.
306 Brandon, Monogamy, p. 77.

The bitter Red Pill

Men's need for love is as immense, as it is deeply suppressed. We have already discussed how women accomplish this suppression, with their roles as mothers and by policing sex in their youth. It is a condition that also affects them to a degree, because they "never feel there is enough love to go around"[307]. This complaint can recall the parricide who complains that she is an orphan. Women, however, can at least rely on the love of their children. They count on it from very early on, when they are still girls, and they feel that when they have kids of their own they will never be alone and loveless. Not so for men. On the one hand, work does not leave them time to enjoy their children, even if they are lucky, don't divorce and keep living in the same house. On the other hand, they are not programmed biologically to derive as much pleasure from their children as women do. It has been found e.g. that marriage reduces the "male virility hormone"[308], testosterone, and that fatherhood reduces it even more. And of course, having someone else take care of them is perfectly normal for women, something they have been accustomed to all their lives - and which they demand of their children. For the male standards, this is indecent.

With all the social programming inflating men's need for love, the fact that *a man will never be loved by a woman as much as he needs* seems unthinkable. The "Red Pill" theory and men's movement is built precisely around this truth. Its name comes from the red pill in the movie *Matrix*, which painfully unplugs you from the Matrix and makes you see reality. A whole internet community of men who started with PU ended up with the Red Pill Theory. In the relevant forum on Reddit, their "meeting point", messages of gratitude regularly appear, going like this:

> "*Title: Thank you to all of you. Thank you so fucking much.*
>
> I never had a father in my life who could give me guidance and teach me how the world, and women really works.

---

307 Baumeister, Is there anything good about men?, p. 206, citing My Mother, My Self
    by Nancy Friday.
308 'Harvard Gazette: Marriage lowers testosterone'.
    http://news.harvard.edu/gazette/2002/09.19/01-testosterone.html

In the past year, I turned from a guy that repulsed women, into one that has multiple plates [note: "spinning plates" are women interested in you, that you keep around], has girls constantly complimenting him on how he is (mostly things I learned from TRP) and knows how to hold frame. What I learned here not only made me more successful with women, but with friends, in business and in every aspect of my life. It also dramatically raised my self-esteem and self-respect.

I'd have been fucked without theredpill.

All of this fucking works. No one who has swallowed the red pill can ever say that we don't speak the truth.[...] Theredpill is the father I never had. Swallowing the red pill is on the top 3 best things that have ever happened to me.

And to think that I came here by pure chance. If I never stumbled here accidentally - I might have been one of those guys whom at 32 marries a post-wall slut and gets cheated on.

I doubt that I'm the only one whose life has been dramatically improved by stumbling here purely by chance.

I could never thank all of you enough.

My current plates, and my future girlfriends are/will also be very grateful to what all of you have taught me - into the man I became because of everything in here."[309]

Is is perhaps a paradox that the moment a man stomachs that women are not here to love him, and loses this doggy look "please love me", he instantly becomes attractive... The problem with this approach is that you cannot fake it. You really need to believe it, and forever lose hope that you will find someone to love you. And this is not easy. "This pill tastes bitter (as fuck)."[310]

---

309 https://www.reddit.com/r/TheRedPill/comments/2fm6xo/
    thank_you_to_all_of_you_thank_you_so_fucking_much/
310 https://www.reddit.com/r/TheRedPill/comments/2dgvf9/
    step_one_swallowed_the_damn_pill/

So, what is the Red Pill about, in practical terms? It is a pragmatic approach of the sexual market, which focuses on your self-improvement: doing the things that benefit you directly while being incidentally attractive to women. Increase your status in an area that interests you, exercise to feel good while building a nice body, cultivate your social skills in order to derive more pleasure from your social interactions while being charming at the same time. Learn *game* in order to seal the deals that come your way. But don't invest massive time and effort for any single woman. Above all, avoid emotional investment in a woman, and avoid commitment – marriage, of course, is out of the question. Don't invest anything you can't afford losing, and always be in a position to walk away. Be self-centered, enjoy the things you like, and let women come to you[311].

Before discussing whether things could actually be different or whether the Red Pill is the only feasible solution, let's first examine how things got so messed up in the first place...

---

311 https://www.reddit.com/r/TheRedPill/comments/49ip0l/
      the_price_of_settling_is_too_high/d0s7k4d/

Part 4: From Prehistoric to Historic Society: What Went Wrong?

Woman with a digging stick. Photographer: S. Kinoshita, 1937

Introduction

In previous chapters we presented the ways in which women are advantaged against men, and how the root of women's supremacy is biology. Women are in a position to exchange sex for resources, while men are not. But perhaps the picture that emerged from our analysis so far is a bit gloomy: if women are prostitutes by biology and men willing to kill to have sex, then the future of humanity is bound to be grim, as some believe it was in the past. But if we look still further back, in *pre*history, we realize that things were not so dismal. Not that women's biology was different – women were always in a position to take advantage of sex – only that society could be different with the same biological foundation.

Let's start from the beginning.

Chapter 30: Challenging the Dominant Model

Paternity certainty and jealousy

A cornerstone of the (reactionary) dominant model of sociobiology is the belief that men care above all for the certainty of their paternity. Paternity and marriage are considered so unquestionable that the whole model bends and twists like a snake in order to stick all the conflicting facts concerning sexuality around it.

But we don't need to look very far to find evidence to the contrary:

> "The Marind-anim people of Melanesia believed [that] semen was essential to human growth and development. They also married quite young, and to assure the bride's fertility, she had to be filled with semen. On her wedding night, therefore, as many as ten members of her husband's lineage had sexual intercourse with the bride, and if there were more men than this in the lineage, they had intercourse with her the next night…. A similar ritual was repeated at various intervals throughout a woman's life.
>
> Welcome to the family. Have you met my cousins?
>
> Lest you think this a particularly unusual wedding celebration, it seems the ancestors of the Romans did

something similar. Marriage was celebrated with a wedding orgy in which the husband's friends had intercourse with the bride, with witnesses standing by."[312]

The most modern views of evolutionary biology also depart from the hypothesis of paternity certainty:

"Many Pleistocene mothers probably had boyfriends. But each woman's boyfriend may not have been the father of any of her offspring.... Males may have given some food to females and their offspring [but] anthropologists now view much of this behavior more as courtship effort than paternal investment. Viewed from the broad sweep of evolution, it is unlikely that male hominids did much direct fathering. In almost all mammals and all primates, females do almost all of the child care, with very little help from males. Males could never be sure which offspring really carried their genes, whereas females could be certain."[313]

In Amazon tribes, as well as in other places of the world such as in remote New Guinea, there is a perception that scientists call "partible paternity"[314]. They consider that "a fetus is made of accumulated semen", so a woman engages in sex with many men. "She'll solicit "contributions" from the best hunters, the best storytellers, the funniest, the kindest, the best-looking, the strongest, and so on—in the hopes her child will literally absorb the essence of each." Regarding men's attitude towards this arrangement, "far from being enraged at having his genetic legacy called into question, a man in these societies is likely to feel gratitude to other men for pitching in to help create and then care for a stronger baby. Far from being blinded by jealousy as the standard narrative predicts, men in these societies find themselves bound to one another by shared paternity for the children they've fathered together."

Regarding the issue of jealousy, Desmond Morris has some useful observations from our more familiar Great Britain. He observed a professional soccer team for months, an experience he describes in his book *The Soccer Tribe (1981)*. It seems that players did not pass only the

---

312 Ryan, Sex at Dawn, ch. 9.
313 Miller, The Mating Mind, p. 190.
314 Ryan, Sex at Dawn, Ch. 6.

ball to each other. "If one of them scores (sexually), he is not possessive, but is only too happy to see his team-mates succeed with the same girl."[315] The difference between these players and ordinary mortals is that, on the one hand they had a sense of community and companionship, and on the other, being famous, they had countless sexual opportunities.

A similar lack of jealousy can be observed in the Maasai war tribes, where all men of an age group have the right to engage with all women in the same age group (with the women having the right to refuse their attentions). The only thing you have to do if you covet "the wife of thy neighbor" is to leave your spear outside her hut and enter. If in the meantime her husband returns, he will see the signal and discreetly turn away, seeking to do the same in some other hut.

It emerges therefore that male jealousy is not an inescapable biological behavior. Neither is it a pathological condition, as mainstream psychology maintains. It is a social phenomenon, having as its main reason the strangulation of the average man's sexual opportunities[316]. If she has made you work so hard to get her, isn't it normal to be enraged when she gives it to someone else for free?

The current notion of paternity, with all its expected behaviors and the emotions that surround it, originates in the agricultural class societies of the past. In today's world with frequent divorces, the notion is challenged in practice, albeit from a negative perspective: instead of heading towards a more modern and manageable form of paternity, we now have a "fatherless society", with extremely negative consequences for the children. Instead of children having many fathers, as in "partible paternity", they have none, and are left to hate mom's boyfriends one after the other...

Bonobo: a different model of sexuality

Chimpanzees are the genetically closest species to humans. While no

---

315 Morris, Desmond. *The Soccer Tribe*. London: Jonathan Cape (1981).

316 Female jealousy has different characteristics from the male one, and is more related to "emotional infidelity" and its concomitant danger of losing the partner together with the material support he provides. See the discussion in Buss, The Evolution Of Desire, p. 127-128.

chimp is monogamous, the sexuality of bonobo chimps, a species that lives in Congo, is of particular interest.

Sex in bonobos is a free-for-all due to the great sexual receptivity of the females. The sexually satiated bonobos have low stress, have sex for pleasure and share their food. The end result is that they have very low male aggression: "The abundance of sexual opportunity makes it less worthwhile for males to risk injury by fighting over any particular sexual opportunity."[317]

Sex is not a prize for the winner who climbs to the top, but it is widely available to all. It is the binding element of the community. This is very different from what we have come to consider normal in our society, that sex is something rare and exceptional.

Chapter 31: Sex and Economy in Prehistory

Human's sexuality in prehistory was similar to bonobos. Let's look at the social dynamics around economy and sex that characterized the hunter-gatherer, evolutionary-defining period of the human species.

People lived in groups numbering 30 to 150 individuals. Robin Dunbar has found that there is a relation between a primate's brain and its average social group size[318]. As in other primates, man has a cognitive limit to the number of people with whom he can maintain stable social relations. These are relations in which everyone knows everyone else, as well as the ways in which everybody relates to each other. Dunbar, extrapolating from his observations in primates, suggested that for the human this number is around 150. Evidence from anthropology support this working hypothesis; for example, the first neolithic villages found by researchers had a population of 150. Army units are organized in similar numbers. Modern studies have confirmed "Dunbar's Number" with data

---

317 Ryan, Sex at Dawn, Ch. 6.
318 Wikipedia, Dunbar's Number. https://en.wikipedia.org/wiki/Dunbar%27s_number

from social networks.

In prehistorical times, men's main occupation was hunting, while women took care of the children and gathered plant foods. The group's eating table was common. Sex was also a common activity. Preferences always existed, obviously, but sex was basically free. Men were required to bring the meat to the group, and women to provide sex.

Let's see how this arrangement survived until today in the tradition of a hunter-gatherer tribe:

> "The Kulina of Amazonia have a ritual known as the dutse'e bani towi: the "order to get meat." Don Pollock explains that the village women "go in a group from household to household at dawn, singing to the adult men in each house, 'ordering' them to go hunting. At each house, one or more women in the group step forward to bang on the house with a stick; they will serve as the sex partners of the men of the house that night, if they are successful in their hunt. Women in the group ... are not allowed to select their own husband."

> What happens next is significant. Feigning reluctance, the men drag themselves from their hammocks and head off into the jungle, but before splitting up to hunt independently, they agree on a time and place outside the village to meet later, where they'll redistribute whatever they've bagged, thus ensuring that every man returns to the village with meat, guaranteeing extra-pair sex for one and all. Yet another nail in the coffin of the standard narrative.

> Pollock's description of the hunters' triumphal return is beyond improvement:

> At the end of the day the men return in a group to the village, where the adult women form a large semicircle and sing erotically provocative songs to the men, asking for their 'meat.' The men drop their catch in a large pile in the middle of the semicircle, often hurling it down with dramatic gestures and smug smiles.... After cooking the meat and eating, each woman retires with the man whom she selected as her partner for the sexual tryst. Kulina engage in this rit-

ual with great humor and perform it regularly."[319]

Hunting, especially in prehistory, was a collective affair. Even the worst hunter was useful in order to guard one's back, so that you would not get attacked by a lion. Or a clumsy hunter might get lucky, for example as he holds his spear up, a mammoth might trip and fall and get nailed on it. The good hunter might be unlucky for some days and catch nothing. The unlucky one could have been your friend, your cousin, or might have given you a gift recently, so you wouldn't have the heart to leave him without a prey – and thus without sex. Besides, next time he could catch something and you might not, while maybe last week you cooperated and risked your lives together to kill an auroch, an experience that brought you closer together... When then meat is a currency for sex, the unpredictable and collective nature of hunting makes sharing it beneficial for men.

Let's now make a working assumption that someone is the best hunter by far, and that he likes to get all the women exclusively for himself. He is also very handsome, and all women prefer him to such a degree that they want to have sex only with him, ignoring all the others. The solution to the problem in this simple society, is equally simple: one night that he's asleep, you break his head with a large stone and throw him to the crocodiles. The day after, everyone can have sex again! If this scenario sounds arbitrary,

> "Consider the case of the Pitcairn Islanders. In 1790 nine mutineers from HMS Bounty landed on Pitcairn along with six male and thirteen female Polynesians. Thousands of miles from the nearest habitation, unknown to the world, they set about building a life on the little island. Notice the imbalance: fifteen men and thirteen women. When the colony was discovered eighteen years later, ten of the women had survived and only one of the men. Of the other men, one had committed suicide, one had died, and twelve had been murdered."[320]

A reactionary like Matt Ridley cites the example above to support his

---

319 Ryan, Sex at Dawn ch. 9.
320 Ryan, The Red Queen, p. 202.

theory that violence and sexual competition are inherent and inescapable for the human species, and therefore that monogamy which sets limits is the only viable system. In reality, this example shows exactly the opposite: that the competitive ethos that characterizes class society and influences modern people is a social construct, and it would have led our species to extinction in its infancy if it had been man's natural state.

This said, in primitive societies, it is quite likely that the best hunter did have more sex than the others. (An anthropologist of the '70s turned the worst hunter in a tribe he was studying to the most attractive man... by giving him a rifle and teaching him how to use it). There was no possibility to accumulate food, and there was no inheritance of wealth, therefore the truly capable men could have more sex, according to their provision to the group. This arrangement leaves plenty of space for evolution to proceed. Much more if we consider that women tend to be attracted to the most masculine men during their fertile days, and are more likely to reach orgasm and give them the extra fertilization bonus[321]. But never could one man have exclusiveness, to the degree that the rich and powerful of the class era do, where "simple agricultural societies often see harems of up to one hundred women per top man."[322]

Which means did man possess to ensure sexual equality in prehistoric societies?

We already mentioned one, with the example with the crocodiles: the exile of the lone Don Juan to a quiet and verdant place. Even today, when laws and Interpol exist, and that in any case it is hard to escape to a nearby jungle should you get noticed, there are cases where the sexually disdained kills the rival lover. It is not difficult to imagine similar hotheaded situations in the past.

And what happened with the woman of the tribe who systematically shunned you? How did you handle this?

First, there were other fruit-bearing trees around. But let's indulge in the idea that you only wanted *one* of the women in your tribe, because it will give us interesting insights. Just as nature has equipped woman with a

---

321 Buss, The Evolution of Desire, p. 232.
322 Ridley, The Red Queen, p. 194.

blessing that is an indisputable advantage, i.e. her milder sex drive, it has equipped man with an advantage to counter it: his superior physical strength. The average man has the physical strength allowing him to kill – or rape – the average woman with his bare hands.

The discussion in the scientific community of whether rape is a biological reproductive strategy for humans is vast and difficult, so we will not try to exhaust it here. We will only mention that it *is* a reproductive strategy for countless species on the planet, from insects to primates. If you are a woman you might find this discussion alarming – and you have every reason to be freaked out, because rape restricts your reproductive freedom. If you are a man... well, again, you might be freaking out too, because ever since monogamy was established, your possibilities to find at least some homely woman to relieve your sexual hunger are quite enough, and you tend to take them for granted. But the situation for the males of the human species, especially if we bring to mind the pre-Homo Sapiens, ape-like humanoids, was different. In species where sex is not free, males that are not selected by a female and are unable or unwilling to exercise violence to get sex, are genetically eliminated because they will be leaving no offspring. Because of that, many anthropologists believe that rape was very common in the past. But this, for the more recent human species, is unlikely. It would mean that women are stupid. Or that they would have to constantly remain in female groups for protection, as e.g. argued by Geoffrey Miller: "The same group-protection effect would have guarded females against sexual predators. Ancestral women could protect one another from harassment and rape, just as other female primates do."[323] In this case, though, even going to the bushes to defecate would be terrifying business.

Sure, living in fear is probably one biological strategy. But what's really so wrong about letting someone of medium biological quality copulate with you? On the one hand, he has reached reproductive age. And when the probabilities for that are 50-50, he's not really of such an inferior quality. Furthermore, if he was really a piece of scum he would have graver problems than getting sex: the other men of the tribe would have driven him away. On the other hand, and that's something that often

323 Miller, The Mating Mind, p. 191.

mainstream anthropologists seem to forget, *early humans didn't know that sex lead to pregnancy*. Pre-Homo Sapiens species didn't know it, and Homo Sapiens probably only found out in the last 20.000 years. So copulation was just that, not a prelude to pregnancy. Combine that with the fact that early human females where un-fecund most of the time, either due to pregnancy and breastfeeding, or due to their anovulatory adolescence. We already mentioned that the rate of conception per copulation for humans is 1 in 1000. Consider also the factor of group cohesion, food sharing, etc. All the above elements make it rather more natural for women to adopt the strategy that "sex is free-for-all but more so for my loverboy", than "sex is only for him – and I have to live in fear".

With the development of language and the degree of communication it provides, human communities had more collective solutions to implement to maintain the sexual balance. Some observations from modern tribes are indicative:

> "There is the distinction between equality of opportunity (meritocracy) and equality of outcome (egalitarianism). Hunter-gatherer tribes are intensely egalitarian about certain issues like sharing meat equally, articulating their views during tribal discussions, and preventing anyone from becoming a tribal 'chief.' Yet they are often meritocratic about sexual reproduction."[324]

For the average man, of modern or of older times, "meritocratic" sexual opportunities are good enough. For example, in hunter-gatherer tribes where the institution of marriage exists, it is extremely rare for a hunter to have more than two wives. If the typical modern man had half the sexual opportunities of the most successful men, the world would be very different and we wouldn't have to be discussing all this.

Let's take another example to show how goods, like sex, can be common. Imagine you were living in a village, and a new neighbor moved next to your house. One day, she comes and asks you for two eggs that she needs, to make a crème brulée. She has brought you a pumpkin from her garden as a gift. The following week, you run out of flour, and ask her

---

324 Miller, The Mating Mind, p. 337.

for some, but since you are in a hurry you don't give her something in exchange. But the following day you give her a bottle of milk from the goat. On another occasion, she brings you some mussaka she cooked. And so on, until you end up not keeping exact "score" of these exchanges: you give and take freely. If at some point you realize that she exploits you, you can take measures, such as stopping to give her things for free or insulting her. And exactly this knowledge, viz. that there will be consequences, as well as the knowledge that you will spend all your lives as neighbors, is enough to result in the continuance of this free giving and taking.

Let's take one more example about commons, this time from the gaming world. Clash of Clans is a popular strategy game for mobile devices, with millions of users. You build a base with defensive weapons and fortifications, and attack other players' bases. At a stage in the game you enter one of the thousands of existing clans. Your clanmates can fill your clan castle with extra soldiers, which you can use for defense or attack. Accordingly, you are expected to give soldiers to them. The total number of units you give and take is recorded, so that your clanmates can see it – but the units you give to *each* clanmate separately can only be seen if he happens to be online at the time of donation, and are not recorded. The dynamic of donations unfolds as follows: as a newbie in a clan, you are expected to give back about as many soldiers as you get. The older ones frequently check your donations to make sure you don't take advantage of them, and will complain or kick you out if you cheat. As you get "older" and they get to know you, supervision becomes looser. With people with whom you have exchanged soldiers often, you end up not checking things at all, and just give them support when they ask for it. Those people will often give you particularly valuable soldiers and you will do the same. Finally you start to assume that your clan will cover your needs in soldiers, and you will cover for them. The trust that has built up relieves you from the trouble of keep track of logistics, increases effectiveness and leads to a sense of community and intimacy.

In the same way, in primitive communities women gave sex easily, just as the men shared their food. The growing awareness among anthropologists that in many societies women also hunted[325] (small game), completes the picture of the meat-for-sex contract: sex was not the *only* way for women to obtain meat, it was just the *easiest*. No big deal.

The picture above is of course very generic. The balance of the sexual economy has always been dynamic, and during certain periods it tilted towards the one or the other side, with the "sex stopcock" opening or closing depending on the circumstances. Cultural differences are observed not only in human societies, but even in the societies of primates, groups of dolphins, herds of hyenas and even lower animals. In this regard, it is futile to define what would be a "pure", "natural" human society. The social arrangement around sex has always varied in time. But the basic conditions where such that the balance was kept: on the one hand, there was no possibility for wealth accumulation, and on the other hand, groups were small. Each member could perceive what was going on and exercise the part of social control that corresponded to them, defending their personal interest as well as the interests of the group.

The abolition of flirting

When we discussed biology in Part 2, we noticed that flirting imposes a huge cost on the species, because females use the capacity for prodigality as a quality indicator. *The whole arrangement of sex in the early days of the human race can be viewed as seeking to eliminate that cost.* Flirting remains a procedure, but it is relativized: it gives you a bonus in sex, but is not a necessary prerequisite for getting it from women. The economy that ensues, the saving of energy, is what allowed the human species to colonize the highest level of evolution, for example feeding on the most precious foods, meat, fruit and vegetables instead of leaves and tree bark. Despite the lack of terrifying jaws and sharp claws, and being much weaker than even chimpanzees half his size[326], man has no natural enemies. While individuals in other species were busy with their internal

---

325 'New Women of the Ice Age | DiscoverMagazine.com'.
    http://discovermagazine.com/1998/apr/newwomenoftheice1430#.UOMLgHfSls8
326 'How strong is a chimpanzee, really?'.
    http://www.slate.com/articles/health_and_science/science/2009/02/how_strong_is_a
    _chimpanzee.html

competition for reproduction, man, having found the solution in free sex, developed his capabilities and his technology and cooperated in hunting other species to extinction[327]. (Note that for the primitive man the world was vast and endless, so there is no point in blaming him for lacking an ecological conscience, as we understand it today). Running with your comrades after a mammoth to hunt it down might sound scary, but it is incomparably preferable than running away form a mammoth trying to hunt *you*. On the other end, the male sea elephant, who is by 90-95% completely excluded from reproduction, has absolutely no motive to develop cooperation and care for the interest of the group...

See how fascinating is the situation that unfolds once flirting is abolished as a prerequisite for sex:

What men did when sex was given to them freely, was to deal at their leisure with how they could ensure... more and better sex! Big game hunting, cooperation, greater physical abilities and sports, altruism, as well as all form of arts, everything that makes us humans, emerged more as *runaway flirting abilities* than survival skills[328]. If you are going to do some *prodigious waste* to signal quality, it is more beneficial for the species, in the long term, for this type of waste to be a creative one, rather than an effort to kill your rival. A famous songwriter was scientifically right when he said that "the ultimate goal of art is to get a girlfriend"... Some scientists, like Geoffrey Miller in *The Mating Mind*, argue that even language, as well as the human brain itself with its unprecedented capabilities, are products of this process of displaying fitness while at the same time benefiting the species.

An observation for *all* human skills, in science, art, sports, IQ, language – anything, is that in men there is much greater heterogeneity than in women. As (feminist) Helen Fisher admits, "There's many more male geniuses in the world – and there's also many more male idiots in the world."[329] (Incidentally, this explains why there are men in every

---

327 'Humans, Not Climate, to Blame for Mass Extinction of Ancient Species : Biology : Nature World News'.
http://www.natureworldnews.com/articles/7406/20140604/humans-not-climate-to-blame-for-mass-extinction-of-ancient-species.htm
328 Miller, The Mating Mind, p. 251.
329 Fisher, Helen. *Why we love, why we cheat*. TED Talk.

pinnacle of society – and not some "female oppression"). It is a basic attribute of sexually selected traits that "they show conspicuous differences between individuals"[330]. Men are much more subject to being sexually selected or rejected, they are winners and losers, whereas women are much more "in the middle". Biologists acknowledge this difference by labeling the male as the "genetic sieve". The evolution from animal to human happened through the man, not the woman, with the positive traits being selected more and prevailing, while the weaker ones were condemned to genetic oblivion. In fact, evolution in all animals proceeds via the male. This finding is not intended to applaud the male. It is really a terrifying process, to be hanging between triumph and disaster.

The terms under which the game of reproduction is played defines the result of evolution.

You can't really put two starving men in front of a juicy steak, stage a literary contest for who gets it, and expect to come up with a Nobel-prize-winner for Literature. Stealing the steak or bashing in your opponent's head while it is focused on his manuscript is much more effective as a strategy, than trying to write a masterpiece. You'll come up with a gorilla. The starving nations of Africa have not come up with the most efficient food-producing techniques. You have to give some slack for beauty to emerge. Likewise, the human intellect has not been produced by dog-eat-dog sexual competition. It is the product of positive differentiation in a social environment of cooperation, solidarity and sexual equity.

Chapter 32: What Went Wrong: the 8.2 Kyr Event

How then did we end up in our current situation?

---

http://www.ted.com/talks/helen_fisher_tells_us_why_we_love_cheat/transcript?language=en#t-2660
330 Miller, The Mating Mind, p. 14.

> *'Why farm? Why give up the 20-hour work week and the fun of hunting in order to toil in the sun? Why work harder, for food less nutritious and a supply more capricious? Why invite famine, plague, pestilence and crowded living conditions?' – Harlan[331]*

The point in time when history went wrong was the Agricultural Revolution, which anthropologist Jared Diamond has called "The worst mistake in the history of the human race"[332].

When Marx was writing his studies on capitalism the information was scarce, and the explanation given for the Agricultural Revolution, i.e. that agriculture multiplied man's food, was probably logical and expected. But today we know that things were not so. The transition to agriculture was accompanied by hunger, disease, and poor health. Life expectancy fell dramatically, from 32 years down to 20[333]. Palaeopathological studies in human skeletons confirm that people's nutrition worsened, and starvation was common in the first farming communities, unlike in tribes of hunter-gatherers. The conclusion is that the transition to farming was not a progressive choice, but a compulsory regression.

Let's see how it came about.

Why would I become a farmer?

The first thing to note is hunter-gatherer tribes that have survived today know about farming, but they have no reason to engage in it. As one forager puts it, "Why should we plant, when there are so many mongongo nuts in the world?"[334] Similarly, pre-agricultural groups knew about farming long before they eventually made it their main food source. So the crucial question is not when was agriculture *discovered*, but *when it became the prevailing system and why*. These questions leads us to the first farming communities and the cradle of modern civilization, Mesopotamia.

331 Harlan, J. R. *Crops and Man*.USA: American Society of Agronomy (1992).
332 Diamond, Jared. *The Worst Mistake in the History of the Human Race.* DiscoverMagazine, May 1987. http://discovermagazine.com/1987/may/02-the-worst-mistake-in-the-history-of-the-human-race
333 Wikipedia, Life Expectancy. Accessed 19 Jan. 2015. https://en.wikipedia.org/wiki/Life_expectancy
334 Ryan, Sex at Dawn, ch.5.

Step one: permanent settlement

A parameter that is key in determining for the evolution of human civilization, and which only recently has begun to receive the attention it deserves in the scientific community, is climate.

The last ice age ended 12,000 years ago. The climate became warmer and humid. In the fertile valley of Mesopotamia, these conditions created a real garden of Eden. While previously hunter-gatherers were forced to move when food was exhausted in an area, they could now settle in one region permanently. Susan Squire describes it beautifully:

> "Let's say that sometime between 10,000 and 8,000 BCE, in the vicinity of the Mediterranean Sea, a wandering tribe hacks its way through dense underbrush. Upon emerging, these nomads stop dead in amazement. They stand at the edge of a field fertile beyond imagining, a vast edible tableau of golden grains and wheat begging to be harvested, and promising to yield more than enough food to feed everyone for a year. The air is warm, the soil is rich, the sun glitters. Why not stay for the night—and the next, and the next? The gatherers get busy gathering; the hunters, having investigated the verdant forests surrounding the open land and found them full of well-nourished animal life, get busy hunting (and saving time, too, without fruitless hours and days spent tracking elusive prey). Pretty soon the group concurs that chasing the food supply when it's right in front of you, replenishing itself as fast as it's consumed, no longer makes sense. The wandering days are over. The group settles down."[335]

So the first permanent settlement didn't mean that humans became farmers. They remained hunter-gatherers. But now they could stay in the same place, for generations upon generations.

Step two: the cold

And just when everything was going fine, and people were living in what would later survive in myths and collective memory as "paradise", came

335 Squire, Susan. *I Don't: A Contrarian History of Marriage*. USA: Bloomsbury (2008). Prologue.

the cold. In climatology, this is known as the 8.2 Kyr event, because it happened 8200 years ago, around 6200 B.C.[336] Due to the collapse of the great glaciers that covered North America, and the consequent disruption of the Mexico Gulf Stream, the temperature dropped significantly, around 3 degrees Celsius, and severe drought prevailed. This event lasted two to four centuries. These centuries pushed humanity into a new world. It was the lever that led the train to change track.

Result: Paradise Lost

The Garden of Eden dried up, the animals dropped in numbers. The old way of hunting and gathering while being permanently settled, did not work anymore. Humans had either to abandon food-collection, and work hard cultivating the earth, or leave the land of their ancestors and become nomads. "In fact, [humans] seem to have gone in both directions. Some used their knowledge of plant and animal life to undertake the planting of seeds and the domestication of herds, others reverted to the life style of their nomadic ancestors. We do not know on what basis individual groups made their choice"[337] ... although, since moving was easier for men than for women with children, we can assume that societies in which men had the upper hand became hunter-gatherers, while those in which women had more power became farmers.

Let us now follow the development of the farmers, who were to become our ancestors.

Sex and economy in history

The emergence of class society

We saw that sexual relations in prehistorical times were closely knit with the form of the economy. This was also the case in historical times.

---

336 Before it there was another, heavier cold period, Younger Dryas, that lasted 1700 years, from 12,800 until 11,500 before present. So the transition to farming we describe here happened probably in two "waves", in a culturally spiral fashion. For more information, see Brian Fagan: *The Long Summer. How Climate Changed Civilization.* USA: Basic books (2004).

337 Harman, Engels and the Origins of Human Society.

With the consolidation of the agricultural economy came the replacement of "primitive communism" by class society. The important issues concern *how* this transition happened. "Why did [people] accept the rise of ruling classes? Why did those rulers come to exploit rather than serve the rest of society?"[338] It is interesting to follow the comparative arguments. In what follows, we will be closely following the arguments presented Chris Harman, in his article on *"Engels and the Origins of Human Society"*, which brings Engel's famous book up to speed with current knowledge about early humans.

A first answer blames people's "greed". Ironically, this was initially proposed by communist Friedrich Engels himself[339], and yet it is the main argument of conservatives and reactionaries to today.

A "more marxist" answer, from Engel's Anti-Duehring, that even more ironically is now the mainstream systemic view, refers to "the initial advantages to society as a whole of having the surplus set aside in such a way that it could not be immediately consumed by the producers.... But this does not explain why a group which had not previously exploited and oppressed should suddenly start doing so, nor why the rest of society put up with this new exploitation and oppression."

The "classical Marxist view" is summarized as follows: "A group discovers it can increase the total social wealth if it concentrates resources in is own hands, organizing others to work under its direction. It comes to see the interests of society as a whole as lying in its own control over resources. It defends that control even when that means making others suffer."

Observe that the last is not very far from the first two. In practice, it explains man's "greed" in economic terms. Still, it seems that something is missing. Sure, when classes were consolidated, such dynamics of greed, control, exploitation and its ideological justifications did unfold. But what is it that promoted them from the outset?

Given that the first class oppression had to do with the sexes, in order to

---

338 Harman, Engels and the Origins of Human Society.
339 "As Gailey points out, his explanation in *The Origin* seems at points to amount to just blaming greed – some people found they had a surplus in their hands and used it to the detriment of others.", Harman, Engels and the Origins of Human Society.

answer the question we first need to examine the theories about the origin of the "oppression of the woman".

"The world historic defeat of the female sex"?

The emergence of class society is supposed to be "the world historic defeat of the female sex", as Engels put it. Let's look at the arguments.

The argument of heritage

> "[Engels] says men came to produce both the food and the tools of production, that this necessarily gave them ownership rights and control over the surplus, and that they wanted to pass on ownership to their sons, not to their wife's relatives. But he does not show why they should suddenly get this desire after thousands of years in which their closest relationships were with their sisters' children."

Mosuo, in the mountains of China, is a tribe that managed to avoid the institution of marriage. Men and women have free sex. This tribe is a living confirmation of what evolutionary psychology predicts, that "where paternity certainty is so low and inconsequential ... men do indeed raise their sisters' children as their own."[340]

The argument of the new state organization

> "[Others] have emphasized the impact of the rise of the state in smashing the old lineages in which women exercised their influence. The state subordinates the rest of the society to the newly emerging ruling class. But that means destroying "the relative authority and autonomy" of the old kin communities. Insofar as they survive, it is as transmission belts for imposing the demands of the state and the ruling class on the mass of people. And this involves taking not just productive, but also reproductive decisions away from the members of these communities. Women, as the biological reproducers, lose out.

> But this account, by itself, does not explain any better than

---

340 For more, see Ryan, Sex at Dawn, Ch. 9.

Engels' why women should not have an equal share of power and influence with men in the new ruling class and state – nor why women should usually also be reduced to a subordinate role among the exploited class. It explains the collapse of the old order, but not the gender hierarchy that exists in the new."

The argument of the plow

The argument of the plow is very popular. It was proposed by Gordon Childe: Initially women were those engaged with agriculture, and that gave them an important place in production and therefore the distribution of power.

"All this changed, however, once the plough replaced the hoe and the digging stick as the major agricultural implement. Stock keeping was already a male sphere, and the plough turned arable farming into one as well, sharply reducing women's place in production: 'The plough ... relieved women of the most exacting drudgery but deprived them of their monopoly over the cereal crops and the social status that it conferred.'"

However, "an account just in terms of the plough and cattle farming is not sufficient, since classes emerged in the New World a millennium and half before the European conquest led to introduction of the plough." Furthermore, "Most of the men who carried through the burden of these new productive activities did not become part of the dominant class. Most ploughmen did not become princes and most soldiers did not become warlords, and neither of them made up the priesthood which often came to constitute the first ruling class and which never got involved in heavy work of any sort."

What really happened: The female coup d' etat

We saw that the spreading of agriculture and the rise of class society happened in a period of grave ecological crisis and mass hunger. What do you do when you are hungry? You use whatever means you have to survive. Men only had their working power. Women, besides that, also had their vagina. *This was the defining factor for the rise of social classes.*

As we have seen, sex was always a "possession" of the woman. She could exchange it for food. In the long periods of the "abundance of enough", this exchange had a socialized form: the man could consider sex almost free when he did his duty to hunt and provide meat to the tribe. The day-to-day nature of the hunter-gatherer economy did not allow for big deviations from the model.

With farming, however, things changed. In the Great Hunger, men could no longer bring enough food. Women increased the pressure on them by cutting them off from free sex. *This "female coup d' etat" was what led humanity to class society.*

The sex-for-food contract took on a new form. Sex was no longer taken for granted. Neither was food. But now, since agricultural products could be stored and accumulated, they could be exchanged with sex. Previously, the small size of groups allowed men to exercise control, so that nobody could acquire too much power. In a group around Dunbar's Number (150), social control is "easy", it doesn't require that you waste too much time or gray matter. It is almost "automatic". And systematic deception is difficult or even impossible. As the saying goes, "You can fool all the people some of the time, and some of the people all the time, but you cannot fool all the people all the time."

But the growth of the community meant that the most unscrupulous could count on the credulity of the others and escape control, so as to ultimately secure the now expensive sex for themselves. Marx and Engels were not ignorant of this process: they talked about "brutal sensuality" as a factor that propelled class society.

The accumulation of wealth (i.e. food) was obviously important and served as life insurance in difficult times. But it was even more important to ensure sex. Besides, equal societies can manage accumulation in a communal basis, so that in a crisis no one starves – or they all do. Only women were *not* equals, they were always sexually superior. Why give away your vagina for free, when there is a chance to die of hunger? You will give it to the one who can pay with food. The "objectification" of the female body benefited the woman, not the man. If they had the choice, men would sell their penis, and "objectify" their own sex. The appropriation of the means of production by *some* men was the answer to the appropriation of the means of reproduction by *all* the women.

This is the era when marriage was consolidated as an institution. With the specter of hunger threatening everyone, women played the trump card, demanding lifelong feeding for them and their children in exchange for their sexual availability. It is no coincidence that the first form of marriage was polygamy. Women elbowed each other to be included in the harems of the rich. Apart from feeding, they now needed protection from the other men, since the female *coup* inevitably brought about men's wrath.

Chapter 33: The History of Marriage

Marriage has thus its origin in that era. As an institution it embodies the overturning of the prehistoric gender balance in favor of women. In anthropology there is no broad consensus on its definition, but *its basic feature is man's obligation to support a woman until the end of her life.* "In return for his support, they are prepared to let him make use of their vagina at certain given intervals"[341], as Esther Vilar pointedly writes. Even when the woman becomes old and loses any attractiveness, man's obligations remain.

The ancient religious texts reveal to which extent which marriage was an institution favoring women.

> "A wife was seen as being of high value, and was therefore, usually, carefully looked after. Early nomadic communities in the middle east practiced a form of marriage known as beena, in which a wife would own a tent of her own, within which she retains complete independence from her husband; this principle appears to survive in parts of early Israelite society, as some early passages of the Bible appear to

---

341 Vilar, The Manipulated Man.

> portray certain wives as each owning a tent as a personal possession (specifically, Jael, Sarah, and Jacob's wives). In later times, the Bible describes wives as being given the innermost room(s) of the husband's house, as her own private area to which men were not permitted; in the case of wealthy husbands, the Bible describes their wives as having each been given an entire house for this purpose."[342]

In Talmud there is "a requirement for a man to provide food and clothing to, and have sex with, each of his wives." Indeed, despite strict laws against adultery, it seems that then, as now, women had their cake and ate it: "The literary prophets indicate that adultery was a frequent occurrence, despite their strong protests against it, and [the] legal strictnesses." Both the husband for the money, and the lover for the sex. It is not a coincidence that Jews, a society of archetypal "Patriarchy", accept as a token of Jewism *the mother's nationality, while that of the father is ignored.*

The protection enjoyed by women in divorce, with alimony, is not a new phenomenon either.

> "In ancient Egypt, divorce entailed heavy financial penalties for the husband, but none for the wife. Both Hindu and Muslim law oblige husbands to support their divorced wives. In other cases, she has the right to be maintained by her children. In Europe beginning in the Middle Ages, divorce was very difficult to achieve for both men and women. As a result, legally speaking a man might never be released for the duty to support his wife, even if the couple had long ceased to share a house and a bed, even if she had turned to prostitution, even if they had been formally separated by an ecclesiastical court. In this sense, if perhaps in no other, the declaration 'till death do us part' was quite literally true."[343]

Polygamy

Polygamy, as the first form of marriage, came about due to the better

---

342 Wikipedia, Marriage. Accessed 19 Jan. 2015. https://en.wikipedia.org/wiki/Marriage
343 Van Creveld, The Privileged Sex.

social position of women: many women could ascend socially and take advantage of the wealth of the few men of the elite. In the first class societies women didn't have to marry the poor, they could share the rich. The fact that King Solomon had 1000 women instead of only one meant that 999 more women would live like a queen, while 999 men would spend all their lives without a woman.

In the Incas kingdom,

> "The sun-king Atahualpa kept fifteen hundred women in each of many 'houses of virgins' throughout his kingdom.... Beneath him, each rank of society afforded a harem of a particular legal size: Great lords had harems of more than seven hundred women. 'Principal persons' were allowed fifty women; leaders of vassal nations, thirty; heads of provinces of 100,000 people, twenty; leaders of 1,000 people, fifteen; administrators of 500 people, twelve; governors of 100 people, eight; petty chiefs over 50 men, seven; chiefs of 10 men, five; chiefs of 5 men, three. That left precious few for the average male Indian whose enforced near-celibacy must have driven him to desperate acts, a fact attested to by the severity of the penalties that followed any cuckolding of his seniors."[344]

> "for violation of [women of the royal family] the law directed that the culprit's wife, children, servants, and relatives, as well as all the inhabitants of his village and all their flocks, should be put to death "without leaving a suckling nor a crying baby, as the saying is". The village was to be pulled down and the site strewn with stones."[345]

Polygamy, perhaps counter-intuitively, is the ideal system for a woman who wants to have a man exclusively to herself: there are so many unmarried men, that she has countless options. Unless of course what she wants is a rich man *exclusively* to herself...

Despite the romantic hype around modern marriage, in reality women prefer polygamy. "'Which woman would not rather be John Kennedy 's third wife than Bozo the Clown's first?' said one (female) evolutionist."[346]

---

344 Ridley, The Red Queen, p. 173.
345 Betzig, Despotism and Differential Reproduction, p. 60.
346 Ridley, The Red Queen, p. 185.

Studies in primitive tribes where polygamy still survives support this conclusion.

> "Among the Kipsigis of Kenya, rich men have more cattle and more wives: Each wife of a rich man is at least as well off as the single wife of a poor man, and she knows it. According to Monique Borgehoff Mulder of the University of California at Davis, who has studied the Kipsigis, polygamy is willingly chosen by the women: A Kipsigis woman is consulted by her father when her marriage is arranged, and she is only too aware that being the second wife of a man with plenty of cattle is a better fate than being the first wife of a poor man. There is companionship and a sharing of the burden between co-wives."[347]

In Western society, women's preference for (male) polygamy expresses itself in the countless opportunities for extra-marital sex that men of high status have, taking Bill Clinton as a prime example. "Men in positions of power tend to practice polygyny: legitimate polygyny where it is allowed; functional polygyny where it is not."[348] For women it is something like a roulette: they give a chip (sex) in order to get the chance to hook a good catch and secure him for themselves.

Monogamy

If polygamy is a system that suits, firstly, all women and, secondly, men of the *upper* classes, its abolition suits the *majority* of men. One way to do it is to abolish marriage totally as a form of relationship with exclusive character and lifelong duration. In other words, the prevalence of free sexual (and emotional) relationships. Another way to abolish it, which emerged historically, is monogamy. With it, women maintained marriage as an institution, along with the benefits it conferred them, but were forced to expand the portion of men to whom they became sexually available, to include the lower classes.

Regarding men's attitude to monogamy, the first thing to note is that in every society the elite maintained polygamy for as long as it could. "[I]n the

347 Ridley, The Red Queen, p. 185.
348 Townsend, What Women Want – What Men Want, p. 236.

six large, highly stratified early states, commoners were generally monog-amous but ... elites practiced de facto polygyny. Those states included Mesopotamia, Egypt, Aztec Mexico, Inca Peru, India and China."[349]

The issue, therefore, with the predominance of monogamy is that it cancels the rich man's privilege to exercise institutional polygamy. When the rich "resigned" from this privilege it was out of necessity to secure social peace. The fact that the social pressure from the poor towards the rich to abolish polygamy was strong is evidenced by exhortations in ancient religious texts "for the marriage to remain monogamous"[350].

The exact process of its abolition is the work of historians. And as Matt Ridley writes, "No historian can yet explain what changed, but guesses include the idea that kings came to need internal allies enough that they had to surrender despotic power."[351] What is certain is that if it is difficult in today's society of "equal opportunities" to justify striking wealth gap between the rich and the poor, it would be a hundred times more difficult if in addition to dazzling wealth someone had a harem of dazzling women to display, and the poor had no women at all. That is why in societies where polygamy still exists (e.g. some Arabic countries), the pretext of equality has more or less been abandoned.

The concept of marriage today

In Western societies, most children are already born outside of wedlock. The child, not marriage has become the factor that creates the family. From this perspective, the discussion about marriage actually corresponds today to the issue of procreation, either as a conscious choice or as an assumed risk of having a pregnancy "by accident". Most women today work outside the house, so the support of their husband is a complement, typically not essential. But the support of a child continues to be a huge burden. Men are forced to bear it, willingly or not, contrary to their interest. A huge 25% of children worldwide are born with an unintended pregnancy, without their parents having planned it - and since

---

349 Wikipedia, Monogamy. Accessed 19 Jan. 2015.
        https://en.wikipedia.org/wiki/Monogamy
350 Wikipedia, Monogamy.
351 Ridley, The Red Queen, p. 206

the woman chooses to keep it, that means without being chosen by the father. Women, as we saw,[352] derive much more satisfaction from procreation, while men pay for it more expensively.

The system benefits from women's emotional need for procreation, because that way it reproduces itself inexpensively. Even the poorest of women consider unthinkable not to have children, and in any case a realistic assessment of the ability to raise their children properly, as a criterion for childbearing, is very un-womanly. Women scratch the back of the system, providing it with ready cheap labor, and the system scratches their back providing them with alimony, easier jobs, greater security and better living standards than men.

Chapter 34: The Greatest Victim of the War of the Sexes

"The first casualty of war is innocence." – Platoon (movie)

Class society is the predominance of women over men in the war of the sexes, with the collaboration of a small percentage of men of the upper class. In previous chapters we saw that life expectancy in the Upper Palaeolithic was 33 years. With the Agricultural Revolution it collapsed to 20, and increased to 31 only in the early 20th century. In those few thousand years, which correspond to a moment in terms of evolution, women were able to reverse the natural balance of the sexes, and go on from living 5 years or 15% less than men, to living much more.

The era of the domination of women, the era of inequality, although marked by wars and human misery, has managed to make us conquer space, reduce child mortality (and thus increase life expectancy), along with other benefits brought by modern technology. Because of this, many conclude that it was a progressive era – including Marx himself. But we cannot forget that it was men (not women) who should get the credit for

352 See Part 3, Chapter 28:Why do people have children?, p. 155.

almost all the of the progress.

This said, the era when men predominated, the era of gender equality, Pre-history, was incomparably more important. It was the era during which human evolved into a creature that was no longer an animal. Man managed to limit competition and increase cooperation within the species. Women, when allowed, always chose "the best" as mates, de facto creating competition. If the female strategy had prevailed in human evolutionary history, women would be happy around the more powerful men in the group, and the rest would wander in the periphery, celibate and frustrated. We would have become gorillas, in other words, and we would probably be threatened with extinction by a different species which boasted free sex.

The first casualty of the sex war is intimacy.

The most dramatic effect of the female coup d' etat, i.e. of the abolition of free sex, is the loss of intimacy. While male hunters felt mutual companionship which allowed them to control female sexuality by limiting competition between men, in class society female sexuality was left unchecked, destroying male companionship. While in the era of hunter-gatherers women granted a privileged treatment to the most capable hunters and the ones who could emerge as the *natural* leaders, something that was positive for our species, when the Agricultural Revolution took place, women started preferring the most ruthless men, those who sought power by all means, who took advantage of the reduced capabilities for democratic control of the wider societies, in order to deceive. men's sexual strategy favored collectivity and equality – allowing for a positive differentiation. Women's sexual strategy favored greed, unbridled individualism and exploitation.

When intimacy was lost from the male community, it was lost from society overall. It is difficult to appreciate your wife as a human being when you have been forced to work hard, step on dead bodies, and pay dearly to possess her. In a world where antagonism is the rule, even your own children are considered rather as extra wealth producers for the family, than as yet fragile human beings needing your love and protection.

The loss of intimacy is perhaps the biggest problem that modern humans face. It is what they call *"loneliness"*.

As for the violence that marks class society, there is no longer any mystery surrounding it: "the deprivation of physical sensory pleasure is the principal root cause of violence"[353]. Men were not only deprived of sex, but they were also compelled to violence.

Chapter 35: Athenian Democracy as an Exception

According to Claudine Leduc, a feminist who studied ancient Athens, "Women were the chief victims of the invention of democracy"[354].

> "Leduc makes the very interesting point that it was in the more socially conservative city-states, such as Sparta and Gortyn, that women could be citizens and own property in their own right;... In Athens, which was socially more innovative and inclusive with respect to male foreigners, the locus of citizenship remained the (male-headed) household, and women passed from father's to husband's household, treated not so much like chattels as like children."[355]

The superior social position of the woman in the authoritarian regime of Sparta, compared to Athenian democracy, is not a paradox. Athenian democracy was the victory of the free citizens against the oligarchy. Since women always had special relationships with the ruling class, restricting the power of the aristocracy and restricting the power of women went hand in hand. This does not mean that the position of women in Athens was worse than the position of men, it just was not so blatantly better, as in Sparta.

As shown above, women's power is based in their sexual superiority and

---

353 Prescott, James W. *"Body Pleasure and the Origins of Violence"*. The Bulletin of the Atomic Scientists, November 1975, pp. 10-20.
http://www.violence.de/prescott/bulletin/article.html
354 Leduc, Claudine. 1992. "Marriage in Ancient Greece." In *A History of Women: From Ancient Goddesses to Christian Saints*, ed. Pauline Schmitt Pantel. Cambridge, MA: Harvard University Press (1994).
355 Seabright, The War of the Sexes, Ch. 4 (comment no. 13).

their control over reproduction. Athenian democracy targeted these two areas. Of all the measures taken by Solon, who is considered the founder of Athenian democracy, perhaps the most important was that he filled Athens with good and cheap brothels.

"At some point during his career, Solon perceives that too many married men are plunging heedlessly into too many adulterous liaisons with questionable characters of either sex – it's not the adultery that bothers him, it's the heedlessness – which seems to be causing family chaos. The antidote to chaos is order, and that's just what Solon creates in the extramarital universe. Deciding that domestic life would improve if men's needs for casual sex could be met cleanly, safely, efficiently, and without fuss, he develops a network of whorehouses stocked with male and female slaves, known as concubines. Although Solon's brainstorm may or may not improve Athenian family life, the brothel business soon becomes an indispensable accessory to sexual life. It suits the Athenian government, which profits from men's patronage. It suits the patrons, who can be good citizens and please themselves at the same time. And because it simplifies – clarifies – men's relations with women, it suits the prevailing aesthetic. What is current practice for the Israelites would be anathema for the Athenians, with their apparent distaste for emotional and domestic sturm und drang. Multiple bedmates, definitely; multiple wives, no way.

... If it works half as well as it sounds, the Athenians win the gold medal for wife control in the Western Olympics, twenty-five centuries running. Among the champions is Demosthenes, the orator who famously summarizes the code about two hundred years after Solon establishes prostitution: "We keep hetaera for our delight, concubines for the daily needs of our bodies, wives so that we may breed legitimate children and have faithful housekeepers."

Maybe this is why the men of Athens are so productive. With their sexual needs identified, compartmentalized, and fulfilled by a dedicated service team assigned to each one, they can be laser-focused on the work that turns the classical age into a golden one."[356]

Women didn't have it so bad in Athens: they had a dowry, protection, and if they wanted they could be educated and live an independent life as heterae. "As long ago as ancient Athens it is possible to find cases in which men, but not women, were put on trial and punished for adultery."[357] The strongest man in Athens, Pericles, casually acknowledged that "my wife rules me."

As today, so then, the position of women was a combination of the typical female preferences with what was more convenient for them in these circumstances. Indeed, the waiver on the part of women of adult responsibility was related with the wide-spread homosexual relations of the ancient world. We could say that there were not so many *real* women to fall in love with, so the only real persons available were other men.

The notion that women were "victims of democracy" can only be understood as an anachronism, as the view of a modern bourgeois, for whom "oppression" seems a bigger problem than hunger and war – precisely because she has never come close to either. It was infinitely preferable to be a woman in Athens than a man in Sparta, where you were a soldier from 7 to 60, i.e. practically all your life. "[S]o crass was the contrast between the "Spartan" life of men and the luxurious ways of women that Aristotle blamed it for the city's decline"[358]. In fact it was better to be a woman in Athens than a man in Athens too, as the male "privileges" and civic participation were paid for with the obligation to go to war, which was not a rare occurrence, a thing which feminist historians tend to forget or deem an irrelevant detail.

And, of course, if we extend our discussion to the tens of thousands of slaves on whom the economy was based and who numerically outnumbered the free citizens[359], the advantage of being a woman becomes glaring: instead of working in the Laurium mines[360], were life

---

356 Squire, I Don't.
357 Van Creveld, The Privileged Sex.
358 Van Creveld, The Privileged Sex.
359 Wikipedia, Slavery in Ancient Greece. Accessed 19 Jan. 2015.
    https://en.wikipedia.org/wiki/Slavery_in_ancient_Greece
360 "Countless male slaves, but very few female ones, worked in the silver mines of
    Laurion from which classical Athens derived much of its wealth." - Van Creveld, The

was brutal and short, you worked in the house, and you often became the mother of your owner's child, with all the privileges this entailed.

It is tempting to say that women were so much "victims of democracy" as were aristocrats – that is, as much as they should be. In reality, both of them were much less so.

Privileged Sex.

Part 5: Towards a Solution

Hieronymus Bosch, The Garden of Earthly Delights (detail), ca 1500.

Chapter 36: Rage, Sex and Violence

Rage

As discussed in the previous chapters, we know that the typical reaction of men to feelings is... to avoid them[361]. Pleasure in life, though, comes through emotions, and men's tendency to avoid feelings costs them dearly. Even negative emotions are preferable from the deadening lack of emotion, and "women, in general, feel both positive and negative emotions more strongly than do men. And, sex differences aside, emotional life is richer for those who notice more."[362] Women "live more" than men because society is made to suit them, and they are allowed to live emotionally. Men, finding that an "intuitive" way of living does not work, are forced to overemphasize logic over emotion[363], which has a psychological and physiological cost: stress. It is as if women are comfortably driving a car in their country on the right, while men are obliged to drive in the UK, on the left, constantly on edge and never managing to adjust and relax. Women *don't think, they "feel"*. Using Kahneman's terminology, we can say that women don't much need to activate their higher, "effortful" thought System 2. The lower and automatic System 1 brain processes are enough to navigate the world, letting their soul to be relaxed and free to sensually enjoy it.

There is great confusion among average people as well as in the scientific community about women's "emotionality". The oft-repeated phrase "women are more emotional" does not really explain anything, although it implies that there is a biological predisposition for women to feel emotions more intensely. But there are many indications to the contrary: "Boy babies are more trouble. They scream and cry more often than girl babies, and louder too. (Incidentally, this well-documented finding has been recognized as an important challenge to the conventional claim that females are more emotional than males.)"[364] In reality, men operate less emotionally because, from their infancy, they are trained in devitalizing their emotions. Even though no mother does it consciously, the basic aim of this process is to block male sexuality. How can you be cool, relaxed, and leave your emotions flow freely, when they tell you to urgently have sex with a woman, and she says no? What will you do, rape her?

---

361 See Part 2, Chapter 10, p. 75.
362 Goleman, Emotional Intelligence, Ch. 4.
363 "In the male brain, most emotions trigger less gut sensation and more rational thought", observes Louann Brizendine. The Female Brain, p. 123.
364 Baumeister, Is there anything good about men?, p. 13.

For men, sex precedes emotional involvement – at least for those who have matured beyond adolescence. "It's sex first, then relationship, not the other way around.[365]" In fact, this is true for women too: a woman will find a way to have sex with you if she really desires you, and won't put you on hold because she is trying for something to happen with someone better right now[366]. The vast majority of men are forced to endure female tests, with the usually vain hope that at some point they will have sex.

> "Dating is the females' boot camp for males. Here ... he becomes conditioned to sitting at her feet, leash in mouth, tail wagging, anticipating the slightest hint of a sexual favor. His female drill instructor is the end product of 6000 years of survival of the fittest. While he is usually there just for fun, she's working."[367]

> "Through persistence, a woman gradually convinces a man to compromise his primary reproductive goal of unfettered access to a variety of women—a dream he relinquishes reluctantly, and one for the loss of which he never really forgives her."[368]

Nora Vincent, in *Self-Made Man*, after writing that she became a "momentary misogynist" from her experience in flirting as a man, continues:

> "I saw my own sex from the other side, and I disliked women irrationally for a while because of it. I disliked their superiority, their accusatory smiles, their entitlement to choose or dash me with a fingertip, an execution so lazy, so effortless, it made the defeats and even the successes unbearably humiliating. Typical male power feels by comparison like a blunt instrument, its salvos and field strategies laughably remedial next to the damage a woman can do with a single cutting word: no."[369]

For these reasons, the main male emotion since the withdrawal of free

365 Tomassi, The Rational Male.
366 Ibid, "Iron Rule of Tomassi #3".
367 Shannon, The Predatory Female, p. 38.
368 Shlain, Sex, Time and Power, p. 348.
369 Vincent, Self-Made Man, ch.4.

sex is *rage*. As Herb Goldberg wrote in 1976, "[Man] is now being told that he is afraid of the woman. What he is really afraid of are his own impulses of anger and rage toward her over being increasingly abandoned, frustrated, and caught in binds – all of which he can't express directly"[370]. This rage is the steam that has been moving the whole of society for the past few millenia. It is what the ruling class transforms into war, workaholism, male self-sacrifice, guilt and other destructive and self-destructive tendencies.

Sex and Violence

James W. Prescot, in his famous study *"Body pleasure and the origins of violence" (1975)*[371] examined the relationship between physical affection and violence in 49 primitive communities. He focused on two issues, physical affection to babies and sexual freedom, especially before marriage. One finding is that there is a correlation between lack of affection and corporal punishment on the one side, and adult violence on the other, something that for today's understanding is self-evident. The most interesting part of his study, however, is the exceptions he identified: societies that were violent although being affectionate towards babies, and societies that had low levels of violence despite being strict to children.

> "When the six societies characterized by both high infant affection and high violence are compared in terms of their premarital sexual behavior, it is surprising to find that [all] of them exhibit premarital sexual repression, where virginity is a high value of these cultures. It appears that *the beneficial effects of infant physical affection can be negated by the repression of physical pleasure (premarital sex) later in life*. The seven societies characterized by both low infant physical affection and low adult physical violence were all found to be characterized by permissive premarital sexual behaviors. Thus, *the detrimental effects of infant physical affectional deprivation seem to be compensated for later in life by sexual body pleasure experiences during*

---

370 Goldberg, The Hazards of Being Male, p. 52.
371 Prescot, Body pleasure and the origins of violence.

adolescence."[372] [emphasis in the original]

The scientific understanding of the time, highlighted by the (in)famous experiments of Harry Harlow on monkeys, was that the lack of motherly affection led to neurotic behavior. This was Prescott's starting point. His study, however, led him to a "revision of the somatosensory pleasure deprivation theory from a one-stage [infancy] to a two-stage [infancy and adolescence] developmental theory where the physical violence in [all of the] cultures could be accurately classified."

The psychoanalytic tradition that emphasizes the importance of the early years in the formation of personal (and by extension social) characteristics is very strong. Maybe that is why Prescott insists on referring to both developmental stages, infancy and adolescence: "The percent likelihood of a society being physically violent if it is physically affectionate toward its infants and tolerant of premarital sexual behavior is [zero] percent." In practice, as the exceptions that he found show, *just the sexual liberality during the years of youth has sufficient predictive power for a society's violence,* without having to examine childhood at all.

We have discussed sex extensively in this book. We saw that women hold the key to it, not men. As said earlier, "when men have the edge, sex is cheap and abundant. When women hold the advantage, sex is rare and expensive. Men prefer sex to be free and easy; women are better off when it is precious."[373]

All the above suggest that although men have been traditionally blamed for the great problem of violence in the world, the female sex is accessory before the fact.

"Disorder is not sent down by Heaven, it is produced by women." – *Confucius.*

This does not imply that women have been doing it consciously. Nobody is willingly evil. As we have explained, at the start of this process women

---

372 Due to errors in the data, the original study shows 1 out of the 49 tribes not conforming to the general results. When the error was corrected, there were no exceptions left.

373 Baumeister and Twenge, *Cultural Suppression of Female Sexuality.*

reacted traumatically to an external (environmental) event, i.e. hunger, by withholding sex. When the problem was so big that men could not solve it (e.g. by hunting mammoths, or developing the appropriate technology in time), the sexual restriction persisted, traumatizing men even more and making them violent. Only a tiny part of this violence returned to the female sex that initiated it, while the biggest part was displaced elsewhere: to other men, leading thus to class societies, to expansionist wars, to enslaving people. *Although stress for an individual is a normal and beneficial response to an emergency situation, when it becomes chronic it becomes a pathological problem. Similarly, the societies that limit sex are societies living in a state of permanent emergency, societies which appeared in critical historical periods and which have not "yet" returned to a normal relationship between the sexes.*

Beyond violence: human relations

Almost everyone considers violence a symptom of disease. The conservatives claim it is a disease of the individual, progressives a disease of society. In this sense, it is not extravagant to generalize Prescott's conclusions on the reasons of violence to explanations for the wider psychological and social ills. The most important thing to note is the key role of an adequate sex life during youth for the psychological makeup of individuals. This is something that modern psychology, amazingly, denies. The prevailing theory, called Attachment Theory, claims that how comfortably and naturally someone relates to other people is based exclusively to the relationship one had with one's parents during the first years of one's life, ignoring the subsequent years. Attachment Theory has become the basic tool for analyzing relationship problems. Prescott's study, however, shows that a supportive and loving mother, might be able to give her son a good start, but she cannot protect him fully from the frustrations of the relentless sexual war he will experience during his adolescent years. Not all male wounds have their root in childhood. In fact, most of them are inflicted at the age of sexual awakening.

Here is how PUA Neil Strauss describes it:

"I have a theory that most naturals [i.e. natural seducers] ...

> lose their virginity at a young age and consequently never feel a sense of urgency, curiosity, and intimidation around women during their critical pubescent years. Those who must learn to meet women methodically, on the other hand … generally suffer through high school without girlfriends or even dates. Thus, we're forced to spend years feeling intimidated by and alienated from women, who hold in their sole possession the key to releasing us from the stigma blighting our young adult lives: our virginity."[374]

Many therapeutic approaches are based on the therapist assuming the role of a "second parent", who undertakes to teach the patient, by means of a safe attachment, the correct ways to control one's emotions, which his parents didn't manage to teach him. At the level of society, many women truly benefit from a similar process, since many men are willing to "play dad", providing them with protection and positive experiences. When the sexes are reversed, however, when a woman finds herself protecting a man, this scheme does not work. The feelings of "incest" that awakens in the woman kill both sex and relationship. As a result, society does not offer remedial experiences to men. Each man is left alone to find ways to mend the wounds he endured from a hasty weaning and parental violence as a child, and the violence of sexual deprivation as a youngster.

A necessary discussion about Violence

We need to clarify some things about violence.

For every individual, there are acceptable and unacceptable forms of violence. Prisons are a form of violence, the police and their use of guns constitute violence, war is violence, but all those examples are widely accepted by most people. This suggests that, in principle, violence is not unacceptable. What is unacceptable is the "unfair" use of violence. Apparently, the dominant ideology rarely reminds people that the above tools of the system are still a form of violence, even if it is "justified"; instead, it supposedly "condemns violence, wherever it comes from". The hypocrisy of this attitude emerges clearly in the report from the US

---

374 Strauss, The Game, ch.8.

Senate on the tortures committed by the CIA. The US Secret Service threatened terrorist suspects with electric drills, performed virtual executions, virtual drownings, in many cases they deprived them of sleep for at least 180 hours, and anally raped them with several instruments[375]. Khalid Sheik Mohammed, "the self-admitted mastermind of the Sept. 11 attacks ... was subjected to ... simulated drowning 183 times"[376]. George Bush "defended these inhuman practices stating that all that happened were necessary to protect citizens". 58% of Americans approve these tortures.

Useful insights about some positive aspects of violence can be inferred from scientists' efforts to determine how cooperation evolves in social species. A "selfish", i.e. non-cooperative behavior appears at first glance to be more efficient for the individual, so the emergence of cooperative behaviors is a puzzle for scientists. Let's follow this discussion, as Christakis and Fowler present it in *Connected: The Surprising Power of Our Social Networks*[377].

Political scientist Robert Axelrod showed that the "tit for tat" strategy is more efficient than always cooperating, i.e. sacrificing some benefits in favor of someone else, and also more efficient than always being selfish: "In tit for tat, you cooperate the first time you meet someone, and thereafter simply copy what that person did the last time you interacted with him... If someone cooperates, then reciprocate that cooperation the next time around. If someone does not cooperate, punish him next time by withholding cooperation. Simple, but effective." But what happens when a conscientious guy, who uses tit-for-tat, finds himself in a society with many selfish individuals who never cooperate? The first time he meets someone he will cooperate, and the other will reap the benefits of this cooperation, but will never reciprocate. Selfish individuals in a

---

375 'Wikipedia, Senate Intelligence Committee report on CIA torture, Accessed 2 Aug. 2018,
https://en.wikipedia.org/wiki/Senate_Intelligence_Committee_report_on_CIA_torture
376 'New poll finds majority of Americans believe torture justified after 9/11 attacks - The Washington Post'.
http://www.washingtonpost.com/world/national-security/new-poll-finds-majority-of-americans-believe-torture-justified-after-911-attacks/2014/12/16/f6ee1208-847c-11e4-9534-f79a23c40e6c_story.html.
377 Christakis, Nicholas A, and Fowler, James H. *"Connected: The Surprising Power of Social Networks"*. New York: Little, Brown and Company (2009). Ch. 7.

society of cooperators, if it is large enough, profit from it. This leads to another possibility: "Rather than attempting to cooperate and risking being taken advantage of, a person could fend for herself." Mathematician Chris Hauert proposed this extended model and termed these people "loners".

> "Using some beautiful mathematics, Hauert and his colleagues showed that in a world full of loners it is easy for cooperation to evolve because there are no people to take advantage of the cooperators that appear. The loners fend for themselves, and the cooperators form networks with other cooperators. Soon, the cooperators take over the population because they always do better together than the loners. But once the world is full of cooperators, it is very easy for free riders to evolve and enjoy the fruits of cooperation without contributing (like parasites)."

The emergence of free-riders pushes cooperators to adopt the "loner's" strategy. "Because of the free-rider problem, cooperation is not guaranteed to succeed."

> "To deal with free riders, another type of person is needed: punishers. People everywhere feel the desire to enforce social norms they see being violated. Some people honk when a car cuts them off in traffic, even though the honk does not change the outcome. Others risk confrontation by asking people smoking in a no-smoking area to stop. And on many occasions, innocent bystanders are willing to testify in court to crimes they have witnessed, even though this potentially exposes them to retribution. These people all pay a small cost themselves to impose a cost on someone who does not cooperate. And this is a different kind of connection. Cooperators connect to others in order to create more; free riders connect in order to leach off those who create; and punishers connect in order to drive away free riders."

What Christakis and Fowler showed is that "small groups of interconnected, interacting cooperators and punishers could coevolve in a world of people who otherwise keep to themselves, and *this pushes the whole population toward higher overall levels of cooperation and connection*" [emphasis added]. They also note that the balance among the different types of behaviors does not necessarily mean that different persons apply one strategy: it holds equally when each person applies a mix of strategies in specific proportions. Someone, for example, could behave as a cooperator 60% of the time and as punisher 40% of the time, etc.

So we see that the possibility of "fair" violence (punishment) is not only useful, but necessary for social evolution. "Many studies have shown that punishment is an effective way to sustain cooperation in groups."[378] The issue is who uses it and to what purpose. It is significant that in all the democratic periods in history, from ancient Athens to the short-lived revolutions of the medieval peasants, from the Paris Commune to the first years of the Russian Revolution, the entire body of the people was armed. Democracy is a revolutionary regime, it is the regime of the many against the few and powerful. It needs constant vigilance and the ability to use violence against those who constantly try to get rid of it.

A similar solution was reached by nature for safeguarding equality between the sexes. It is up to men to maintain it when it is threatened by the sexual strategy of women, and men's physical strength, i.e. their ability to exercise physical violence, was ultimately the weapon given to them for this purpose. (This, of course, refers to the evolutionary period of the human species. In the large, organized societies of the historic era, the perpetrator of violence is overwhelmingly the State, not individuals).

Mass rape in the Middle Ages: a glimpse into male rage

In earlier chapters, we showed that after abolishing free sex, women needed to seek the protection of the powerful to escape the rage of other men. In reality, the emergence of a ruling class that, hoarding the right to exercise legal violence could offer precisely this protection that women sought, was both a consequence and a prerequisite for the female *coup d' etat*. The two processes were dialectically linked. Without the ruling

---

378 'More Trouble with Testosterone | Psychology Today'.
http://www.psychologytoday.com/blog/the-moral-molecule/201001/more-trouble-testosterone

class to protect them, women couldn't stage their coup, and without the female coup, there was no real reason to become a ruling class.

The degree of protection provided by the ruling class to women is highlighted in the following historical example, cited by feminist Silvia Federici[379], where this protection is negated. Around the 14th-15th century, the constant uprisings and the militancy of the lower classes had come to threaten the power of the ruling class. It was the "golden age of the European proletariat" which led to the abolition of serfdom. Naturally, the first thing demanded by the poor men when they were to leave poverty behind, was sex. They were no longer willing to remain celibate while the ruling class enjoyed all the women, either as wives or as "maids". A sexual outlet was initially afforded them through the "institutionalization of prostitution, implemented through the opening of municipal brothels soon proliferating throughout Europe". But this was not enough. In France and in Venice, under the obsessive fear of the rich against popular uprisings, and due to their belief that "if the poor gained the upper hand they would take their wives and hold them in common", "the municipal authorities practically decriminalized rape, provided the victims were women of the lower class". As a result,

> "the gang-rape of proletarian women became a common practice which the perpetrators would carry out openly and loudly at night, in groups of two to fifteen, breaking into their victims' homes, or dragging their victims through the streets, without any attempt to hide or disguise themselves. Those who engaged in these "sports" were young journeymen or domestic servants, and the penniless sons of well-to-do families, while the women targeted were poor girls, working as maids or washerwomen, of whom it was rumored that they were "kept" by their masters... On average half of the town male youth, at some point, engaged in these assaults, which Rossiaud describes as a form of class protest, a means for proletarian men – who were forced to postpone marriage for many years because of their economic conditions – to get back 'their own,' and take revenge against the rich."

How the feminist historian views this situation is revealing. The author

379 Quotes are from Federici, Caliban and the Witch, pp. 46-49.

laments that "proletarian women, [were] so cavalierly sacrificed by masters and servants alike". She considers that these "vicious sexual politics that gave [the most rebellious male workers] access to free sex" was a way of the ruling class to win them over, and "[turn] class antagonism into an antagonism against proletarian women".

However, this outburst of rage against women, especially when it involved 50% of the poor male population, was not just a result of diversion. Such rape rates occur only in times of war, where the women that are raped are clearly on the "other" camp, and "the social psychology of 'in-group'/'out-group' operates to an extreme"[380]. The mass rapes described above suggest that there can be no real solidarity between men and women of the lower classes when the latter despise the former and provide sexual "favors" to the ruling class. Federici's claim that "the legalization of rape created a climate of intense misogyny" is naive at best. The de facto decriminalization of rape did not *create* misogyny, it just opened a window to reveal a pre-existing male rage.

In modern history, there are numerous other examples of similar kinds of violence against women. In France, mistresses of German officers during the WWII were summarily executed after the liberation. In every war, the punishment for cooperating with the enemy, i.e. for treason, is death. It is simply a reflection of the common sentiment about justice that sleeping with the enemy is a punishable offense.

Male and female violence

Let's look at another case of male violence, taken from Herb Goldberg's *The Hazards of Being Male*[381]. Roger R. had three children, the second of which was a hyperactive boy

> "who would get up at 6:30 every morning and go full speed ahead into late evening.... The incident that caused Roger to go into a violent rage took place after a particularly hard week at work. Roger was relaxing, watching a football game while his son kept jumping all over him, asking him to play. Suddenly, Roger had what he called a 'blackout.' 'I just

---

380 Moxon, The Woman Racket, p. 285.
381 Goldberg, The Hazards of Being Male, p. 61.

> grabbed Seth and started beating him and I couldn't stop. If Sylvia hadn't been around to hear the kid screaming, I might have killed him. Afterward, when she got me away and I saw the bruises on his body I started to cry. I couldn't believe what I had done.'"

After some sessions with a psychologist,

> "the underlying resentments that had been brewing inside of him for years and were the long-developed cause of the Sunday incident, came pouring through. Roger had gotten married when he was nineteen because Sylvia was pregnant.... His wife was only the second woman he'd ever had sex with. The first was a 'back-seat job.' Right after the wedding he went to work full-time, attended college in the evening, and put his remaining energies into trying to be a good father and husband.... Roger had long envied the single men he knew. He daydreamed constantly about sex.... [L]ike many people in our culture, [he] got married and had children many years too soon and for many of the wrong reasons. His growth stopped when he got married. Unlike the common notion, marriage didn't mature him – it stunted him.... [He] became a father not because he really wanted to but because he felt too guilty not to.... Like most middle-class men ... he had been taught that he had to take responsibility for sexually 'impulsive' behavior, if the woman so insisted. He was, in fact, legally responsible. He tried everything to fit happily into his role and continually repressed his resentful feelings until they could no longer be contained. His son finally became the target of eleven years worth of rage and frustration."

The case of Roger R. is exemplary. At the heart of male aggression one finds sexual frustration. The example above was an isolated violent outburst in which the unlucky recipient of his rage was his child. In other cases, having a defenseless target for aggression displacement is a sufficient reason for some men (and women) to have children. Besides, isn't hitting your children legal, while hitting your spouse isn't? Hitting your child mustn't be such a bad thing, then[382]... In other cases, aggression might be displaced against the "enemy" of your country, an

---

382 Irony is often a proper weapon against the powerful and the system.

underling in your workplace, your competitor, a stranger who will overtake your car in a manner which you find improper...

A feminist nicknamed *The Femitheist* became popular on the internet in 2012 when she proposed the "International Castration Day". She argued that men's high testosterone was to blame for their high rate of criminality compared with women[383]. Since then she has... refined her theory, arguing that the solution is to reduce the male population to 1-10% (sic). This extreme view reflects a widespread perception that men are biologically more inclined to be violent than women, independently of social conditions.

The first mistake of this approach has to do with ignorance of how testosterone affects aggression. In laboratory experiments it has been found that testosterone is indeed necessary for aggressive behavior[384]. Animals that had testosterone removed are unable to exhibit it. Moreover, animals that have received testosterone well above the normal limit, e.g. four times the normal rate, exhibit abnormally intense aggression. However, when testosterone is within the normal range, it does not influence aggression. We can liken it to gasoline in a car. With no gas there is no motion, and when gas overflows there can be an explosion. But when the tank is at the lower limit or nearly full, there is no impact on the car's ability to move. If someone's testosterone is "anywhere from roughly 20 percent of normal to twice normal"[385] the degree of aggression with which he will react to an external situation does not change. It is external situations which push the individual to become aggressive, which in turn elevates testosterone levels. Sapolsky is very clear: Given the hypotheses "(a) testosterone elevates aggression; (b) aggression elevates testosterone secretion; (c) neither causes the other", he emphasises that "There's a huge bias to assume option a, while b is the answer. Study after study has shown that when you examine testosterone levels when males are first placed together in the social group, testosterone levels predict nothing about who is going to be

383 'The Woman Who Thinks Reducing the Male Population by 90 Percent Will Solve Everything | VICE United States'. http://www.vice.com/read/is-reducing-the-male-population-by-90-percent-the-solution-to-all-our-problems
384 Sapolsky, The Trouble with Testosterone, ch. 11.
385 Sapolsky, The Trouble with Testosterone, ch. 11.

aggressive. The subsequent behavioral differences drive the hormonal changes, rather than the other way around."[386]

What determines one's level of violence is one's frustration, not testosterone levels or even gender. One can quote an example where female violence is greater than male violence with our familiar and amiable Bonobos. "Accounts exist of bonobos confined in zoos mutilating one another and engaging in bullying. These incidents may be due to the practice in zoos of separating mothers and sons, which is contrary to their social organization in the wild.... Severing the lifelong alliance between mothers and their male offspring may make them vulnerable to female aggression."[387]

Another source of aggression is, simply, power. Noam Chomsky has called the US the "ultimate bully", stressing that after the WWII it has been involved in hundreds of wars, more than any other country. The powerful use violence simply because they can. There is a difference between the violence of the powerful and that of the oppressed, with the first being much more effective while the second is often self-destructive.

Correspondingly, female violence is both more extensive and more effective than men's, although "traditionally, men did not recognize [its] existence..."[388]. A first grade teacher commented on the difference in aggression "as it appeared at an early age: ... Boys were more physically aggressive than girls, but... they were like teddy bears. Their behavior was fairly direct and active. In contrast... the girls who were aggressive tended to be 'mean and devious.'". From early on, girls are free to explore all form of aggression. In contrast, although "there [are] no significant differences by sex in core, lower, or upper body measures of strength for younger boys and girls"[389], boys are taught that "you shouldn't hit girls", implying that hitting boys is more OK. Maybe that's the reason why girls hit boys up to 20 times more than vice versa[390].

In puberty, we can witness what doctor Leonard Shlain calls "pubescent

---

386 Sapolsky, The Trouble with Testosterone, ch. 11.
387 Wikipedia, Bonobo. Accessed 19 Jan. 2015. https://en.wikipedia.org/wiki/Bonobo
388 Goldberg, The Hazards of Being Male, p. 15.
389 'Products - Data Briefs - Number 139 - December 2013'. Accessed 21 Oct. 2014.
    http://www.cdc.gov/nchs/data/databriefs/db139.htm
390 Farrell, The Myth of Male Power, p.206.

reverse sexual dimorphism": "Girls are larger, taller, heavier, and in many cases as strong as or stronger than boys of the same age... Mother Nature has conveniently equipped the girl with the physical means to defend herself",[391] and this occurs in a period when boys "are least able to control their urges".

As the years advance and boys become stronger, female aggression changes tack: "[B]y age thirteen, a telling difference between the sexes emerges: Girls become more adept than boys at artful aggressive tactics like ostracism, vicious gossip, and indirect vendettas."[392] Henceforth, indirect, hidden forms will characterize the repertoire of female aggression. The legendary female *nagging*, i.e. passive-aggressiveness, is so insidious and efficient that a typical women's magazine called "Wedding" came to write that it was "worse than cheating" for the health of one's relationship. Mainstream psychology, of course, offering reciprocal service to its best clients (women) fully justifies it as a purely defensive, not offensive weapon: "[Male-dominated society] has resulted in hysteria becoming the only weapon of women for the expression and claiming of her desires towards the omnipotent world of men, but also, at the same time, for her revenge ... With the intelligence of the unconscious woman found the counterweight to the male 'superiority' in hysteria, which was a way of protection but and revenge at the same time."[393]

Consistent with the female principle of the disclaimer of responsibility, nagging assumes no responsibility for aggression making it impossible to deal with it and perpetuating the relationship's problems. It is a blackmail aiming at the perpetual prevalence of the woman – or the deterioration of intimacy and the disintegration of the relationship.

---

391 Shlain, Sex, Time and Power, p. 141.
392 Goleman, Emotional Intelligence.
393 Riemann, Fritz, *Grundformen Der Angst*, 1997.

Chapter 37: Social Runaway

We have already described the runaway process in biology, where a feature evolves out of proportions, following its own, autonomous course. Similar dynamics appear in human societies. Class society, as we've seen, was an emergency situation, that ensured the survival of women over men, as well as the survival of a few men of the ruling class over the majority, in times of hunger. It was not a conscious, calculated choice. That is, it was a "natural" form of social organization only in a state of intense crisis, where hunger and death were a daily issue.

That kind of society has long since become a hindrance to the development of human abilities, but it persists because it still has momentum. Beyond the ideological mechanisms of its reproduction, i.e. education, religion, prevailing moral codes, there are very real, material mechanisms at play. There are "vested interests". However, as we have underlined in our analysis, the most important mechanism of systemic reproduction is not to be found in monetary economy, but in sex.

Progressives realize that you cannot have political and social democracy without economic democracy. But they have a hard time understanding that you cannot have economic democracy without first having sexual democracy.

The system serves the upper classes because it gives them the opportunity to live in luxury. This is especially true for the women of these classes, who, beyond luxury, also enjoy a life of laziness – while the men often need to work. But what is more important for these men by far is that they enjoy the greatest sexual freedom they can imagine in this world: "power is the ultimate aphrodisiac", as Henry Kissinger put it. In other words, the rich and famous do not have to chase after women, women chase after them.

The greatest impediment to the overthrow of the system is that it serves not only the ruling class, but also 50% of the world's population, i.e. women. Almost all of them during the first, defining decades of their lives, enjoy the sexual power afforded by their control of the sex market.

They get more "strokes", to use Berne's terms, as their power consolidates. To put it simply, it is more enjoyable to be complimented and desired all day, than if you have sex once and are ignored afterwards. But the commercialization (for money or for "strokes") of such a fundamental commodity as sex leads to the commercialization of the human relations and society.

Despite this, society today is actually oppressive for women as well – at least for a vast majority of women. They may not be working in the worst professions, as men do, work is often unpleasant even for them. They also live in a society of alienation that they have created, and when their sexual capital is depleted, when they are approximately 35-40, they begin reaping its bitter fruits.

"And who could forget her opening comment in therapy? 'Ever since I turned thirty I've noticed that when I enter restaurants, no one stops eating to look at me. I'm devastated.'"

- Irvin Yalom, The Schopenhauer Cure

Women have of course their children they can suck the life out of, but for the less ruthless women this might create a degree of uneasiness and leave a sense of dissatisfaction, as they are forced to live on a low existential level so as not to realize this behavior. And of course, by blocking sex they strangle men's ability for love, in the same way that depriving someone from food destroys his ability to enjoy the other pleasures of life, which he could, in turn, offer to others. Women are thus deprived of the pleasure of having a free and whole person love them.

Trying to convince women to give up their power is as difficult as convincing capitalists to give up capitalism. "Coincidentally", the first socialists tried to do exactly this, arguing that capitalists themselves would gain from the abolition of capitalism at the level of human relationships. Then Marx showed that this idealistic approach was hopeless, and that class war was inevitable. In this sense, an ideological appeal to women about the advantages for them and society as a whole that a cease of their keeping sex a hostage would have, is directly opposed to their daily experience which consist in enjoying men's interest and providing. Moreover, women today *are* in practice sexually liberated. It is *men* who are not liberated, and sexual liberation makes sense only for them.

Chapter 38: The Need for a Restriction to Female Sexual Selectivity

The revival of liberation ideologies marked by May '68 coincided with the feminist revolution that had already begun. Although the latter, as explained above, expressed rather a need of the system than of the women, the result of the collusion between the two movements was to consider "female sexual liberation" as an "integral part of the war to liberate society". In reality, women, after trying "sexual revolution" for two to three decades, have found that it didn't suit them and took it back. A Time Magazine cover from 1984 proclaimed "Sex in the '80s: The Revolution is Over"[394]. Whomever saw Greek beaches in the '80s, with female tourists bathing topless and bikinis being an exception, easily realize the contrast with today, when the situation is reversed and the exception is now to be topless.

The end of the sexual revolution was due to modern women gradually realizing what women in older times unconsciously knew: that sexuality belongs to them exclusively, and that they can do whatever they want with it. And what they want is to give it to the rich and powerful in exchange for money and power. Today, the argument that female prostitution (in the more general sense of the term) is due to poverty and woman's oppression, collapses like a house of cards. John Townsend, who studied female students of the upper-middle class, found that they preferred men above them to an even greater degree than women of the lower classes[395]. Another study, also on female students of the upper

---

394 Extremely interesting is the picture about female suicide in the US, which shows a spike exactly at the times of "female liberation", 1960-1984, and recession since then. On the contrary, male suicide spikes precisely in the decade after 1984. See Stevenson, The Paradox of the Declining Female Happiness (Figure 7).

395 "If she comes from a professional, upper-middle-class family, she generally expects to marry a man who can provide a similar or superior lifestyle—even though her

classes, found that 9% had made an "attempt to trade sex for some *tangible* benefit. [emphasis added] … Dire need was not the motivation of these college women. As the study's author noted, 'It's more about getting what you want than getting what you need, unless you think everyone needs a $200 Louis Vuitton bag.'"[396]. And if we move beyond the "tangible benefits" and examine reasons like "I wanted to get a raise – I wanted to get a promotion"[397], the percentage of women who prostitute themselves skyrockets.

With the advent of reliable contraception, another myth collapses, one which was plausible, and until recently all-powerful: that women restrict sex necessarily to avoid getting pregnant. In fact, they just restrict sex towards the average man – even if they are "average" themselves. If they find the "proper" man, they can go after sex quite pressingly. In 1993, Warren Farrell invited women to take up part of the risk of flirting, "to be equally responsible for taking sexual initiatives and risking sexual rejection rather than lecturing only males on how not to do it wrong"[398]. But even in a traditional country like Greece, women aggressively flirt whomever they really desire – even if they will almost never expose themselves explicitly. They will just do it for the top 1% of men with very high "mate value": those who are physically very attractive when women are in their pre-marital, "exploratory" mode or in the married, lover-seeking mode, and the very successful men when women have entered the "marriage mode". By comparison, men's options can only slant "downwards", with women who are "worse" than they are. This difference in scale is what makes the position of women qualitatively different than men's.

Based on these facts, the notion of a "fully liberated" society where "everyone" (including women) will be free to choose their sexual partner is really terrifying for most men – i.e. those in the bottom 90-95% of attractiveness and those in the bottom 50-80% of the economy. As things

own earning power may be minimal. Women from the working class might prefer to marry up if they could, but they might also be content with finding men who are successful within their own class." - Townsend, What Women Want – What Men Want, p. 161.

396 Buss, Why Women Have Sex, Ch. 8.
397 Buss, Why Women Have Sex, Ch. 8.
398 Farrell, The Myth Of Male Power, p. 263.

stand, at least most of them will expect to find a woman to marry them, even if this means them becoming providers and risking going through a divorce. The fact is that women's sexual freedom, or more appropriately women's sexual *power*, not only needs no expansion, but it is overinflated and needs to be cut down to size. Warren Farrell, although sympathetic to feminism (at least a "mature" version of it), says it clearly:

> "The old belief that men have the power and women are powerless leads predictably to a battle between the sexes. How? The perception of women as powerless makes us fear limiting the expansion of women's power. Fear of limiting the power of the sex with the greatest spending power, the greater beauty power, the greater sexual power, the greater net worth among its heads of households, and the greater options in marriage, children, work, and life creates the corruptness of absolute power which will ultimately lead to a much bloodier battle between the sexes"[399].

For those preaching a society of equality, dealing with sexual inequality is inescapable. They cannot bypass the issue of how men are to ensure adequate sex. Geoffrey Miller puts it thus:

> "The discriminatory nature of sexual choice undermines all egalitarian Utopias. Women might like the idea of all men being able to have equal amounts of sex, but no individual woman would be willing to forgo her power of sexual choice to allow an unattractive, unfit man to copulate with her. In the realm of human sexuality, no one would agree to the maxim 'from each according to his abilities; to each according to his needs.'"[400]

Whomever has not swallowed whole the neoliberal axiom that the rich should be given free rein to expand their riches, and who believes that their restriction is for the benefit of society, may be in a position to understand that there is a corresponding situation with women and sexuality. Feminist sociologist Cathrine Hakim declares openly that women posses more "sexual capital"[401] (or "erotic capital") than men.

399 Farrell, The Myth Of Male Power, p. 255.
400 Miller, The Mating Mind, p. 337.
401 Hakim, Catherine. *Erotic Capital, Eur Sociol Rev (2010) 26 (5): 499-518.*

and that "given the large imbalance between men and women in sexual interest over the life course, women are well placed to exploit their erotic capital." It is a very interesting attempt to socially and morally legitimize female (generalized) prostitution, against the "patriarchal" and "pseudo-ethical" ideology that "inhibit women from exploiting their erotic capital to achieve economic and social benefits." We could, of course, counter that men have a greater "capital of physical strength" that they should use, ignoring the "pseudo-ethical" and legal barriers of "matriarchy", in order to expropriate women's greater "erotic capital". But perhaps things don't have to get that bad.

In any case, it becomes clear that there is a war. And up to now it has been one-sided, with women stubbornly defending their historic coup to appropriate for themselves all the sexuality of the human race. Men must pick up the glove. The goal is *a social, and not personal, management of the female "erotic capital" - with the participation of men*, because women do collectively manage their sexuality, restricting one another.

Unfortunately, this war cannot always be waged painlessly or along political correct lines.

The male war for sexual liberation

In a war it is important to know your real enemy. Is it really women? Ultimately, no.

The inequality in the distribution of wealth in favor of the ruling class is huge. Although women benefit when compared to men, they would benefit even more from economic equality. As we argued earlier, women are humanity's petty bourgeois. They have it better than men, but they eventually live a life which is depressing and unfree. When the petty bourgeois compare their life to those "above" they feel wronged. But then there is worse, those "below", so they figure that "it's not so bad", and they cannot be easily convinced to get into trouble for a social change. If it is unthinkable for the petty bourgeois to give up his little store to a communal economy, it is equally unthinkable for women to

http://esr.oxfordjournals.org/content/26/5/499.abstract

give up their full control over sex. "Whoever wants it all, loses what little she has", they think proverbially. Only proletarians have nothing to lose – except their chains.

For women, a society where men will not have to "pay" for sex seems dangerous: how will they and their children live? They will probably be obligated to have jobs they would rather avoid. They will be denied of the bliss created by men's heightened interest: if men are free to choose, why would they choose them? They will choose the prettiest...

On the other hand, men's fear of sexual liberation, the fear of being alone, which makes them still support marriage to a degree, has recently started to be replaced by another fear: that their wives ditch them and take the children with them, as well as the house and half their wages. For more and more men it becomes clear that they have nothing to lose from a liberated society – except their celibacy. With the exception of course of the men of the ruling class, who fight fiercely to maintain their privileged position in women's preferences.

It all comes back to the beginning of the class society, and to the reasons for its appearance. It emerged from a huge crisis, where survival was at stake. Societies that adjusted to the preferential survival of women over men prevailed. The (male) ruling class was a reaction to this situation. Current technology, however, could feed and cover the basic needs of everyone. *The restriction that women keep imposing on sex is the reason why economy is not geared towards human needs, but is instead based on sheer competitiveness.* The most typical example of this process is American football. The images of men clashing on the field barely differ from images of stags clashing with their antlers. The only difference is the doe do not wear shiny mini-skirts and don't shake their breasts during breaks to keep reminding people what awaits the winner – and the winner only. "To increase desires to an unbearable level while making the fulfillment of them more and more inaccessible: this was the single principle upon which Western society was based"[402], writes Michel Houellebecq. *For capitalism, if hunger is the whip, women are the carrot.*

---

402 Houellebecq, Michel. *The Possibility of an Island.* USA: Alfred A. Knopf (2006).

If you have ever wondered why a super-rich man, who seems to have it all, wants to become even richer, the answer is: sex – even if somewhere on the way this has become sublimated. Luxury and opulence are not the deeper motive. As a mogule once put it, "If women didn't exist, all the money in the world would have no meaning."

The issue is that attraction for women is based on status, and the status is always relative, so it can always be higher. *The runaway competition of class society is the result of female sexuality left unchecked.*

Let's illustrate the relative value of luxury vs sex with a mind exercise. Imagine you can choose one of two free vacation packages for life. Pack A offers a 10-day yacht cruise in an exotic island every year. Cocktails, music and party on the beach, hot wet bodies under the sun, nights by the sea around a fire. But there is a catch: there are no women around! All the aforementioned bodies under the sun are male (with lots of hair on their chests), the guys around the night fire by the sea are all bearded, and the captain, the officer and the crew of the ship are all men.

Now Pack B takes you to an anonymous and drab apartment block in a former Soviet country. The food is cabbage, every day. No sun, no sea, no cocktails. But every year the finalists for the Miss World beauty contest gather there, and have a wild 10-day party with plenty of wild sex.

For every heterosexual, unmarried or non-guilt ridden man, the choice is obvious...

The different relative value of luxury vs sex for men and women is highlighted by the difference in the participation of men and women in the highest positions in society. The smaller percentages of women in these positions (for example, women are only 4% of the CEOs in the list of the top 500 companies of Standard & Poor's) correspond to the extent that all people (men and women) crave luxury. The overwhelming, additional percentage of men in high posts (along with the effort and sacrifices that these posts entail) is due to the status and the consequent attractiveness and sex that these positions confer.

Men are enemies of women in the same way as workers are enemies of the petty bourgeois: they need to expropriate them in order to free them. For as long as women will insist in their alliance with the system, enjoying an easier, careless life in exchange for the reproduction of the working class, for as long as they will accept being the system's "carrot", hoarding sex and turning it into a rare occurrence, they will be de facto enemies of men. In a war, your enemy's soldiers are de facto your enemies, for as long as they fight against you. You can call for truce and a sense of brotherhood, but this does not mean that you shouldn't be fighting them. Even if men's real enemy is class society, in order to liberate themselves they need to fight both its institutions as well as those that benefit from it, i.e. the capitalists... and women.

Chapter 39: Towards the Solution: The New Sex Contract

The basic Sex Contract, "meat for sex", has been in place for so long that it has embedded the basic psychology of the sexes. The rectification of balance and social peace predicates the rectification of this contract, somehow. In the modern era, however, at least in Western society, the problem of food and the satisfaction of other basic needs has been solved by technology. Women take them for granted, and don't feel they have to "pay" for them with sex. They use sex more for their "cake" than for their "bread". Women can today buy the meat from the butcher, but men are still bound to ask women for sex.

A neo-conservative solution proposes a "return to the past", where women were in the house and did not work, so that they were financially dependent on their husbands. Although in recent years this is revived as a proposal from some circles, it is both impossible and wrong: we saw that it represented the culmination of female superiority in previously difficult economic and labor market conditions, and not some kind of balance of the sexes.

Prima facie, the equation "meat for sex" appears then impossible to solve today. In the big picture of modern society, what is so important that men have to offer, for women to agree to provide sex? The answer is: peace.

In all its manifestations. Elimination of crime, exploitation, war. Women would understand that better with a wording like "conditions under which every woman could raise her children with comfort and in safety".

All human behavior can be analyzed in two dimensions, survival and reproduction. When the survival needs are adequately covered, it is solely the behaviors around sex that define society. That's why sex is the key to changing society.

Let's take the example of an extreme social phenomenon, war, and let's see its relation with sex. "In order to kill the enemy, our men must be roused in anger", says Sun Tzu. No anger – no killing. You can manage to create *a little* anger with propaganda. But a *paranoid* anger is needed if men are to be sent to kill and get killed. "A rational army would run away" says Montesquieu. This anger has been systematically cultivated all their lives by sexually frustrating them. The system only needs to obscure the real cause of anger, to block the venting outlets towards the real culprits, and to point the anger towards the "enemy".

To the question "what motives initiate a war?" anthropologist Jared Diamond answers: "In the New Guinea Highlands, common answers are 'women' and 'pigs'." As for the reason for "New Guineans ranking pigs on a par with women as causes of war, recall that pigs to a New Guinean are not mere food ... they are the main currency of wealth and prestige, and are convertible into women as essential components of bride-price... The Yanomamo and many other peoples similarly report women as a or the major cause of war. "[403]

Sexually satiated men cannot be sent to war.

For as long as men are deprived from the sex they have been programmed by nature to crave, there is no chance that peace and social justice will prevail. Men with the physique of a Nicolas Sarkozy will always desire women with the physique of a Carla Bruni. If the only way to have them is to serve the system by cutting down the pensions of the elderly or the wages of the young, that is what they'll do. Kissinger, fully aware of the benefits of power, said "Now when I bore people at parties, they think it's their fault". There will always be guys ready to launch a

---

403 Diamond, Jared, *The World Until Yesterday*, Ch.4.

war in a Middle Eastern country for a hundred or so fellatios. Not all men are ruthless, of course. Most men might instead keep a moral stance, refraining from harming the weak, even if it will lead them to social stagnation, low status, and as a final result, complete or relative celibacy. But "brutal sensuality", to remember Marx, has a much more decisive effect on society than moral integrity. Moral principles were never a factor attracting women.

One can perceive where the difficulty lies: sex for meat is a direct transaction, one which is very comprehensible and rather "intuitive", while sex for peace is much more complex – and requires a more conscious reflection.

In practical terms, in order to restore the balance between the sexes there are two basic social areas which require reform – or better, a revolution: the status quo on procreation, and the sexual life of the young.

Chapter 40: Reproductive Rights for Men: Towards the Abolition of Marriage and Liberation from Procreation

Men's reproductive rights

It should be self-evident, at least for those who consider themselves to be progressive, that men should have the same reproductive rights as women. They should be able to "decide freely and responsibly the number, spacing and timing of their children and to have the information and means to do so"[404]. In practice, this also means to "have the right to relinquish all future parental rights and financial responsibility" in case of an unplanned pregnancy, firstly outside marriage, but within marriage as well, since women have a corresponding right to abort.

---

404 From WHO's definition of Reproductive Rights. Referred in Wikipedia,
      Reproductive Rights. Accessed 19 Jan. 2015,
      https://en.wikipedia.org/wiki/Reproductive_rights

In the '70s Herb Goldberg had already suggested a simple and practical way to do it:

> "I propose that any couple intending to have a child sign a contract formalizing this mutual desire. In the absence of such a contract the male must be given the prerogative of demanding an abortion unless he is released from any financial or legal responsibility if the woman insists she wants the child despite his request to terminate the pregnancy. Otherwise whenever birth control measures fail the male becomes a potential victim because he is legally responsible without having made the decision to have a child."[405]

Unfortunately, instead of moving in this direction, society moves towards the exact opposite. Courts impose on men the obligation to financially support their wife's children even if they are proven not to be their own[406].

It is interesting at this point to contrast paternity fraud with rape. Geoffrey Miller argues that rape is a *reproductive* crime, not a crime against survival: "For rape to be viewed as a serious crime from a survival rights viewpoint, for example, it must be characterized as 'a crime of violence, not sex' – a description that raises many difficulties in cases of date rape. By contrast, a sexual choice viewpoint leads naturally to the view that even non-violent rape is a serious crime, because it violates human rights to exercise sexual choice."[407] The corollary of this principle, if we apply it impartially in the case of men, is that paternity fraud should be considered a crime which is equally important as rape. The relative large number of women worldwide who bear someone else's child should be serving time in incarceration. Instead, this scam, one which has devastating consequences for men and children, is fully legitimized by the system which needs its subjects to reproduce by any means – including the sacrifice of males.

How would the sexual dynamics between the sexes move if men were

---

405 Goldberg, The Hazards of Being Male, p. 156.
406 They are relieved of the obligation only if the DNA test is done until the first or second year of the child's life. http://www.divorcecorp.com/child-custody-2/child-support/child-support-dna-test
407 Miller, The Mating Mind, p. 428.

given reproductive rights?

An immediate consequence would be that the "attractiveness" of the rich would be reduced, because they could no longer get trapped for marriage or alimony with a pregnancy. It would also reduce the attractiveness of "bad boys" who might offer exciting emotional experiences but who do not count as dependable fathers. Sex would be freer, for its own sake, and a corresponding culture would be cultivated. Of course, there is the possibility that women would further limit the sex they give away, as a result of this pressure on them to take full and exclusive responsibility for an unplanned pregnancy. However, this is not necessarily a bad thing. To the extent that women's ulterior motives for having sex are revealed, men will feel freed to turn to the cheaper, better and more honest sex offered by prostitutes.

Joint custody in divorce

By ensuring reproductive rights to men, many of the problems related to child custody in divorce cases would cease to exist. In the meanwhile, we cannot ignore the issues that arise from the existing situation.

The pseudo-scientific myths that justified the system's decisions to give child custody almost always to the mother have started to collapse[408]. Studies have shown that "children in joint-custody arrangements had fewer behavioral and emotional problems, higher self-esteem and better family relationships and school performance compared with those in sole-custody situations"[409]. But it will take continued struggles on the part of men for joint custody to become the norm, for alimony to be abolished, for fathers to be able to spend as much time with their children as mothers, and for women not to have the right to take them away to another city.

In this respect, joint custody should be the starting point, a right and not one more obligation for the man. He needs, as we've seen, to devote

---

408 Parenting Time & Shared Residential Custody: Ten Common Myths. The Nebraska Lawyer, Jan/Feb 2013. http://www.acfc.org/acfc/assets/documents/Articles/Nebraska%20Lawyer%20Magazine.pdf
409 'Joint custody might be best option for children of divorce, study finds'. American Psychological Association. http://www.apa.org/monitor/jun02/custody.aspx

incomparably more effort and money than women to satisfy his elementary sexual and emotional needs. Therefore, he is often trapped between his desire to be with his children and his need of a woman. If loneliness and emotional hunger eat away his vitality, it makes no sense to keep a lifeless presence next to his children. It is then better to limit the quantity of time spent with his children and increase the quality of each moment. And if the father cannot understand that he has a duty to take care of his own self, and keep himself happy, maybe he can better understand that his children have a right to have a happy father. The ultimate conclusion of this reasoning is that a father and his children have the right to enjoy each other, even in the cases when the father, either because it was not his choice or he does not have the economic means to do so, has renounced all financial responsibility. Research has shown, and some sociologists have begun to realize, that it is important that a man be a father to his children even if he cannot afford to pay for alimony. "'Deadbeats' can still be good dads"[410].

In the perspective of reproductive strategies, it is clear that the situation for women and men in divorce is fundamentally different. A woman with children has fulfilled the greater part of her reproductive strategy. A divorced man, who has children needing his resources, both the material ones and quality time with him, has a huge handicap regarding his capacity to ensure enough sex and satisfactory emotional relationships with other women. Instead of men paying for alimony, the fair thing would be for women to pay for the dating expenses of the man they threw away with divorce. Of course, due to female domination, this proposal sounds absurd, while the female expectation for the man to finance a woman's reproductive strategy at the expense of his own is considered normal.

Child welfare and sexual exchanges

Ideally, every woman should have the right and the opportunity to bring children to the world if she wishes to do so, and to raise them in a safe environment. Covering the basic (and other) needs of her children should

---

410 'How 'deadbeats' can still be good dads - Ideas - The Boston Globe'.
   http://www.bostonglobe.com/ideas/2014/12/05/how-deadbeats-can-still-good-dads/
   EdiXe3spvu7hSOIhDJXWfJ/story.html.

be guaranteed by society, so that every child starts off in life with equal opportunities. Men, as demonstrated by centuries of history, are willing to contribute to this end, by taking up the burdens corresponding to them, and even by taking up the lion's share of these burdens. But men should not do this without getting what they deserve: sufficient, quality sex. What should a celibate man feel like when he pays taxes for the health and education of the children he never had the chance to father?[411] Why risk his life in a war to defend his country when this means defending the right of the rich to keep bedding the women that despise and reject him?

The expropriation of sex by women breaks down social cohesion. It strips the system naked, revealing that at its core, compulsion is the ultimate means it uses in order to function. The oppressed, i.e. men, have no interest in supporting it. Until they can get enough sex, the only rational attitude for men is to be anchorites or revolutionaries. Until very recently, before the feminist revolution changed things, women's sexual strategy was well hidden. Then, the average men could, if grudgingly, tolerate wage labor in order to have a woman in bed, since it was (supposedly) inconceivable for a woman to have sex out of wedlock, and there was no other option. But ever since women decided to rid themselves of these strictures, and those ordinary guys see them by the hundreds partying with the rich and the top 1% of the most handsome men during their 20s, why should they work like slaves to purchase one single piece of merchandise in their 30s, who's second-hand and rather worn-out?

The only way to have a harmonious society, that will ensure women's right to procreation, is by ensuring men's right to sex. As we have seen in Part 3, where we discussed the anovulatory cycles, sacred prostitution was one such arrangement during the historic times. It was a very practical way for women to pay back men for the fact that in a savage and insecure era of constant wars, they were provided with a protected life. Many of the prostitutes were priestesses in temples. The respect that such a post commanded shows the recognition that they were performing an important social function. In some nations, women gathered their

---

411 Of course this money is only a minor part of the unfair taxation system. Essentially, taxation is about burdening the lower classes, especially men, to finance the infrastructure that the rich men use in order to get richer – and more attractive.

dowry in this way, relieving their father from the duty.

Sacred prostitution and the practices of the Maasai, where men have a right to many women, are customary ways to restrict the female sexual veto. The big issue is how something to similar effect can be achieved in modern society.

The most important goal: sexual life of the young

The interventions described above which concern adults is only a symptomatic treatment of the problem. The social mores and the legal framework impose female domination on men externally, but the most important factor which supports it is internal, located in the very soul of men. We do not mean their innate need for female intimacy. We mean the intensification of this need that women effect, firstly through their role as mothers, and secondly with the control of sex during their adolescence and youth. Despite mainstream psychology's focus on the role of the mother, it is the latter which, as we have seen, plays a more crucial role for man. Therefore, *changing the sexual landscape of youths is the absolutely most important battle in the war of the sexes.*

In youths the problem of relationships and sex is even greater than in adults. Here, there is no institution like marriage to define the framework for relations. There is only the social dynamic, which is overwhelmingly in favor of women and the spoiled boys of the ruling class and against the average man. Women and the rich are the ones that emerge from youth with a mentality of abundance, that normalizes their sense of entitlement. In contrast, the majority of the poorer boys end up with a mentality of scarcity which will undermine their efforts for all their life.

The idea about the change that is needed is simple: sex for boys and young men should be taken as much for granted as it is for girls. For this to happen, we need to bring about a full sexual saturation of boys during their age of sexual awakening and their first youth. The ruling class and women fear, and rightly so, that a mentality that sex is free and you don't have to struggle for it will make men disobedient. "Then try getting men to do anything", they say. Try to make them work in crappy jobs for peanuts. Try sending them to war. And try making them support a woman and her children for all their lives, dutifully sacrificing their manliness and their humanity in the process.

Women and the rich have the same self-righteous expectation from non-rich men: why can't everyone mind his own business and be happy about it? Why demand more than what we give them?

It is true that the looser sexual mores of the post-feminist era initially helped men get more sex. But it is just a drop in the ocean. Girls retain the right to a sexual veto. They are the choosers, and this results in a huge inequality in the distribution of sex. Since in the medium term there is no prospect for this situation to change, the only realistic solution is prostitution (again). A broad social legitimization of prostitution could give a sexual outlet to boys – as it did in older times. With the abolition of the sexual monopoly of their female peer, boys will be in better position to set the terms in their emotional and sexual relationships.

Chapter 41: Other Considerations

This book is not intended as a complete program for male and social liberation. It aims to define a framework to understand the situation between the two sexes, and to set the key criteria for social change. In this section we would like to briefly examine some additional aspects of the issue. The topics addressed briefly below are not secondary, but require thorough analysis to be treated properly, and that is something that diverges from the general purpose of the book.

Who is the subject of these social changes?

In any discussion about social change the most important factor is the subjective: who is going to do all this? Apparently the answer should turn towards men. But they are not a uniform social body. There is a great difference between poor and rich men in how they experience the war of the sexes. Furthermore, the majority of women, despite their feelings to the contrary, do not really benefit from the situation, since it keeps the whole society imprisoned. In other words, they could potentially be allies of men.

In any case, it is clear that men should realize the collective nature of their sexual oppression: it is a social, and not only a personal problem. Awareness is the first step towards action.

The Left should stop being opportunistic, it should stop supporting women when they attack men (as e.g. in the issue of prostitution). It is true that, in part, the Left is sincerely fooled, and really believes that women are disadvantaged. But it is also, in part, being blatantly opportunistic, attempting to win over the women who are claiming even more benefits, while men, at least until recently, watched on helplessly.

Changes at the level of social conventions

Social conventions are more important than institutions, because they prove that a principle has been incorporated more organically in society. The set of social conventions for each sex needs drastic change. The general direction, as we have already pointed out, is to assign extra burdens on girls and women, and relieve boys and men.

An example is the expectation of responsibility from boys. While for their proper psychological development children have the right to be irresponsible, up to the point of being unjust, boys are crushed early on by the expectation to assume "their" responsibilities. They must keep their word, weigh their words. Girls, on the other hand, have their parents (especially their fathers[412]) to solve their problems, and their status and attractiveness are virtually unaffected by behaving in a light-hearted, irresponsible fashion.

---

412 Brizendine, Louann. *The Male Brain.* New York: Broadway Books (2010). ch.5: "Dads bond with their daughters by helping to solve their problems and fixing things that are broken, whether it's their dollies or their financial portfolios. Fathers also bond with their sons by helping them, but research shows that this "help" often centers on making the boys stronger and tougher."

Another example is the "sexual double standard" we discussed in Part 3. We saw that not only has it disappeared against women, but it has been reversed, and men that "cheat" (an unfortunate term) are judged more harshly than women who do the same. Based on our analysis, however, a married man who has a mistress is just trying to rescue what he can from his right to his reproductive strategy, which he sacrificed by marrying his wife. Nora Vincent was surprised by a phenomenon that for every man is perfectly normal: "The oddest thing about all this dirty talk [about titty bars and porno mags] and hiding strip club visits from their wives was the absolute reverence with which they spoke about their wives and their marriages."[413] Men don't compare their women, and a man going with another woman is not an insult towards his wife.

His wife, on the other hand, having secured for herself a husband "above" what would normally correspond to her, chooses a lover who has an even higher "mate value" than her husband. It is perhaps natural to want the best she can have, but in this case her action is accompanied by ingratitude and insult. Female infidelity is a cynical and painful reminder to men that marriage was a defeat, not a chivalrous concession.

Until the day men have the same sexual opportunities as women, until the day the average man can go out for a night and sleep with three or more women of equal or higher attractiveness, until that day, men should have a right to sleep with other women. When and if women lose the overwhelming sexual dynamic currently in their favor, only then will we be able to discuss their rights over other men.

Some women choose what they perceive as a dignified stance regarding sexual freedom by having a child "on their own". They may even consider it a right attitude towards men, since they do not burden a man directly (except indirectly, through the benefits provided to her by society as a whole with the taxation of men). It is not correct, however, for their child, whom they deprive of a father, and who has every right to hate them for it.

In the end of the day, sexual policing may backfire at women. Some prisons are so strong that even the guards cannot escape.

---

413 Self-Made Man, ch.2.

Feminism

Feminism and the most conservative women's movement such as that of Phyllis Schlafly are two different manifestations of the same system, as is the case with the Democratic and the Republican Party, with whom they are respectively associated. Both movements side with women and oppose men. Feminism expresses a strong confidence in the system, and considers that since it managed to squeeze the men dry at work, it can do the same to women without losing their capacity to bear children. Until recently this assumption was proven to be correct. On the other hand, the conservative women's movement expresses the fear that a change in the traditional way of exploiting men could bring about a complete collapse of the system. "What man wants to risk a financial and emotional commitment, buy a ring, and assume a mortgage on a house, when he will rank only number three in the heart of the woman he loves?" [after the baby and the career][414] asks Schlafly. In recent years, one may see a glimpse of hope that the conservatives' fear may come true.

Feminism, despite having been wholeheartedly in the service of the system ("How feminism became capitalism's handmaiden – and how to reclaim it"[415] is the title of feminist Nancy Fraser's article), at least does not mock men that with their work, diligence and devotion women may appreciate and love them. In the pre-feminist era, "Appreciation kept the slave a slave"[416], as Warren Farrell characteristically put it, and by withdrawing appreciation, however painful that may be, women are setting men free from their emotional shackles.

Historian Martin van Creveld describes how Simone de Baeuvoir became a feminist: "Like many other feminists from Mary Wollstonecraft on down, de Bauvoire grew up in a middle-class family whose male head found it hard to provide and became the object of his wife's resentment. Determined never to be in her mother's position, the

---

414 Schlafly, Feminist Fantasies.
415 Fraser, Nancy. *How feminism became capitalism 's handmaiden - and how to reclaim it.* The Guardian, 14 Oct. 2013.
    http://www.theguardian.com/commentisfree/2013/oct/14/feminism-capitalist-handmaiden-neoliberal
416 Farrell, The Myth of Male Power, p. 359.

dutiful daughter decided to stand on her own economic feet..."[417] At the psychological background of every feminist exists this internalized fear to trust a man. From it stems their hostility towards women who manage to secure a man for themselves to protect them. However, supporting women's "independence" – for their own reasons – feminists can become tactical allies to men. They support e.g. the obligation of women to work and not be dependent on their man, while at times a few feminists have advocated the abolition of alimony[418]. The male sex can only enthusiastically concur when discussing female independence, supporting for example female enlistment in the army, so that they responsibly assume their share in defending their country and not rely only on men; supporting joint custody so that women have more time for their career, etc. *With the exception, of course, of their exclusive right to control sexuality.*

As difficult as it is, it is however easier to win over a feminist to the struggle for gender equality (i.e. men's liberation) than a traditional, conservative woman. Feminists at least accept it in words, and if they maintain the capacity for rational thought there is a chance that sometime they will understand men's arguments. Besides, brilliant individuals in the men's movement, like Esther Vilar, Warren Farrell, Christina Hoff Sommers, started off as feminists.

Chapter 42: Sexual Liberation and Social Emancipation for All

"Your children are not your children. They are the sons and daughters of Life's longing for itself", writes Kahlil Gibran. It would probably destroy the poetic effect, but we could say the same for the *vagina*.

---

417 Van Creveld, The Privileged Sex.
418 "An end of alimony would force each able-bodied person to be financially responsible for themselves... With opportunity comes responsibility." 'An End to Alimony Would be Good for Women - Forbes'.
http://www.forbes.com/sites/emmajohnson/2014/10/29/an-end-to-alimony-is-good-for-women

The man learns early on that his self does not belong to him. It is spanked by the parents, insulted by the boss and a brutalizing job, tortured by the unfulfilled sexual passion, and above all, used by the country as cannon fodder whenever needed. When half of the population, i.e. men, have so little control over their existence, is it not socially acceptable to give full control to the other half, i.e. women. It constitutes unfair and unequal treatment. A country that imposed military duty only on blacks, relieving whites, would be a racist country, not a country with antiwar sensitivities "coincidentally" expressed towards the whites.

Even in the theoretical case that the above disadvantages of men were to be undone, for as long as women retain the right of sexual veto there can be no equality and justice. The two sexes evolved in parallel, with each taking up from its biology a different role in the case of the human species. Women took up the burden of birth. The cost that men took up is what Roy Baumeister calls "striving for greatness"[419]. *Restlessness*, which is innate in the male psyche, is what is responsible for all the human conquests. This male restlessness, fortunately or unfortunately, will not subside. Man has evolved to derive pleasure from risk, and even from danger. And his sex drive is in-wrought with this part of his psychology. Women cannot claim "all these were nice when we needed you, but now change your psychology and satisfy yourself with crumbs". As much as he would like, man is not made to be happy in a house, with a little wife and wage labor, the "wedded life of leaden boredom, which is described as domestic bliss"[420], to quote Engels.

Despite Hollywood's mythology, women don't have sex only for love and romance. They have sex to make their girlfriends jealous, to get back at their ex, and for a bunch of other petty reasons. For 237 different reasons, according to a study by Meston and Buss[421]. If sex is a tool for such mundane things, why can it not be used as a tool for great ones, such as social peace?

The female *coup d' etat*, the appropriation of sex through the right to

---

419 Baumeister, Is There Anything Good About Men?, p. 72.
420 Engels, Friedrich. *The Origin of the Family, Private Property and the State.*
421 Meston, Cindy M and Buss, David M. *Why Humans Have Sex.* Archives of Sexual Behavior, Vol 36, Issue 4, Aug. 2007
     http://link.springer.com/article/10.1007/s10508-007-9175-2

veto, can be likened to what Marx called primitive accumulation in capitalism, exemplified by the enclosure and appropriation of common lands and the expulsion of serfs from these privatized areas. As capitalists believe that they have an inalienable right to their property while overlooking the initial injustice that created it and ignoring the injustice that maintains it, so do women regarding their right to veto.

Liberation is therefore primarily men's business. But women have nothing to lose either, at least those that are not lazy and don't have a problem working in a job that can offer them some form of satisfaction. They may live their youth as princesses, but the misery of the society they created and preserve will eventually catch up with them. Why reign in an unhappy world, when you can live together as equals in a happy one?

The revolutionary theories of the 19th and 20th century had capital as their epicenter, while remaining conscious that they essentially referred to human relations. The revolutionary theory of the 21st century can only have as its focus, along with capital, sex.

Author's Note

This book is the result of three years of research and writing – along with decades of involvement and experience with gender politics. As you have seen, it makes some quite strong points, in trying to make clear which are the central issues in the War of the Sexes. As the author, I had a double aim when writing it: to help men make better decisions for themselves, leading to a more satisfactory life, and at the same time to give them sound knowledge to use as ammunition in the war of making a better world.

If you think that the book accomplishes its targets, I ask you to contribute by spreading the word: quote the book in your social media, or, even better, *write a review*. It can be only one or two lines, but it will greatly help in making the book more visible to other men searching for answers.

Adam Leonas

Appendix: Tables

Sexual Assault victims in England-Wales 2011

Estimated numbers of victims of sexual offences (thousands) in the last 12 months among adults aged 16 to 59, average of 2009/10, 2010/11 and 2011/12 CSEW[422]

Offence	Males	Females	All
Any sexual offence (including attempts)[1]	72	404	473
Most serious sexual offences (including attempts)	12	85	97
Rape (including attempts)	9	69	78
Assault by penetration (including attempts)	4	31	34
Most serious sexual offences (excluding attempts)	9	62	70
Rape (excluding attempts)	6	52	58
Assault by penetration (excluding attempts)	4	21	25
Other sexual offences	68	369	436
Unweighted base[2]	20.69	24.2	44.9

(1) Subcategory figures will not add up to the figures above them because respondents may have been victims of separate incidents of different types of sexual offence.
(2) The bases given are for any sexual offence the bases for the other measures presented will be similar.

---

422 Source: Office for National Statistics, UK, http://www.ons.gov.uk/ons/rel/crime-stats/an-overview-of-sexual-offending-in-england---wales/december-2012/index.html

Life Expectancy in India and Greece

Table 6: Life expectancy in India[423]

Year	Men	Women	Difference	Percent
1960	43.3	41.5	-1.8	-4.2%
1970	49.8	48.5	-1.3	-2.6%
1980	55.4	55.3	-0.1	-0.2%
1990	58.1	58.7	0.6	1.0%
2000	60.7	62.6	1.9	3.1%
2010	63.63	66.71	3.08	4.8%

Table 7: Life Expectancy in Greece[424]

Year	Men	Women	Difference	Percent
1960	67.3	70.5	3.2	3.4%
1970	70.1	73.6	3.5	5.0%
1980	72.3	76.5	4.2	5.8%
1990	74.5	79.5	5	6.7%
2000	75.5	80.6	5.01	6.8%
2010	77.9	83	5.01	6.4%

---

423 'India - Life expectancy at birth'. Accessed 13 Aug. 2014.
   http://www.indexmundi.com/facts/india/life-expectancy-at-birth
424 Source: http://www.worldlifeexpectancy.com/country-health-profile/greece

Bibliography

Books

Baker, Robin. *Sperm Wars: Infidelity, Sexual Conflict and Other Bedroom Battles.* London: Fourth Estate (1996).

Baumeister, Roy F. *Is there anything good about men?: How Cultures Flourish by Exploiting Men.* USA: Oxford University Press (2010).

Ben-Shahar, Tal. *Happier: Learn the Secrets to Daily Joy and Lasting Fulfillment.* USA: Mc Graw Hill (2007).

Benatar, David. *The Second Sexism: Discrimination Against Men and Boys.* USA: Wiley-Blackwell (2012).

Berne, Eric. *Games People Play: The Psychology of Human Relationships.* USA: Penguin Books (1964).

Betzig, Laura L., *Despotism and Differential Reproduction: A Darwinian View of History.* USA: Routledge (2017). First Edition: 1986, Transaction Publishers.

Blumstein, Phillip and Schwartz, Pepper. *American Couples: Money, Work, Sex.* USA: William Morrow (1983)

Brandon, Marianne. *Monogamy: The Untold Story.* USA: Praeger (2010).

Brian Fagan: *The Long Summer. How Climate Changed Civilization.* USA: Basic books (2004).

Brizendine, Louann. *The Female Brain.* New York: Broadway Books (2006).

Brizendine, Louann. *The Male Brain.* New York: Broadway Books (2010).

Bucay, Jorge and Salinas, Silvia. *Amarse con los ojos abiertos.* 2009.

Buss, David M. *The Evolution of Desire: Strategies of Human Mating.* USA, Basic Books (2003).

Christakis, Nicholas A, and Fowler, James H. *Connected: The Surprising Power of Our Social Networks.* New York: Little, Brown and Company (2009).

Dawkins, Richard. *The Selfish Gene.* UK: Oxford University Press (2006).

De Beauvoir, Simon. *The Second Sex.* UK: Jonathan Cape (1956).

Diamond Jared, *The World Until Yesterday*, Penguin Books (2013).

Engels, Friedrich. *The Origin of the Family, Private Property and the State.* Australia: Resistance Books (2004).

Farrell, Warren. *The Myth of Male Power.* USA: Berkley Books (2001).

Farrell, Warren. *Why Men Earn More: The Startling Truth Behind the Pay Gap.* USA: AMACOM (2005).

Federici, Sylvia. *Caliban and the Witch: Women, The Body and Primitive Accumulation.* New York: Autonomedia (2004).

Fisher, Helen E. *The Sex Contract: The evolution of Human Behavior.* USA: William

Morrow & Co (1982).

Friedan, Betty. *The Feminine Mystique*. USA: W.W. Norton and Co. (1963).

Glover, Robert A. *No More Mr Nice Guy!: A Proven Plan for Getting What You Want In Love, Sex and Life*. USA: Barnes & Noble Digital (2001).

Goldberg, Herb. *The Hazards of being Male: Surviving the Myth of Masculine Privilege*. USA: Signet (1987).

Goleman, Daniel. *Emotional Intelligence: Why it can matter more than IQ*. UK: Bloomsbury (1996).

Gottman, John with Declaire, Joan. *Raising an Emotionally Intelligent Child: The Heart of Parenting*, USA: Simon & Schuster Paperbacks (1997).

Greer, Germaine. *The Female Eunuch*. Harper Perennial Modern Classics (1970).

Harlan, J. R. *Crops and Man*. USA: American Society of Agronomy (1992).

Hoff Sommers, Christina. *Who Stole Feminism: How Women Have Betrayed Women*. USA: Simon & Schuster (1994).

Horstman, Judith. *The Scientific American Book of Love, Sex and the Brain: The Neuroscience of How, When, Why and Who we Love*. San Francisco: Jossey-Bass (2012).

Houellebecq, Michel. *The Possibility of an Island*. USA: Alfred A. Knopf (2006).

Kahneman, Daniel. *Thinking, Fast and Slow*. New York: Farrar, Straus and Giroux (2013).

Kalben, Barbara Blatt. *Why Men Die Younger: Causes of Mortality Differences by Sex*. Society of Actuaries, 2002.

Kinsey, A. C., Pomeroy, W. B., & Martin, C. E. *Sexual behavior in the human male*. Philadelphia: Saunders (1948).

Meston, Cindy M, and Buss, David M. *Why Women Have Sex: Women Reveal the Truth About Their Sex Lives, from Adventure to Revenge (and Everything in Between)*. USA: St. Martin's Griffin (2010).

Moore, Robert L. and Gillete, Douglas. *King, Warrior, Magician, Lover: Rediscovering the Archetypes of the Mature Masculine*. USA: Harper SanFrancisco (1990).

Morris, Desmond. *The Soccer Tribe*. London: Jonathan Cape (1981).

Moxon, Steve. *The Woman Racket: The new science explaining how the sexes relate at work, at play and in society*. UK: Imprint Academic (2008).

Mystery, with Chris Odom. *The Mystery Method: How to Get Beautiful Women Into Bed*. New York: St Martin's Press (2007).

Pilinski, Michael. *Without Embarrassment*, USA: Kipling Kat Publishing Company (2002).

Riemann, Fritz, *Grundformen Der Angst*, 1997.

Riddley, Matt. *The Red Queen: Sex and the Evolution of Human Nature*. USA: Harper Perennial (2003).

Ryan, Christopher and Jetha, Cacilda. *Sex at Dawn: The prehistoric origins of modern sexuality*. USA: Harper Perennial (2011).

Schlafly, Phillis. *Feminist Fantasies*. USA: Spence Publishing Company (2013).

Seabright, Paul. *The War of the Sexes: How Conflict and Cooperation Have Shaped Men and Women from Prehistory to the Present*. New Jersey: Princeton University Press (2012).

Shannon, Lawrence. *The Predatory Female: A Field Guide to Dating and the Marriage-Divorce Industry*. USA: Banner Books (1985).

Shlain, Leonard. *Sex, Time and Power: How Women's Sexuality Shaped Human Evolution*. USA: Viking Penguin (2003).

Smith, Helen. *Men On Strike: Why Men are Boycotting Marriage, Fatherhood and the American Dream – and Why It Matters*. USA: Encounter Books (2013).

Squire, Susan. *I Don't: A Contrarian History of Marriage*. USA: Bloomsbury (2008).

Strauss, Neil. *The Game: Penetrating the Secret Society of Pickup Artists*. USA:

ReganBooks (2005).

Sun Tzu, Sun Pin, D.E. Tarver. *The Art of War: Sun Tzu's Classic in Plain English with Sun Pin's: The Art of Warfare.* USA: iUniverse Star(2002).

Symons, Donald. *The evolution of human sexuality.* New York: Oxford University Press (1981).

Tomassi, Rolo. *The Rational Male.* Nevada: Counterflow Media LLC(2013).

Townsend, John Marshal. *What Women Want – What Men Want: Why the Sexes Still See Love and Commitment So Differently,* New York: Oxford University Press (1998).

Van Creveld, Martin. *The Privileged Sex.* Israel: DLVC Enterprises (2013)

Vilar, Esther. *The Manipulated Man.* USA: Pinter and Martin Ltd. (2009).

Vincent, Norah. *Self-Made Man: One Woman's Year Disguised as a Man.* USA: Penguin Books (2006).

Scientific Articles, Reports and other publications

Angel, Lawrence J. (1984) *Health as a crucial factor in the changes from hunting to developed farming in the eastern Mediterranean.* In: Cohen, Mark N.; Armelagos, George J. (eds.) (1984) *Paleopathology at the Origins of Agriculture* (proceedings of a conference held in 1982). Orlando: Academic Press. (pp. 51-73).

Baumeister, Roy F. *Ego Depletion and Self-Control Failure: An Energy Model of the Self's Executive Function.* Self and Identity. 1 (2): 129–136, 2002.

Baumeister, Roy F. *Gender and erotic plasticity: sociocultural influences on the sex drive.* Sexual and Relationship Therapy, Vol. 19, No. 2, May 2004
http://www.hawaii.edu/hivandaids/Gender_and_Erotic_Plasticity__Sociocultural_Inf
luences_on_the_Sex_Drive.pdf

Baumeister, Roy F. and Twenge, Jean M. *Cultural Suppression of Female Sexuality.* Review of General Psychology 2002, Vol. 6, No. 2, 166-203.

Baumeister, Roy F. Catanese, Kathleen R. Vohs, Kathleen D. *Is There a Gender Difference in Strength of Sex Drive? Theoretical Views, Conceptual Distinctions, and a Review of Relevant Evidence.* Personality and Social Psychology Review August 2001, vol. 5, no. 3, 242-273.
http://citeseerx.ist.psu.edu/viewdoc/summary?doi=10.1.1.186.5369

Bertrand, Marianne, Claudia Goldin, and Lawrence F. Katz. *Dynamics of the Gender Gap for Young Professionals in the Financial and Corporate Sectors.* American Economic Journal: Applied Economics 2: 228–55. (2010).

Clemens, Ben. *Men and Women's Support For War: Accounting for the gender gap in public opinion.* E-International Relations, Jan 19 2012.
http://www.e-ir.info/2012/01/19/men-and-womens-support-for-war-accounting-for-the-gender-gap-in-public-opinion

De Beauvoir, Simone. *Sex, Society, and the Female Dilemma.* Saturday Review, June 14, 1975.

Del Guidice, Marco, Booth, Tom and Irwing, Paul. *The Distance Between Mars and Venus: Measuring Global Sex Differences in Personality.* PLOS One, 2012.
http://www.plosone.org/article/info%3Adoi/10.1371/journal.pone.0029265

Diamond, Jared. *The Worst Mistake in the History of the Human Race.* DiscoverMagazine, May 1987. http://discovermagazine.com/1987/may/02-the-worst-mistake-in-the-history-of-the-human-race

Dube, Oeindrila, Harish, S.P. *Queens*. Journal of Political Economy V.128 N.7, University of Chicago, June 2020.

Dutton, Donald G. and White, Katherine R. *Male Victims of Domestic Violence*, New Male Studies, 2013, Vol. 2, Issue 1, pp. 5-17.

Fraser, Nancy. *How feminism became capitalism 's handmaiden - and how to reclaim it.* The Guardian, 14 Oct. 2013.
http://www.theguardian.com/commentisfree/2013/oct/14/feminism-capitalist-handmaiden-neoliberal

Glenn, Norval D and McLanahan, Sara. *The effects of offspring on the psychological well-being of older adults*, Journal of Marriage and Family, Vol. 42, No. 2, May 1981. http://www.jstor.org/discover/10.2307/351391

Hakim, Catherine. *Erotic Capital*, Eur Sociol Rev (2010) 26 (5): 499-518.
http://esr.oxfordjournals.org/content/26/5/499.abstract

Harman, Chris. *Engels and the Origins of Human Society*. International Socialism, No. 65, Winter 1994. https://www.marxists.org/archive/harman/1994/xx/engels.htm

Hill, Alexander K, et al. *Quantifying the strength and form of sexual selection on men's traits.* Evolution And Human Behavior, 2013.
http://www.wellingresearchlab.com/uploads/1/3/5/7/13572010/hill_et_al._2013.pdf

Joan Ditson and Sharon Shay, *A Study of Child Abuse in Lansing, Michigan,* Child Abuse and Neglect, 8 (1984).

Kessler RC, Duncan GJ, Gennetian LA, et al. *Associations of housing mobility interventions for children in high-poverty neighborhoods with subsequent mental disorders during adolescence.* JAMA. 2014;311(9):937-948.

Kreitman, Norman el at. *Association of age and social class with suicide among men in Great Britain*, Journal of Epidemiology and Community Health 1991; 45: 195-202.

Leduc, Claudine. 1992. *Marriage in Ancient Greece.* In *A History of Women: From Ancient Goddesses to Christian Saints*, ed. Pauline Schmitt Pantel. Cambridge, MA: Harvard University Press (1994).

Meston, Cindy M and Buss, David M. *Why Humans Have Sex.* Archives of Sexual Behavior, Vol 36, Issue 4, Aug. 2007
http://link.springer.com/article/10.1007/s10508-007-9175-2

Mezey, Gillian. *Rape – victimological and psychiatric aspects.* The Journal of Hospital Medicine (UK). (1985)

Oesch, Nathan and Miklousic, Igor. *The Dating Mind: Evolutionary Psychology and the Emerging Science of Human Courtship*, Evolutionary Psychology, 2012. 10(5): 899-909 http://www.epjournal.net/wp-content/uploads/EP10899909.pdf

Prescott, James W. *Body Pleasure and the Origins of Violence*. The Bulletin of the Atomic Scientists, November 1975, pp. 10-20.
http://www.violence.de/prescott/bulletin/article.html

Schlafly, Phyllis.*What's Wrong With Equal Rights for Women?* Phyllis Schlafly Report, February 1972.

Stevenson Betsey, Wolfer Justin. *The paradox of the declining Female Happiness.* American Economic Journal: Economic Policy, American Economic Association, vol. 1(2), pages 190-225, August 2009. http://www.nber.org/papers/w14969

Suzanne S. Ageton, *Sexual Assault Among Adolescents*, Lexington, MA, Health, 1983.

Szalay, Frederick S., Costello, Robert K. *Evolution of permanent estrus displays in hominids.* Journal of Human Evolution, Vol. 20, issue 6, June 1991, pp. 439-464.
http://www.sciencedirect.com/science/article/pii/004724849190019R

Vikstrom, Josefin el at. *The influences of childlessness on the psychological well-being and social network of the oldest old*, BMC Geriatrics 2011, 11:78
http://www.biomedcentral.com/1471-2318/11/78

Voyer, Daniel,Voyer, Susan D., *Gender differences in scholastic achievement: A meta-*

analysis. Psychological Bulletin, Vol 140(4), Jul 2014, 1174-1204
https://www.apa.org/pubs/journals/releases/bul-a0036620.pdf

Weizer, Roland. *Sex Trafficking and the Sex Industry: The Need for Evidence-Based Theory and Legislation.* 101 J. Crim. L. & Criminology 1337 (2013).
http://scholarlycommons.law.northwestern.edu/jclc/vol101/iss4/4

'FastStats - *Attention Deficit Hyperactivity Disorder*'.
http://www.cdc.gov/nchs/fastats/adhd.htm.

'*Gender Based Violence, Health and the role of the Health Sector*',
http://siteresources.worldbank.org/INTPHAAG/Resources/AAGGBVHealth.pdf

'*Mortality and causes of death* - Gender Statistics Wiki'.
http://unstats.un.org/unsd/genderstatmanual/Print.aspx?Page=Mortality-and-causes-of-death.

Reported Road Casualties in Great Britain: 2012 Annual Report, Department for Transport
https://www.gov.uk/government/uploads/system/uploads/attachment_data/file/245383/rrcgb2012-00.pdf

UN: World Happiness Report 2013. http://unsdsn.org/resources/publications/world-happiness-report-2013/

'WHO | *The economic dimensions of interpersonal violence*'.
http://www.who.int/violence_injury_prevention/publications/violence/economic_dimensions/en